Nonviolent Insurrection in El Salvador

Nonviolent Insurrection in El Salvador

The Fall of Maximiliano Hernández Martínez

Patricia Parkman

The University of Arizona Press • Tucson

THE UNIVERSITY OF ARIZONA PRESS

This book was set in 10/12 Linotron 202 Times Roman.
Manufactured in the U.S.A.

Library of Congress Cataloging-in-Publication Data

Parkman, Patricia.
Nonviolent insurrection in El Salvador : the fall of Maximiliano Hernández Martínez / Patricia Parkman.
p. cm.
Bibliography: p.
Includes index.
ISBN 0-8165-1062-8 (alk. paper)
1. El Salvador—History—Revolution, 1944. 2. Hernández Martínez. Maximiliano. 3. Passive resistance—El Salvador—History—20th century. I. Title.
F1487.5.P37 1988 88-9432
972.84′052—dc 19 CIP

British Library Cataloguing in Publication data are available.

To my father

Contents

Illustrations

Acknowledgments

I am particularly indebted for access to important primary sources in El Salvador to Rodolfo Ramos Choto, director of the Archivo General de la Nación; Francisco José Burgos, head of the Sección de Archivos of the Ministerio del Interior; and Miguel Angel Gallardo, proprietor of the Biblioteca Dr. Manuel Gallardo.

Special thanks are also due Marie Burba, United States Embassy, San Salvador; Beryl Frank of the Organization of American States; Leonel Gómez of Santa Ana, El Salvador; Andrew McClellan of the AFL-CIO; Italo López Vallecillos, director of the press at the Universidad Centroamericana José Simeón Cañas in San Salvador; and Dr. David Luna of San José, Costa Rica, for help in making valuable contacts, illuminating conversations, and friendly advice.

Most of my research in El Salvador was supported by a fellowship from the Secretariat for Technical Cooperation of the Organization of American States.

The preparation of this manuscript for publication was made possible by a postdoctoral fellowship in the Program on Nonviolent Sanctions in Conflict and Defense, The Center for International Affairs, at Harvard University. I am deeply grateful to its Program Director, Gene Sharp, for his encouragement and support over many years; to Susan Abrams and Anne Fitzpatrick for editorial assistance; to Jennifer Bing, Peggy Wright, and Brad Bennett for many hours of help with the mechanics of producing the manuscript; and to Gregg Bates, Philip Bogdonoff, Bob Irwin, and Christopher Kruegler for their sympathetic ears and cheerful assistance with the mysteries of the word processor.

Finally, I am grateful to George Lakey for starting me on the adventure of studying nonviolent struggle in Latin America and to Professors William F. Sharp, Clement Motten, and Arthur P. Schmidt for patiently seeing me through the dissertation that was the basis for this book.

Nonviolent Insurrection in El Salvador

Introduction

In the first week of May 1944 the people of El Salvador's capital city silently demanded the resignation of dictator Maximiliano Hernández Martínez by staying home from work. On May 9, a little more than two months after the inauguration of his fourth term, President Martínez stepped down.

His downfall set off a chain reaction in Central America. The events leading up to it were well covered in the Guatemalan press and in at least one antigovernment newspaper in Costa Rica.[1] Opponents of the other Central American dictators took heart.

The influence of the Salvadoran strike in Honduras may be conjectured from a handbill written in San Salvador and brought into Honduras in late May or early June 1944:

> I have just felt and struggled in the prodigious Revolution that freed the people of El Salvador. . . .
>
> This glorious and magnificent act of our Salvadoran brothers should serve as an example and encouragement to you, oppressed people of Honduras. . . .
>
> Women of Honduras: imitate the woman of Cuscatlán who in this struggle has been the most heroic and self-denying. Students, professionals, workers, working people in general, let us prepare ourselves for the peaceful strike which is the only action that can overthrow the tyrant of tyrants, Tiburcio Carías Andino. . . .[2]

On June 23, university students, teachers, and lawyers in Guatemala City initiated another massive shutdown, consciously modeled on that of El Salvador, and on July 1 the president of Guatemala, Jorge Ubico, resigned.[3]

Meanwhile, in Nicaragua students planned their first demonstration against

President Anastasio Somoza García when news of student demonstrations in Guatemala and Honduras reached Managua, and the slogans on the signs they carried included

> "The Students of Nicaragua are with the Democratic Students of Central America"
> "We Shall Sustain Democracy in Central America, Cost What It May"
> "The Students Persecuted by Ubico Call for Vengeance"
> "The Students of Honduras Will Put Down Carías."[4]

Carías and Somoza survived the upsurge of protest, as attempts to organize strikes on the scale of those that shut down San Salvador and Guatemala City failed in Honduras and Nicaragua.[5] Three years later, however, when pitched battles between antigovernment demonstrators and police erupted in Costa Rica, opposition leaders once again drew on the Salvadoran model in calling for a national strike to protest the actions of government forces.[6]

This wave of shutdowns in Central America exemplifies one of the most distinctive elements of a rich but neglected Latin American tradition of nonviolent political struggle. The existence of such a tradition may come as a surprise to many readers, but it has been visible throughout the region (in Brazil and Haiti, as well as the Spanish-speaking republics) at least since the early years of this century. Indeed, Spanish speakers have for years used the expression *brazos caídos* (literally, fallen arms) to specify *peaceful* direct action, as in *huelga* (strike) *de brazos caídos*.[7]

The *huelgas de brazos caídos* described above typify a characteristically Latin American model of political action best described as a *civic strike*.[8] Latin Americans themselves universally call it a *general strike*, but it is something very different from what general strike means in the rest of the world, and indeed, different from other general strikes in Latin America.

The civic strike is not a working-class withdrawal of economic cooperation (i.e., labor) for class ends. Indeed, in Nicaragua in 1944 and Costa Rica in 1947, organized labor supported the governments, not the strikes, which consisted essentially in the closing of business establishments and professional offices.[9] More typically, labor plays a supporting role in a collective suspension of normal activities—economic and otherwise—in which people of diverse social classes unite for a common political objective. In most past cases the principal participants have been students, professionals, shopkeepers, and white-collar workers, including government employees. Members of the upper classes have usually supported—and sometimes led—civic strikes.

Civic strikes may be acts of protest, as in the Costa Rican case cited above or, more recently, the shutdown of Managua following the assassination of newspaper publisher Joaquín Chamorro in 1978. Some civic strikes have functioned as support for military movements against established governments, as in Venezuela in 1958 and Cuba in 1959. In other cases, like those of El Salvador, Guatemala, Honduras, and Nicaragua in 1944, the civic strike has been used or attempted for the purpose of bringing down a government by people who have no military force at their disposal.[10]

The movement that dislodged Martínez was a classic example of such a nonviolent insurrection. The present case study thus illuminates both a significant moment in the history of El Salvador and a wider phenomenon of continuing importance throughout Latin America.

1. Preparation

The shades of our fathers are at rest. The work of the founding fathers has been fruitful. El Salvador, doing honor to its name, as it did a century ago, has been the first to start the course for the second independence of the fatherland. As it did a century ago, the liberating cry arose in this city . . . in this city which already deserves veneration for the glories which are heaped together, not for pretentious boasting, but for the encouragement, emulation, and orientation of the generations to come. Peoples are important for their history. Mysterious destiny, ours, that of being depositories of redemptive ideas. Subtle enigma, that of shutting up in the smallest country of America the greatest ideal, as though the smallness of the sanctuary were sufficient for the greatness of the spirit, and it had no need of the wide landscape where the power of the Leviathans spends its force.[1]

With these words a student leader of the civic strike that unseated El Salvador's president in 1944 began his speech on the day the National University reopened in triumph. His evocation of the founders of the republic is an appropriate place to begin the story of the insurrection of 1944, for generations had prepared the ground from which it sprang. Ideologically, it drew on a tradition going back to the movement for independence from Spain. Socially, it reflected the growing importance of urban groups that emerged as major participants in national life and acquired some experience in organization and nonviolent action during the late nineteenth and early twentieth centuries.

El Salvador was the cradle and stronghold of the ideals of Latin American liberalism in Central America. This movement began as a reaction against the Spanish colonial regime's political centralization, restrictions on economic activity, and entrenched privileged groups. Inspired by political and economic philosophies that emerged in England, France, and the United States in the eighteenth century, it espoused individual freedom and representative government, linked (in contrast to the content of "liberalism" in the twentieth century) with limited, decentralized government and free market economics. Liberalism was the banner of modernity and change, and it appealed most to those who felt thwarted by existing structures.

In colonial Central America (the Kingdom of Guatemala), the most privileged group after the Spanish officials was the aristocracy of large landowners and merchants resident in the capital, Guatemala City. They controlled the kingdom's trade and also "reaped usurious profits by loaning small farmers money against their crops." The landowners of the hinterlands generally resented their domination, but the strongest resistance to it came from the western district that in the eighteenth century became the Intendency of El Salvador.[2]

This region was one of the principal sources of the kingdom's exports: cacao in the sixteenth century and indigo thereafter. Although the indigo planters of El Salvador had wealth, they were excluded from the prestige and prerogatives of the Guatemala City elite. They failed to receive benefits commensurate with the taxes they paid into the imperial treasury, and it was no doubt an additional grievance that Guatemalans owned a large part of the cultivated land in El Salvador—as much as one-fourth in the 1830s.[3] In the last years of the colonial period, the indigo growers organized to defend their interests against the merchant guild of Guatemala.[4]

The first abortive uprising against Spanish rule in Central America took place in San Salvador, the capital city of El Salvador, in 1811. The royal official who took over the rebellious intendency sourly acknowledged the Salvadorans' potential for leadership—or troublemaking, depending on one's point of view. "The Province of San Salvador," he wrote, "owing to its population, the type of population, its location, and the acquired vice in its ideas, will always be the one that sets the tone in this kingdom."[5]

Independence came to Central America in 1821, with a bloodless coup staged by the aristocrats of Guatemala City. For the next half century Central Americans fought not Spain but each other. The Liberals now challenged the surviving laws and institutions of the colonial regime—and of course the Guatemala City oligarchy—in the name of freedom and progress, though in practice ideological lines were blurred and alliances shifted depending upon the specific issues at stake. Liberal/Conservative rivalry led to the breakup of the federal republic of Central America in 1839. The conflict continued within and among the independent nations of the isthmus throughout the ensuing generation of Conservative dominance, and Liberalism remained strongest in El Salvador.[6]

In 1858 the Salvadoran leader Gerardo Barrios initiated the mid-century "series of revolts that transferred power from Conservatives to new Liberals in Central America."[7] The final triumph of the Salvadoran Liberals in 1871

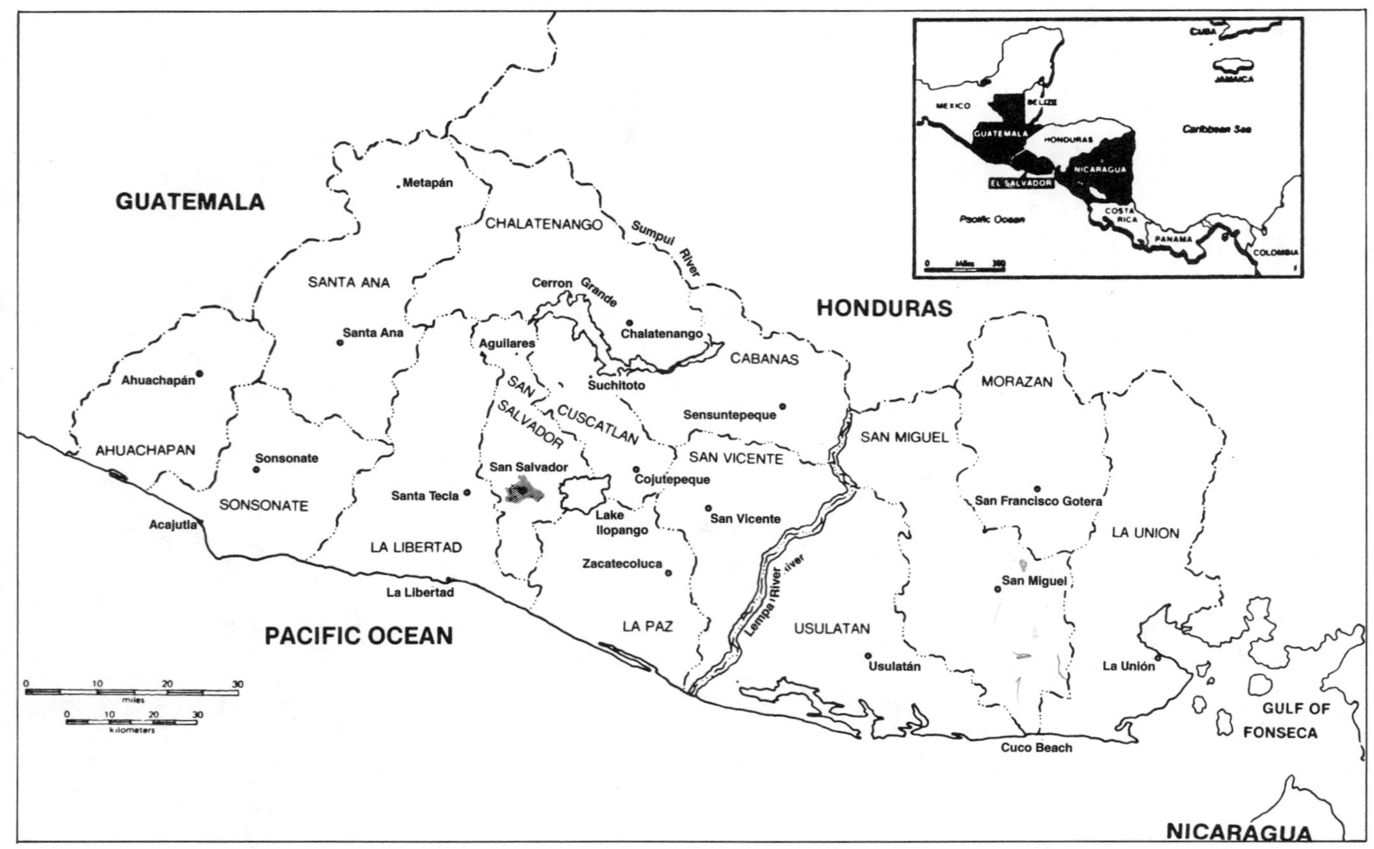

El Salvador. Adapted from Robert Armstrong and Janet Shenk, *El Salvador: The Face of Revolution* (Boston: South End Press, 1982). Used by permission.

brought a thorough-going implementation of their program that went farther than in many other Latin American countries in that period. A secular state recognized divorce and assumed control over education. In the name of economic freedom, a series of laws enacted between 1880 and 1912 abolished village *ejidos* (common land) and the communal lands of Indian communities.[8]

These "new Liberals" were far more committed to promoting economic development in the interest of agricultural entrepreneurs than to the niceties of constitutional government. Presidents continued to establish themselves by armed force and to rule as dictators.[9] The assassination of President Manuel Enrique Araujo in 1913 inaugurated the "dynasty" of Carlos and Jorge Meléndez and Carlos's brother-in-law, Alfonso Quiñónez Molina. These three passed the presidency among themselves, repressed their opponents with notorious ruthlessness, and maintained the country in a state of siege for thirteen of their fourteen years in office. Quiñónez handpicked his successor—*his* brother-in-law, Pío Romero Bosque—and installed him by means of an uncontested election (1927).[10]

Political scientist Dana Gardner Munro, who visited Central America in 1914–16, described Salvadoran political institutions at that time as follows:

> ... opposition to the government is still suppressed with a firm hand, and murders for political purposes are by no means unknown.
>
> ... the presidency is passed on by each incumbent to a successor of his own choosing, and all of the other nominally elective offices are filled in accordance with the wishes of the administration, since the authorities control the elections by preventing the nomination of opposition candidates and by exerting pressure on the voters. Every department is under the absolute personal control of the president....
>
> The Congress has at the present time some degree of independence, and the judiciary is not subjected to the same dictation by the executive as in some of the other countries, but neither is in any real sense coordinate with the latter, nor would be able to resist if a serious difference of opinion arose.[11]

The political values of liberalism—free expression of ideas, free elections, and "alternation in office" (i.e., limiting presidents to one term in office)—became the platform of an oppositionist liberal tradition that Alastair White, in his survey of Salvadoran history, labeled "idealist."[12] The leading figure of this movement, President Francisco Menéndez, presided over the writing of the Constitution of 1886, which was to govern El Salvador (at least theoretically) until 1939. Its democratic principles, "engraved in the consciousness of a strong group of Salvadorans," served as the banner of the insurrection of 1944.[13]

Menéndez's western department of Ahuachapán became a stronghold for the idealists, who supported repeated armed uprisings under the leadership of one of his followers, Prudencio Alfaro, against allegedly tyrannical governments in San Salvador. Though the *menendista-alfarista* tradition probably had more to do with essentially regional and personal rivalries within the landed oligarchy than with political principle, its survival into the twentieth century explained in part why members of prominent Ahuachapán families actively opposed Martínez in 1944.[14]

Alfaro died in 1915, but idealist liberalism lived on in the movement that crystallized around the presidential candidacy of Miguel Tomás Molina in 1922.[15] Although Molina lost the election, the cherished ideals of the liberal opposition triumphed at last during the presidency of Pío Romero Bosque (1927–31), who, despite his ties to the Meléndez-Quiñónez dynasty, lifted the state of siege, respected civil liberties, and in January 1931 presided over the one election in El Salvador's history that is generally recognized as having been free and honest.

By that time new issues had arisen. The election of 1931 climaxed two generations of far-reaching economic and social change that transformed El Salvador and increasingly challenged the traditional liberalism of its ruling elite.

The principal stimulus of change was the expanding cultivation of coffee, which replaced indigo as El Salvador's leading export during the last quarter of the nineteenth century. Latifundia had existed since colonial times, but the capital investment required for coffee production favored larger landowners, and the profits it offered encouraged them to expand their holdings by whatever means they could, particularly in the western highlands where the soil was best suited for coffee growing. This process was facilitated by the abolition of land held in common by Indians and other *campesinos* (people who work on the land; small farmers), which in 1879 still included over one-quarter of the territory of El Salvador. Although the legislation provided for the division of these lands among the members of the communities to which they had belonged, many small farmers were unable to establish their claims or eventually lost the land. Hardest hit were the Indian communities in the region that was most attractive to coffee growers.[16]

As the coffee plantations expanded, campesinos became increasingly dependent on them for access to land for subsistence farming, which they received in return for their services to the landowner, and on wage labor. The social consequences of the coffee revolution were accentuated by accelerating population growth, which took place concurrently. The population of El Salvador doubled between 1892 and 1930.[17]

Change came gradually, but there is evidence that it intensified during the decade of the 1920s. At the beginning of the twentieth century, coffee was still complemented by several other important export crops produced chiefly by small and medium-size growers. Munro observed a sizeable class of small landowners in central El Salvador "who [found] a ready market for their products in the cities, and [were] enabled by the possession of a regular money income to enjoy little luxuries . . . unknown in the more backward parts of the

Isthmus." [18] Moreover, Everett Wilson, in his detailed study of the period between 1919 and 1935, reported "the opinion of some contemporaries" as late as the mid-1920s that small growers produced three-fourths of El Salvador's coffee.

But from 1923 to 1932 coffee's share of export earnings, which had fluctuated between 75 and 80 percent from the late nineteenth century until 1922, jumped to an average of 92 percent. The acreage planted in coffee increased at an accelerating rate, bringing with it shifts in land ownership. The income of non-coffee-producing landowners declined, as did the value of their property. By the late 1920s the trend toward increasing concentration of land ownership was obvious.

Production of food crops fell, and prices for urban consumers increased dramatically. By 1928 El Salvador, which had "previously . . . imported less food than . . . any of the other Central American republics," relied heavily on imports. An influx of displaced campesinos into the cities began to depress urban wage rates.[19]

These disturbing trends combined with other changes in Salvadoran society and the impact of external forces to produce a decade of ferment, during which all of the groups and some of the individuals who were to play major roles in the drama of 1944 appeared on the stage and rehearsed elements of the later action.

At the center of the ferment was the capital city, which "for the first time decisively dominated the nation." Although population estimates before the 1930 census are unreliable, San Salvador unquestionably grew significantly. By 1930 about 90,000 of El Salvador's 1,459,594 inhabitants lived in the capital city, and Wilson estimated that "newly paved roads [to surrounding communities] enlarg[ed] its functional population to about 125,000." Indeed, road building during the decade of the 1920s, together with the completion of the railroad line from the Gulf of Fonesca to Guatemala, knit the country together as never before.[20]

The most powerful actor in the drama was the "oligarchy," which political scientist Chester Lloyd Jones identified in the mid-1930s as the land-owning "upper class . . . , often referred to locally as 'the forty families.' " [21] An observant United States military attaché writing a few years later described some "thirty families" as millionaires, and included them along with smaller landowners and large importers in the 2 percent of the population who comprised El Salvador's "economic and social leaders." [22]

This relatively new elite consisted largely of people who had made their fortunes in the production of coffee. The income and power of some of the larger coffee growers increased through the ownership of the *beneficios* (processing plants) that prepared coffee beans for sale. *Beneficio* owners also functioned as exporters, buying the crops of smaller growers and providing them with credit. In the 1920s they thus controlled "perhaps as much as half" of El Salvador's

San Salvador, 1931 (The Bettmann Archive)

coffee production, and by 1930 five growers controlled over half of the "total appraised *beneficio* values."[23]

Although the oligarchy included a sprinkling of families that had immigrated to El Salvador during the nineteenth century, the production and export of the nation's principal source of wealth always remained in the hands of Salvadorans.[24] Figures from a later period (1939) indicated that foreigners owned some 12 percent of the coffee plantations in El Salvador, as compared with 50 percent in Guatemala.[25] Moreover, Salvadoran capital financed the banks and, to a lesser extent, the railroads that developed in the latter part of the nineteenth century. As a result, El Salvador received less foreign investment than any other Central American country, and Munro described the Salvadoran "land-owning class . . . [as] perhaps the wealthiest and the most enterprising in the Isthmus." Although he also noted that the "upper classes [were] more closely in touch with the outside world and [had] shown a greater tendency to adopt foreign customs and practices than those of the majority of the other countries," the government they staffed displayed a notable independence in foreign affairs.[26] El Salvador was the only Central American country that remained neutral in World War I. The Araujo government protested United States intervention in Nicaragua, and Romero Bosque sent his minister of war to meet the Nicaraguan nationalist guerrilla leader, Augusto Sandino, when the latter crossed El Salvador on his way to Mexico.[27]

Other actors were assuming increasing importance. Wilson, who collated data from the 1930 census and "available directories," classified just under nineteen thousand residents of San Salvador by occupation. Independent businessmen constituted the largest identifiable group, with thirty-seven hundred "merchants" and forty "industrialists." This breakdown also showed an estimated three thousand civilian government employees, twenty-five hundred teachers, and not quite seven hundred people identified with the liberal professions: "lawyers and notaries," engineers, physicians, and journalists. These people, together with their counterparts in smaller cities and towns, constituted the bulk of the "middle sectors," which Wilson presented as an increasingly important force for change in national life.[28]

The younger generation studying at the University of El Salvador played a conspicuous role among the new urban actors. University student involvement in national politics apparently began with a strike in 1890—more than a generation before the first labor strikes—which, although directed at the removal of a professor, embroiled the students in a public conflict over President Francisco Menéndez's alleged attempt to impose the minister of public instruction as his successor. A few months later students protested the military coup that

San Salvador, © 1932 (The Bettmann Archive)

overthrew Menéndez. At least four student strikes in the next two decades evidenced a developing pattern of direct action. Student organizations also dated from the 1890s. At the end of the nineteenth century the student newspaper *El Látigo* (*The Scourge*) initiated a tradition of journalistic combat with the authorities carried on by *Opinión Estudiantil* (*Student Opinion*), founded in 1918.[29]

The "winds of change" that stirred the student generation of the 1920s throughout Latin America came to the National University of El Salvador as well. The university reform movement emanating from Córdoba, Argentina, influenced the new university statutes promulgated by the Romero Bosque administration, which for the first time provided for a student representative on the Consejo Ejecutivo (Executive Council) of the university. The statutes of the Asociación General de Estudiantes Universitarios Salvadoreños (General Association of Salvadoran University Students), adopted in 1931, explicitly embraced the objectives of the Córdoba movement.[30] Like their counterparts elsewhere, Salvadoran students coupled the demand for more control over their education with a lively social concern that found expression in political action and efforts to make common cause with workers—though in El Salvador such efforts seem to have taken the form primarily of rather sporadic and paternalistic attempts at popular education.[31]

Another middle-sector group, the military profession, also grew in importance in the early decades of the twentieth century, though paradoxically this was a period of civilian rule unique in El Salvador's history. Until 1911 generals who came to power by virtue of their personal military leadership usually occupied the presidency of El Salvador. But for the next twenty years all of the chief executives and all members of their cabinets—including ministers of defense—were civilians. Several factors contributed to the change. Once the land formerly held by Indian and other rural communities had been appropriated for coffee growing, the new owners were more interested in the exploitation of their property than in military adventures. Moreover, the Washington Treaty of 1907 ended the frequent wars between Central American countries, and insurgent movements enjoyed diminishing prospects of success as communications within the country improved and the strength of the national army increased.[32]

What Wilson called a "process of military institutionalization" accompanied this separation of military from political leadership. It began with the arrival of a training mission from Chile in the first decade of this century, and by 1918 the army, according to Munro, was "the chief support of the government . . . better trained and better equipped than that of any other Central American country. . . . far larger than the wealth or the actual necessities of the country would seem to justify. . . ."[33]

The creation of the National Guard, a rural police force, in 1912 and the reorganization of the National Police after 1919 augmented the armed forces.

Both drew their officers from the Ministry of Defense's Escuela Politécnica (Polytechnic School), and the National Guard "operated as an adjunct to the army," although its "assignments . . . were determined by the Ministry of Government."[34]

A new officer corps of primarily middle-sector origins came into being during the 1920s.[35] Five years after closing the Escuela Politécnica in 1922, the government founded a new Escuela Militar (Military School) intended to "make military education competitive with instruction given at the National University." The Romero Bosque administration also brought other improvements in the status of the military profession: "... Besides pensions, the regulars received scholarships for their sons and brothers and other considerations unavailable to most occupational groups. The officers' membership in the elite capital social organizations from which they were largely excluded a decade earlier . . . indicated the group's greater social acceptance. . . ."

The founding of the Círculo Militar (Military Club) in 1922 marked the emergence of the military as a self-conscious profession with its own interests to defend. This officers' club proposed, in addition to promoting the "intellectual, moral, physical and economic improvement" of its members, to "increase cohesion and harmony among the officers and to resolve differences between members through the mediation of the organization."

Relations between the officer corps and the governments it served were strained, with two abortive military uprisings during the 1920s. Indeed, Robert Elam, in his study of the role of the military in Salvadoran politics, concluded that the twenty years of civilian hegemony that ended in 1931 amounted to no more than the fragile product of the prestige and political skill of the Meléndez–Quiñónez–Romero Bosque dynasty.[36]

Meanwhile, other sectors of the population were also organizing to defend their interests. Artisans' mutual aid societies (which, reflecting the nature of artisan shops, made no distinction between workers and owners) can be traced to the mid-nineteenth century. The first decades of the twentieth century saw a proliferation of such societies as well as a series of efforts to unite them. Rafael Menjívar found forty-five functioning in 1918, representing not only practitioners of various crafts (shoemakers, masons, carpenters, printers, and barbers) but also railroad workers, commercial employees, and teachers.

That year brought a major advance in the process of federation. Some two hundred delegates met in the first national "Workers' Congress" and set up the Gran Confederacíon de Obreros de El Salvador (Grand Confederation of Workers of El Salvador), which in the 1920s represented about three thousand people.

This was a respectable movement, evidently on friendly terms with the oligarchy. Its representatives made speeches at the 1911 centenary celebration of El Salvador's first rising against Spanish rule, schools operated by the larger societies received government subsidies, and the Federación de Obreros de

El Salvador (Workers' Federation of El Salvador) appeared in the *Guía social* (*Social Directory*) of 1928 along with an elite private club and the Círculo Militar.[37]

But even as the mutualist workers' movement—which still existed in 1944—reached its apogee, a new working class that would organize itself differently was beginning to emerge. By 1920 El Salvador had four large-scale employers of service workers: two railroads and the electric power and streetcar companies of San Salvador. Wilson's occupational survey listed 1,000 railroad workers and 1,300 "motorists" (streetcar conductors and/or bus and taxi drivers). An industrial labor force was also growing. A San Salvador brewery employed 350 people. The first textile factory opened in 1912; by 1936 there were four. In addition, some artisan shops grew to employ as many as 100 workers performing specialized tasks.

Into this milieu, between 1918 and 1920, came new ideological currents that fostered the organization of labor in opposition to capital.[38] Miguel Mármol, a shoemaker who played an active role in the organization of unions and later of the Salvadoran Communist Party, recalled seeing a Panamanian newspaper called *El Submarino Bolchevique* (*The Bolshevik Submarine*) and hearing about the Russian revolution in one of the workers' cultural centers of San Salvador. Radical influences also reached Salvadorans through organizers from Mexico and Guatemala and, from 1923 on, Salvadoran participation in labor conferences abroad.[39]

The appearance of the first unions (*sindicatos*) in 1923 was followed the next year by the organization of the Federación Regional de Trabajadores de El Salvador (Regional Federation of Workers of El Salvador, abbreviated as "FRTS"), whose very name evoked the anarchosyndicalist trade union tradition of South America. It responded to Salvadoran conditions in original ways, however, promoting not only the unionization of the familiar trades, but organizations of tenants and peddlers. Most significant was its drive to organize the campesinos of the coffee region. Indeed, unions outside of San Salvador and Santa Ana (the principal city of western El Salvador) frequently called themselves "Sindicato de Obreros y Campesinos" (Union of Workers and Peasants) or "Sindicato de Campesinos" and consisted largely of agricultural workers. By the late 1920s the FRTS claimed more than forty affiliated unions with a combined membership, according to Mármol, of seventy-five thousand, more than 10 percent of the economically active population.[40]

The Federación Regional participated in international meetings, received literature from several countries, and soon became the battleground of rival ideologies: anarchosyndicalism, which at first predominated, a "reformist" current that Mármol identified with the social democratic Second International of western Europe, and the Marxism-Leninism of the Third International. The latter won out when labor militants who had come to consider themselves Communist took control of the FRTS in 1929. The next year they founded the Partido Comunista Salvadoreño (Salvadoran Communist Party).[41]

The leftward trend of the labor movement in the decade after World War I paralleled widespread discussion of economic and social issues that challenged the individualism of nineteenth century liberalism. On the one hand, increasingly apparent economic and social problems gave rise to discontent with the status quo, while on the other, new ideological currents stimulated proposals for change.

The dislocations arising from shifts in land use were not the only source of concern. Between 1901 and 1930 the Salvadoran government almost invariably ran a deficit. The most obvious victims were its employees, who suffered frequent long delays in the payment of their salaries. The problem stemmed in large measure from the government's heavy indebtedness to both British and Salvadoran bondholders. In 1922 the Meléndez administration undertook to refund this debt with a loan from a New York bank that involved, among other things, the payment of over $1 million annually "to a fiscal agent authorized to collect 70 per cent of the customs duties." By 1931, in the depths of the Great Depression, one-third of the government's revenues went to service the foreign debt.[42]

Public outrage over the loan fed a growing mood of economic nationalism. Alarmed by United States intervention in neighboring Nicaragua, many Salvadorans worried about the penetration of their own economy by foreign capital, of which the longitudinal railroad completed in this period by the United Fruit Company's International Railways of Central America (IRCA) became a visible symbol. Retail trade had already fallen into the hands of other foreigners, namely the immigrants from Palestine popularly known as "*Turcos,*" who began coming to El Salvador around the turn of the century.[43]

These forces, in Wilson's view, gave rise to a sense of insecurity and diminishing opportunities, as well as awareness of social problems, within the middle sectors and impelled them to press for reform. They found inspiration in "the social legislation of contemporary Argentina and Chile" and especially in the Mexican revolution.[44] By the end of the period Marxist ideas gained a few adherents in the university, but except in the FRTS unions they had a minimal impact.[45] El Salvador's indigenous prophet and moralist, Alberto Masferrer, influenced many more Salvadorans. Perhaps the nation's best-known author, Masferrer reached the apex of his career in the 1920s when he edited the crusading newspaper, *La Patria* (*The Fatherland*), and published his most famous work, *El Minimum Vital* (*The Vital Minimum*). His central social doctrine, that every person is entitled to secure possession of the "vital minimum" necessary to maintain health and dignity, challenged laissez-faire liberalism at its moral foundations. Masferrer ceaselessly denounced the misery of the poor, especially the campesinos, calling for "a better distribution not founded in the merits of each one, but also in his necessities; not in chimerical equality, but in real and inevitable fraternity; not in the savage laws of struggle that rule lower Nature, but in the laws of cooperation that rule evolutionary and ascending Nature."[46]

The assumptions of economic individualism gave way to increasing support for government intervention in the economy as demands arose for credit institutions to meet the needs of small and medium-size farmers, industrialization to provide jobs, business opportunities, and more consumer goods, and for public housing, protection of tenants, and labor legislation.[47]

The ferment of this period involved large numbers of people in direct action. Labor strikes began in 1919 and soon won victories. Market women, supported by the banks, demonstrated against changes in currency values in 1922, and the finance minister resigned. That year women also marched in support of Miguel Tomás Molina's campaign for the presidency.[48] Students led a protest against an increase in trolley fares in 1917; twelve years later riders of the Santa Tecla–San Salvador commuter buses boycotted them. In 1930 simultaneous boycotts by electric power subscribers in half a dozen cities impelled fifty power companies to reduce their rates.[49]

El Salvador's ruling oligarchs responded to the spirit of the times. The first labor laws appeared in 1911, and the Romero Bosque administration, besides enacting several provisions for the protection of commercial employees, appointed a labor secretary and set up conciliation boards to mediate labor disputes.[50] The 1919 election saw the first appeals to the interests of campesinos and workers, with candidate Quiñónez promising them "better wages, land, loans, education, hospitals, etc." and both candidates pronouncing themselves in favor of labor's freedom to organize.[51] Quiñónez even created his own short-lived organization of workers and campesinos, the Liga Roja (Red League).[52]

But it was an outsider to the Meléndez–Quiñónez–Romero Bosque political machine who demonstrated the potential of populist politics in a true presidential contest. In the 1931 election Arturo Araujo, a wealthy landowner who for a decade had identified himself with the labor movement, ran as the candidate of an ad hoc Partido Laborista Salvadoreño (Salvadoran Labor Party) with the backing of Alberto Masferrer and a number of labor organizations, particularly "noncommunist splinters of the FRTS."[53] He appealed most to the campesinos, to whom some of his supporters evidently promised the distribution of land.

When the votes were counted, Araujo led a field of five candidates with over 105,000 of the 220,000 votes cast, heavily concentrated in the central and western departments where the rural population was the greatest and most highly politicized. The ruling dynasty's heir apparent, who had looked like a winner with broad support in the city of San Salvador, came in second with only 63,000 votes.[54]

This major upset demonstrated both the genuineness of the government's commitment to a free election and the readiness of masses of Salvadorans to choose for themselves, but it proved to be the last milestone in the advance of Salvadoran democracy, which within the year came to an abrupt end.

2. The Martínez Regime

They say that he was a good president
because he distributed low-cost houses
to the Salvadoreños who were left. . .[1]

On December 2, 1931, an army revolt in San Salvador drove President Arturo Araujo into exile. On December 5 the military directorate that took over the government turned the presidency over to Araujo's legal successor, Vice President and Minister of War General Maximiliano Hernández Martínez. The Martínez era, known to its enemies as "the thirteen-year tyranny," had begun.

Who was this man who ruled longer than any other president in El Salvador's history? What forces brought his government into being and sustained it? What was the nature of his regime and how did it affect the lives of El Salvador's people?

The son of lower middle class parents of predominantly Indian ancestry, Maximiliano Hernández Martínez received most of his formal education at the Escuela Polytécnica Militar (Military Polytechnical School) of Guatemala and devoted his entire professional life to the Salvadoran army, which he entered in 1899. "The principal founder and first president" of the Círculo Militar, he established a reputation as "the Republic's best military technician and the officer who most demanded strict, impartial discipline."[2]

No mere military technician, however, Martínez read avidly on many other subjects. His commitment to theosophy, linked with his belief in telepathy and a variety of magical practices, particularly fascinated his contemporaries. His rigidly strong character inspired both admiration and aversion. One of the severest critics of the Martínez administration, Salvadoran historian David Luna, credited him with impeccable personal honesty, and his administration, which institutionalized the audit of government expenditures, enjoyed a similar reputation. The oligarchy, to which he was always an outsider, nevertheless respected his competence as an administrator. His abstemious personal habits and trim physical condition set him apart from the dissolute officers who had held high office before him, and Luna thought he exercised an almost "hypnotic" power over the army. On the other hand, some found him rancorous and unforgiving. As Luna put it, it was impossible for a person who had fallen into disgrace or become his enemy to reestablish himself or "reach an accommodation." [3]

Martínez's interest in politics became apparent in 1930 when he entered the race for the presidency, from which he subsequently withdrew to become Araujo's running mate. His role in the coup is in dispute.[4]

The officer corps, already restive under Araujo's predecessors, had its own grievances against his administration.[5] Moreover, the rebels acted with broad public support, for the Great Depression had precipitated a major social crisis.

As a result of the steep decline in coffee prices that began in July 1929, many producers let the harvest rot in the fields rather than hire people to pick the coffee beans. Wages for campesinos who could find work at all dropped more than 50 percent. In April 1930 the Federación Regional de Trabajadores de El Salvador circulated a petition demanding a law to "guarantee farm contracts and set minimum pay for agricultural workers" and on May 1 brought eighty thousand demonstrators to San Salvador.

At this point President Romero Bosque's commitment to civil liberties broke down. He reportedly said that although he was willing to permit the organization of urban workers, the unionization of agricultural labor was quite another matter. The government prohibited workers' demonstrations and the publication of "Marxist propaganda." Eight people died when police fired on a demonstration in Santa Ana at the end of the year, and by the time Romero Bosque left office some twelve hundred persons had been "imprisoned for left-wing activities or labor agitation." [6] Repression only drove many campesinos to the verge of spontaneous rebellion. A wave of strikes and protests by rural labor organizations began within weeks of Araujo's inauguration in March 1931.[7]

In the meantime, declining government revenues brought severe cuts in expenditures for public education and pension payments, and government employees again went unpaid. Boycotted by administrators who had served previous governments more to the liking of the oligarchy, the inexperienced Araujo administration proved unable to formulate effective policies, presenting instead a spectacle of mismanagement and corruption.[8] Araujo's decision to seek a new foreign loan sparked riots in San Salvador and Santa Ana, to which he responded by proclaiming a state of siege in July 1931.[9] Moreover, he alienated his mass following by failing to carry out his promises of land reform and

Maximiliano Hernández Martínez (The Bettmann Archive)

by violently repressing labor protests. Salvadorans at every level of society became disillusioned with the results of electoral democracy.[10]

Less than two months after Martínez took office, the simmering conflict in the countryside that had bedeviled his predecessors came to a head. Convinced that a spontaneous uprising of enraged campesinos was imminent, the Salvadoran Communist party attempted to place itself at the head of the revolt by organizing a national armed insurrection.[11] Hastily organized and fatally crippled when the government discovered the plot and captured its most important leaders, the insurrection that broke out on January 22, 1932, was a fiasco. Only some predominantly Indian communities in western El Salvador took up arms, and government troops reestablished control of that region in three days. Thomas Anderson, after examining the evidence carefully, concluded that no more than one hundred persons died at the hands of the rebels. But the military retaliated with mass executions of campesinos in the affected areas that took thousands of lives. Assertions as to the number of victims range from two to three thousand to as high as forty thousand. Anderson concluded that eight thousand to ten thousand would be "a reasonable estimate." [12]

Although this indiscriminate massacre undoubtedly alienated many lower-class Salvadorans, it consolidated support for Martínez among members of the middle and upper classes. Under pressure of the emergency the National Legislative Assembly on February 5, 1932, elected him constitutional president to finish Araujo's term, and leading liberals joined his government. Having established himself with the oligarchy and much of the urban population as their savior from the horrors of Communist revolution, he launched his career as El Salvador's last, and perhaps greatest, *caudillo* (strong man).

Students of Salvadoran history differ as to the nature and impact of Martínez's rule. Most characterize his regime as an essentially conservative one that strengthened the established export economy, discouraged economic and social change, and in all important respects served the interests of the oligarchy.[13] In sharp contrast, Salvadoran historian Italo López Vallecillos asserted:

> The modernization of the Salvadoran State was initiated with the coming to power of General Maximiliano Hernández Martínez . . . , who, with the collaboration of the petty bourgeoisie of liberal origin and the support of some progressive middle sector coffee growers, managed to introduce a series of reforms of incalculable benefit. The reformism of Martínez . . . [,] although it suffered in many respects from "paternalism" and the "strong hand," obviously hurt the great oligarchy.[14]

Evidence exists to support both interpretations.

The most important legacy of this period was the "bifurcation" of power, which established the military as the nation's governing elite in place of the great landowning families while leaving the latter in control of the major economic institutions.[15] The process began with the substitution of army officers for civilian bureaucrats during the crisis of 1932. Two years later four members of the previously all-civilian cabinet, thirteen of the fourteen departmental governors, and subordinate officials in all branches of the government were military men. For the next forty-five years, with one minor exception, the president was an officer. Most other important positions were occupied either by members of the armed forces or by civilians who did not belong to the oligarchy but were "rather more dependent for their career prospects on their relations with the military."[16]

A thoughtful contemporary observer of Salvadoran society, United States Vice Consul H. Gardner Ainsworth, described the Martínez government as "almost entirely middle class" and thought it shared middle-class "nationalistic pride and . . . devotion to material progress and social betterment."[17] Indeed, many of its actions did respond to concerns that middle-sector advocates had raised during the preceding decade.

The president demonstrated his nationalist sentiments by rejecting offers of Canadian and United States assistance in putting down the 1932 insurrection and refusing the United States permission to station troops in El Salvador during World War II.[18] He also attacked the growing foreign penetration of El Salvador's economy. He took control of the customs revenues that had been preempted for the payment of the 1922 loan, reduced debt payments to about 40 percent of the 1928 level, and until 1941 refused to contract new foreign loans.[19] A series of discriminatory laws forbade "persons of the Arab, Palestinian, Turkish, Chinese, Lebanese, Syrian, Egyptian, Persian, Hindu and Armenian races, even though naturalized" to open new businesses of any type or even to participate in them as partners or to open branches of existing enterprises.[20] By the last year of Martínez's rule, a number of United States observers had become convinced that the government was hostile to foreign investment, citing remarks by government officials, including the president himself.[21]

In spite of its rejection of foreign loans and its shrunken revenues during the depression years, the Martínez regime paid its employees promptly, maintained public expenditures "almost at the pre-depression level," and became famous for the construction of roads and bridges.[22]

Moreover, following precedents set by the Arturo Araujo administration, Martínez responded to the crisis of the depression by breaking decisively with the laissez-faire tenets of the liberal tradition.[23] One of the first acts of his administration was the *Ley Moratoria* (debt moratorium law), which stopped the foreclosure of mortgages on land. In 1934 El Salvador's private banks lost the right to issue their own paper money, and the control of the currency was vested in a new Banco Central de Reserva (Central Reserve Bank). In 1939 a new constitution for the first time gave the state the exclusive right to regulate the coining of money, mail, telegraph and telephone services, and radio broadcasting, and increased the number of enterprises that might be operated as state monopolies.[24]

The Martínez regime also made a bid for the support of campesinos and urban workers, setting precedents of some historic importance, although its performance in the field of social welfare never caught up with its promises. The earliest legislation authorizing the state to construct low-cost housing and to buy land for distribution to landless campesinos dated from 1926, but it was the Martínez administration that took the first practical steps to implement such programs. In 1932 it created a fund for these purposes, the Fondo de Mejoramiento Social (Social Betterment Fund) and an agency to administer it, the Junta de Defensa Social (Board of Social Defense).[25]

The 1939 constitution asserted the obligation of the government to promote credit institutions, cooperatives, and small businesses, and to pass "laws to guarantee equity and justice in the relations between employers and employees or workers."[26] The government attempted to protect artisans by passing laws prohibiting the importation of machinery for the manufacture of shoes, metal articles, bricks, tiles, and certain types of soaps.[27]

One of the most significant achievements of the Martínez regime was the creation of a cluster of semipublic economic institutions that brought the oligarchy and the state into partnership. In 1934 the government addressed the problem of credit for agriculture by decreeing the creation of a mortgage bank, the Banco Hipotecario, which began operating in 1936. The Compañía Salvadoreño de Café (Salvadoran Coffee Company), founded in 1942, bought coffee in order to stabilize prices and also made crop loans.[28]

The Banco Hipotecario undertook a variety of activities not normally associated with banking. Under the 1938 *Ley de Almacenes Generales* (General Warehouses Law), it built and operated warehouses for agricultural products and imported merchandise, as well as the products of several small handcraft industries, which served as collateral for credit to the producers. It also undertook the marketing of various handmade articles, distributed scarce kerosene at the legal ceiling price in rural areas during World War II, and processed quinine for distribution at cost in malaria-infested regions.

Finally, the Banco Hipotecario provided funds and leadership for two significant institutions that appeared near the end of the Martínez era. To meet the needs of small farmers it promoted rural credit cooperatives, organized into the Federación de Cajas de Crédito (Federation of Credit Cooperatives) in early 1943. Along with the credit cooperatives, it was a major stockholder in Mejoramiento Social, a private corporation that in December 1941 took over the assets and the functions of the Junta de Defensa Social.[29]

Mejoramiento Social became the vehicle for a potentially important new departure in economic policy. The Martínez era saw very little expansion of industry in El Salvador. Indeed, the government's pro-artisan policies cited earlier obviously militated against the introduction of mass production. Contemporary advocates of industrial development complained that the administration lacked a definite commitment to industrialization and provided insufficient protection against foreign competition and other hazards for investors.[30] But by early 1944 Martínez had joined their ranks. "If we continue as an agricultural country," he told an audience of his followers, "we will not get out of our present poverty. Rich countries are industrial countries."[31] Mejoramiento Social, according to its president, saw the promotion of industry as an indispensable means of raising the living standard of the masses of Salvadorans. While continuing the land distribution and housing programs of the Junta de Defensa Social and moving into the field of assistance to hand manufacturers that the Banco Hipotecario had pioneered, it also proposed to start a number of manufacturing ventures and then turn them over to corporations in which the public might invest.[32] Construction of the first of these, a large modern thread factory near San Miguel, began in early 1944.

This activity did not simply expand the power of the new elite at the expense of the old, however. All of the new institutions were private corporations whose charters provided for varying degrees of participation by the state. The latter's power over the Banco Central de Reserva was limited to the president's power to veto the directors' selection of the bank president. The government appointed the directors of the Compañía Salvadoreña de Café and one of the four directors of the Banco Hipotecario. It held no stock in either the Banco Central or the Banco Hipotecario, and its financial participation in the Compañía Salvadoreña de Café consisted of a single share held by President Martínez. On the other hand, the Asociación Cafetalera (Coffee Growers' Association), controlled by the large producers, held 75 percent of the shares in the Banco Hipotecario and 900 of the Compañía Salvadoreña de Café's 1,260 shares. In Vice Consul Ainsworth's judgment, the personnel of these institutions enjoyed a tacit understanding with Martínez that they would have a free hand so long as they abstained from political activity.[33]

The net effect was to curtail the power of the few families who controlled the private banks and the *beneficios* while expanding that of the landowning oligarchy as a whole.[34] At the same time, the government "gave the urban classes improved national administration, regular salaries, and better terms for retiring the onerous national debt. . . . [It also] established the military as a civil service and maintained career opportunities for the middle groups by enlarging the functions of government and stimulating business activity."[35]

On the other hand, the benefits Martínez offered to workers and campesinos proved to be largely illusory. The efforts of the Junta de Defensa Social failed to produce significant results. Between 1932 and 1942 it constructed fewer than three hundred houses—while the urban population of El Salvador increased by eighty thousand persons—and in the countryside it created "fewer small holdings of land . . . than were absorbed by large landowners in the formation of extensive haciendas. . . ."[36] Moreover, since it gave preference to campesinos already occupying the land, in most cases it simply "legalize[d] the status of peasant land-holders who had previously claimed the land they worked under informal arrangements based on acts of possession." Many of these lots were of poor quality, and in the absence of adequate provisions for credit or technical assistance, the recipients often could not meet the payments required and lost the land.[37]

Labor unions, both urban and rural, disappeared, for the Martínez regime identified organized labor with subversion and permitted only mutual aid societies, which functioned under police surveillance.[38] A few excerpts from the correspondence of the Ministry of Government illustrate the spirit and character of this surveillance. The governor of Ahuachapán forwarded a leaflet issued by the shoemakers of that city announcing that they had agreed to raise their prices with the comment that "they want to start the kind of demands which give rise to extortionism in peoples. The beginning of UNIONISM, LABORISM, and COMMUNISM in the administration of Pío Romero Bosque and Araujo started like this and led to the tragic end of the year '32."

He subsequently reported having told one of the shoemakers "that they should not hold any meeting without your due authorization." The minister of government responded that it would be a good idea to "observe, in agreement with the Director of Police, the movements of the leaders [and] report any occurrence."[39] The minister also received detailed reports on meetings of workers' societies from governors and the director general of the National Police.[40]

The government sponsored its own popular organization, Reconstrucción Social (Social Reconstruction), which "purported to be comprised of workers 'from the shops and the fields' " and to "deal with unemployment and related social problems."[41] In practice, however, Reconstrucción Social displayed more interest in keeping the workers in line than in promoting their interests and served primarily as an instrument for mobilizing political support for the president.[42] Its principal muscle probably derived from the fact that during World War II it became "the official go-between in the employment of Salvadorean workers for the Canal Zone," requiring every applicant to pay thirty *centavos* (twelve cents) for a certificate that identified the bearer as "a man of order and COLLABORATOR WITH THE GOVERNMENT" who had adhered to Reconstrucción Social. This undoubtedly explains why it could claim thirty thousand members in 1943, although the secretary admitted to Vice Consul Ainsworth that only six hundred paid dues.[43]

Although the Martínez administration gave consideration to labor legislation from time to time, the only new law that materialized in twelve years merely required business establishments in San Salvador to close at 1:00 P.M. on Saturday.[44] The conciliation boards inherited from the Romero Bosque administration began to show some signs of life toward the end of the Martínez era, but they had little impact on the welfare of most working people, and one historian of the Salvadoran labor movement claimed that in many instances labor's earlier gains, such as the eight-hour day and weekly day off, vacations, and overtime pay, became dead letters, while wages dropped.[45]

What all this suggests is that Martínez was not simply the agent of any single sector of Salvadoran society. He was an adroit politician who worked tirelessly within the constraints of that society to garner support where he could and neutralize actual or potential opposition. He was a classic Latin American dictator, personally dominating his government.

Although he clearly owed his position to El Salvador's assertive new officer corps, he kept this new elite under firm control. He promptly removed officers who had opposed the coup that brought him to power and did not fall in line with his government. Others were held in line by means of a notorious spy system coupled with a form of blackmail, putting officers caught in any financial transgressions on notice that the evidence against them would remain in the president's desk for future reference. A 1935 revision of the military code imposed the same penalties for merely proposing or planning an uprising as for carrying one out.[46]

During the 1940s Martínez staffed the most strategic military commands with officers who had come through the ranks, whom he apparently trusted more, and removed to more remote posts those who had received training in the Escuela Militar or abroad. To counterbalance the regular armed forces he maintained a "personal detective force," and in 1941 he created a small, poorly armed militia made up of members of his Pro-Patria party.[47]

Civil administration received equally careful attention. According to a long-time friend and admirer of Martínez, members of the National Assembly, cabinet members, governors, village mayors, and civilian administrators consulted him about every action they took, even the hiring or firing of the humblest employees.[48] A critic complained that no bills came before the National Legislative Assembly without the president's prior approval.[49] Indeed, after the 1933 election that body consisted only of administration supporters.[50]

Martínez augmented the traditional powers of the presidency by suppressing the autonomy formerly exercised by municipal governments. Mayors became appointees of the national executive, and the municipalities lost their revenues.[51] A few random reports of the Ministry of Government, which had the responsibility for local administration, suggest the extent to which control was centralized. It authorized the municipality of San Salvador to purchase three pianos for its public schools and the municipality of San Rafael Cedros to spend up to two hundred *colones* (eighty dollars) for the repair of various tools, and solemnly informed the president of the republic "that there is no typewriter available for the municipality of Azacualpa."[52]

Martínez's grip on all organs of government was reinforced by his control of El Salvador's "only recognized political party," the Partido Nacional Pro-Patria, which in 1943 claimed a total membership of 73,785. These members came primarily from the ranks of public employees and others whose jobs depended upon the good will of the government, though the party evidently exercised less than complete control over such persons. A young engineer told a member of the United States Legation staff that his failure to respond to a "summons" to report to the local Pro-Patria headquarters and enroll "would mean that he would not be considered for any work in the gift of the government . . . practically the only employer of civil engineers in the country." On the other hand, one former government employee recalled that nothing at all happened when she refused to sign up as a member, although her fellow workers had been convinced that she would lose her job. Most civil servants helped finance Pro-Patria through a 1 percent levy on their salaries, but there were "a few branches of the government whose employees refuse[d] to pay" the levy, the identities of which were a well-kept secret "in order to prevent other branches learning of this and doing likewise." [53]

The Pro-Patria machine constituted only one element in a web of controls over the lives of Salvadorans that characterized the Martínez era. The government imposed a state of siege on the eve of the January 1932 insurrection and perpetuated it throughout the next twelve years. It also played on the fears the revolt aroused, labeling critics of the regime "Communist." [54] A 1932 revision of the criminal code imposed varying terms of imprisonment for advocating, "publicly *or privately* [emphasis added] . . . anarchist doctrines or doctrines contrary to the political, social or economic order . . . ," attending a meeting at which any such doctrine was promulgated, or possessing literature containing it. The 1939 constitution gave military courts jurisdiction over civilians as well as soldiers accused of "attempts against the supreme authorities; espionage, treason, rebellion, sedition, and the proposal or conspiracy to commit these." [55]

The university lost its autonomy in 1938, when key appointments became the prerogative of the government. Staffed with supporters of the regime, it no longer permitted the wide-ranging discussion of social issues that it had once fostered. Two years later the state took over the university's cherished right to authorize individuals to practice the liberal professions.[56] The result, according to one critic, was to subject its graduates to the humiliation of a police check to certify their good conduct, and the insecurity of knowing that the right to exercise their professions could be arbitrarily canceled at any time.[57] The government also suppressed the Asociación General de Estudiantes Universitarios Salvadoreños in 1939 and an association of secondary students in 1940.[58] Finally it even suspended the Colegio de Abogados (Bar Association) "for political reasons." [59]

A new press law in April 1933 made editors of all types of printed literature liable for prosecution for printing "willful criticism of officials and public employees, as well as . . . matter subversive of the existing social order." [60] Editors sometimes received orders from the authorities to desist from publication of certain types of material.[61] Moreover, the government permanently suppressed some periodicals, notably *La Patria* and *Opinión Estudiantil*, and temporarily suspended the publication of others, including two respected San Salvador dailies. At least four newspaper editors suffered exile, and the editor of a humor magazine that did not amuse the authorities was summarily imprisoned, although he quickly won his release by going on a hunger strike.[62]

Government functionaries and paid informants also monitored private expressions of opinion, and extrajudicial punishment—evidently varying with the zeal of individual officials and the social status of the offender—was prevalent.[63] Some "malcontents had a way of simply disappearing"; these probably included members of clandestine workers' groups who reportedly died at the hands of the authorities.[64] Others suffered arbitrary imprisonment, sometimes accompanied by physical maltreatment. An opposition newspaper charged in 1935 that many men had spent eight months or more in prison without charges on the mere supposition that they were "Communists." Miguel Mármol, a Communist labor leader imprisoned for some two years during the 1930s without ever coming to trial, reported that the government denied holding him, and prison authorities simply hid him from representatives of the court who arrived with habeas corpus orders. In September 1941 the United States minister heard that five students arrested in July were still "held *incomunicado* and in solitary confinement for having pasted up certain notices in the public streets. The British Chargé d'Affaires, who saw a number of these notices, said that they were crude and comparatively harmless . . . pro-Vatican and anti-Nazi. . . ."[65]

The president's secret police force was "reported to be the best in Central America."[66] After the prominent lawyer, David Rosales, resigned from Martínez's cabinet in 1938, two members of the secret police were posted in front of his home noting who came and went—thereby intimidating potential clients.[67]

In short, while Martínez did not find it necessary to resort to a reign of terror after the early months of 1932, he had at his command a varied arsenal of potential weapons against opponents of his rule that undoubtedly contributed to his success in what Latin Americans call *continuismo*—maintaining himself in office beyond his established term. When the term for which Araujo had been elected in 1931 drew to a close in 1934, Martínez handed the government over to his minister of war and ran for a term of his own. He was elected without opposition the following year. Under the Constitution of 1886 he could not legally serve beyond the end of this term in 1940. In January 1939, however, following procedures that critics condemned as illegal, the National Legislative Assembly decreed a new constitution. It extended the presidential term to six years, preserving the sacrosanct ban on reelection except for the period March 1, 1939–January 1, 1945, for which the Assembly gave itself the power to elect the president and promptly elected Martínez.[68]

Martínez derived his power from internal sources; he was no minion of the United States. Indeed, his government existed for two years without United

States recognition, for the latter attempted until January 1934 to follow the principles of the Washington Treaty of 1923 whereby the Central American states agreed not to recognize governments established by armed force.[69] Martínez, however, disregarded the treaty, and his persistence contributed to the collapse of support for it among the Central American republics that had signed it, as well as the major European powers. When the treaty expired in 1933 it was not renewed. The futility of continuing the nonrecognition policy was apparent when all of the Central American countries formally recognized the government of El Salvador at the beginning of 1934.[70]

United States recognition of the Martínez government in 1934 marked one step in the United States' reassessment of its policy toward the Latin American countries, a reassessment that contributed to the Salvadoran dictator's ability to maintain relative independence. By 1936, disillusioned by the results of its involvement in Cuban and Nicaraguan politics, the Roosevelt administration had defined a policy of "noninterference" in the internal politics of its neighbors, renouncing "any and all techniques of influence for the pursuit of certain former policy objectives . . . the spread of democratic institutions in Latin America and the avoidance of situations usually described as instability, chaos, or anarchy." Consistent with that policy, the State Department firmly rejected suggestions from the United States minister in San Salvador that he be permitted to employ "the moral influence" of his position to discourage the establishment of dictatorial government in El Salvador and Martínez's subsequent moves to perpetuate his rule by changing the constitution.[71]

For his part, Martínez, probably motivated both by a nationalist desire to escape North American domination and by his own authoritarian political philosophy, for some years maintained cordial relations with the Axis powers. El Salvador recognized the Japanese puppet state of Manchukuo and was among the first countries to establish diplomatic relations with the Franco regime in Spain. During the 1930s Martínez turned to Germany and Italy for arms and sent Salvadoran officers to those countries for training.[72] El Salvador's purchases from Germany increased between 1931 and 1939 to about one-third of its total imports, although the United States continued to sell more in the Salvadoran market than any other single country and from 1935 on replaced Germany as the best customer for Salvadoran products.[73]

World War II cut off El Salvador's European coffee markets, with serious repercussions for its economy, and compelled Martínez to draw closer to the United States. By October 1940 he had signaled his shift of allegiance to the Allies, removing a number of pro-Nazis from key positions in the government, and in early December 1941 El Salvador joined other Latin American countries in declaring war on the Axis powers.[74] Zealous North American military representatives in El Salvador continued to express doubts about the genuineness of the president's commitment to the Allied cause, but he enjoyed cordial relations with Robert Frazer, the United States minister during the early war years. Indeed, some observers thought Frazer entirely too friendly with the Salvadoran dictator. United States Military Attaché George Baldwin acidly referred to "the Martínez-Renwick owned Legation of the time of Minister Frazer," and Walter Thurston, who replaced Frazer in January 1943, noted "a tendency here to consider that the Embassy has been too amenable to the influence of General Martínez. . . ." [75] Thus Martínez managed for some time to dominate the relationship forced upon him by necessity.

Yet every element of his strength constituted a point of potential vulnerability. In the end his increasing control over Salvadoran national life provoked a reaction, and the very groups that had benefited most from his rule turned against him.

3. The Opposition

The government that General Hernández Martínez heads initially enjoyed acceptance in the country because it was an honorable and progressive government, but the unlimited ambition of power led him to violate our laws, one by one, deliberately passing over our juridical norms consecrated both by written law and by the custom of a century of independent life, such as presidential alternation. At present it has been converted into a government that presents all the characteristics of a totalitarian dictatorship, a head who, if he does not theoretically have a life term, tries to have it in practice, who governs capriciously without respecting predetermined laws; a group of intimates who are either ruffians employed to intimidate those elements which out of honor and dignity do not participate in their servility . . . or are incompetents, real marionettes in the hands of the tyrant . . . a submissive Assembly and a corrupted Supreme Court, instruments appropriated to give a legal varnish to the atrocities of the despot. . . .[1]

What caused the growth of opposition to Martínez? Who were his adversaries, and how did they organize to challenge his rule?

The first significant group of supporters moved into opposition when his intention to seek a third term became apparent, for alternation in office was one principle of the Constitution of 1886 that had been consistently honored in practice, and Martínez's assault on it threatened to do away with "the last vestiges" of El Salvador's liberal institutions and traditions.[2] In August 1938 Colonel José Asencio Menéndez, undersecretary of defense, lost his job for no apparent reason other than his known opposition to a third term for the president. A rash of resignations followed, including those of Alfonso Rochac, auditor of the treasury, Margarito González Guerrero, chief of the treasury legal staff, Manuel López Harrison, undersecretary of public works, Hermógenes Alvarado, undersecretary of government, David Rosales, undersecretary of public instruction, Max Patricio Brannon, undersecretary of finance, and Agustín Alfaro, auditor general of the republic, as well as the assistant auditor of the treasury and "several minor Treasury officials and judges."[3] Romeo Fortín Magaña, former judge, undersecretary of finance, and president of the organizing commission for the Banco Hipotecario, wrote to the president urging him to respect legality by retiring and to permit a "genuine plebiscite" on the constitutional changes then under consideration by lifting the state of siege and allowing full freedom of debate—a proposal also embodied in a petition to the constituent assembly in November 1938.[4]

The mass exodus of respected liberal members of the government over the third-term issue may account for the view of some observers that the caliber of Martínez's associates declined in the later years of his presidency. Increasingly "autocratic and impatient of opposition," he surrounded himself with "yes-men" and refused to listen to anyone else. "Even the President's staunchest supporters deplore this attitude," United States Minister Robert Frazer reported in 1941, "while not a few of his former well-wishers have actually become inimical to him."[5]

Martínez's increasingly dictatorial behavior paralleled what Robert Elam called a "constriction of the decision-making group" around him. For the most part,

> the carefully chosen civilians and officers given charge of the government in the initial period of the dictatorship either remained in the same posts throughout the period or were transferred to positions of comparable power and prestige. The longer the condition prevailed[,] the less capable and the more reluctant the government was to recruit new administrators.

This exclusiveness not only frustrated the aspirations of would-be office holders but also made for rigidity in the face of changing conditions: "The dictatorship appeared more anachronistic with each passing day; more out of step with the times."[6]

One consequence of paralysis at the top that proved particularly dangerous to Martínez was the alienation of junior officers in the army. Promotions reportedly depended upon "politics rather than on merit or seniority," and one 1938 graduate of the Escuela Militar recalled that by 1944 the higher ranks of the army had become so "saturated" that officers of his age had no hope of promotion.[7] Moreover, the low salaries of junior officers gave rise to chronic discontent.[8] The officer corps thus came to consist largely of outsiders who did not see themselves as part of the establishment, and this, in Elam's view, made the junior officers more sympathetic than their superiors to "the aspirations of the middle and lower classes." Their initial support for the Martínez regime gradually shifted to "ambivalence" and then to opposition as they became dissatisfied with its response to those aspirations.[9]

World War II increased the strains on the aging Martínez regime. Although the benefits it brought El Salvador probably offset the economic problems it created, the war brought unsettling ideological influences and stimulated aspirations to which the Salvadoran government could not adequately respond.

The depression caused by the loss of European coffee markets at the beginning of the war turned into a boom after 1940. El Salvador received funds for road building from the Import-Export Bank of the United States and some five hundred thousand dollars, along with technical assistance, from the United States government for the improvement of sanitation and public health. Salvadorans who went to work in the Canal Zone—more than 10,500 between August 1941 and November 1943—sent home about one million dollars annually, and remittances also came from Salvadorans who found work in the United States.[10] Of greatest importance, whether as a result of wartime conditions or of the Inter-American Coffee Agreement of 1940, the 1940–41 price of coffee exported from El Salvador doubled by 1943–44.[11] Prices of other agricultural commodities rose also, farmers increased their plantings, and a shortage of labor pushed wages up.[12]

The boom had some negative effects. Shortages of imported goods inflated their prices and created bottlenecks in certain facets of the economy.[13] Rising prices of domestic products, particularly food—estimated at around 40 percent during 1943—caused widespread concern.[14] The cost of living rose faster than wages, which, in the opinion of some observers, intensified lower-class discontent.[15]

On the other hand, lower-income Salvadorans probably benefited most from the road-building funds, as well as from the wages paid to Salvadorans in Panama and the United States, and one Salvadoran closely connected with working people recalled the World War II period as a good time because, in contrast to the lean years of the depression, jobs and money were plentiful.[16] The government's Comité de Coordinación Económica (Economic Coordination Committee), created in February 1942 to allocate scarce products and control prices, was able to hold down the prices of a few essential commodities, and United States Consul H. Gardner Ainsworth, hardly an apologist for the administration, concluded that the committee's "fairness and efficiency . . . reflected only credit on the Government." [17] The consensus among North Americans on the scene in the final months of the Martínez regime was that it faced no danger from economic discontent. As one of them wrote less than a month before Martínez fell, "most admit that the country has never been more prosperous, more stable financially, more honestly run as a whole." [18]

The war had a more serious psychological impact. Reports from the fighting fronts normally preempted the front page and one or two others in all of the San Salvador newspapers, and editorial pages regularly featured translations of articles by British and North American political columnists. Labor historian Robert Alexander attached considerable significance to North American propaganda in Central America during this period: people heard again and again that their governments were allied with the United States in "a struggle for democracy and for the rights of the common people." The United States naval attaché in Guatemala testified to the importance of such indoctrination in attributing discontent among Salvadoran workers to "a gradual influx of new ideas resulting from the war." [19] The breadth of United States influence in El Salvador is suggested by the fact that, in the provincial city of San Vicente, two thousand people attended a North American propaganda film accompanied by "an eloquent, pro-democratic speech" from the editor of the San Salvador daily, *La Prensa Gráfica*.[20] In San Salvador a more select public received a regular, perhaps more subtle, exposure to North American influence through the embassy-sponsored Círculo de Buenos Vecinos (Good Neighbor Club), which offered its 250 members, in addition to English lessons and social activities, weekly movies, a library, and lectures.[21]

The arrival of the first North American head of the Escuela Militar in 1941 contributed to the ideological split in the officer corps, as "a nucleus of pro-American younger officers" began to develop. One of the then-young officers who joined the revolt against Martínez in 1944 explained his participation by referring to the "struggle of ideas between democracy and totalitarianism," recalling that for him in those days "life was full of ideals." [22]

Whether or not the ascendancy of democratic ideology (and the concomitant decline in the prestige of fascism as the Axis powers began to lose the war) changed anyone's opinion concerning the best form of government for El Salvador, it unquestionably heartened opponents of the dictatorship. One speaker at the reopening of the university after Martínez fell gave florid expression to sentiments that pervaded the Salvadoran press of the period.

> In the midst of the storm that darkens the world[,] there came like a distant but prophetic echo the voice of Roosevelt, who, encircled with the halo of the greatest moral authority America has known, showed these peoples the road of Democracy as the *desideratum* of all human ideals.
>
> And avid with dreams we read the *Atlantic Charter*[,] which revealed to us the right to live free of oppression, of fear, and of dread.
>
> The national spirit summoned its energies and . . . the new faith was born as a sign of the times.[23]

The respectability of this "new faith" also afforded the opposition opportunities to organize and bid for public support openly in the name of ideals that enjoyed a measure of legitimacy. After all, the president himself "reiterat[ed], ever more emphatically, his professions of democratic principles." [24]

Both the economic boom and the new ideological climate that World War II brought to El Salvador probably contributed to renewed pressure for social reform in the last years of the Martínez regime. The pages of *La Prensa Gráfica* in late 1943 and early 1944 abounded with editorials, letters, and articles attacking the high rents and unhealthful conditions in urban housing and espousing minimum-wage legislation, social security (which in El Salvador meant provision for medical care, not for old age), and other measures on behalf of working people, as well as more active protection and promotion of industry.[25]

A variety of citizen initiatives figured in the news. One group of San Salvadorans petitioned municipal authorities for a "study" of the housing shortage, the Sociedad Salvadoreña de Ingenieros (Salvadoran Society of Engineers) offered its cooperation with a proposed government study of urbanization and construction, and a commission to study the question of social security was named at a national congress of physicians. The first "National Congress on the Child" debated a wide range of social problems and proposed reforms, while the Cruz Blanca, Sociedad Protectora de la Infancia (White Cross, Society for the Protection of Childhood) demanded state intervention on behalf of mothers and children.[26]

The most important sign of the times was a modest renaissance of labor activity. When Reconstrucción Social called a meeting of shoemakers during the early 1940s for the purpose of offering them government assistance in finding work in Panama, Miguel Mármol seized the opportunity to propose that they start their own organization. The government tolerated Mármol's Alianza Nacional de Zapateros (National Alliance of Shoemakers), which emboldened workers in other trades, and in spite of continuing official harassment new workers' societies began to appear.[27] In 1942 labor organizations held their first national congress since the 1920s, although intervention by the director of the National Police compelled them to suspend plans for another the following year.[28]

By January 1944 the Confederación de Sociedades Obreras de El Salvador (Confederation of Workers' Societies of El Salvador), which claimed eight affiliated groups, reported the existence of between eighty and ninety labor organizations.[29] At least eight were revived or founded during 1943.[30] The revived Unión de Empleados de Comercio displayed particular vigor, openly propagandizing for the establishment of a minimum wage "as a basis for Social Security," and undertaking to draft a complete revision of existing protective legislation for commercial employees.[31]

With or without permanent organizations, workers pressed for wage increases during 1943 and met with some success. A clandestine bakers' union got around sanctions against strikes by organizing mass resignations from one bakery after another. Although the minister of defense immediately ordered dock workers who walked out at the port of La Libertad to return to work, the shipping company involved raised their pay.[32] Several groups of workers petitioned public authorities to intervene with their employers on behalf of higher wages, and Ainsworth noted on November 3 that after "a two-months' campaign" in the press, most urban workers did receive increases.[33] Employees of the Santa Ana electric company subsequently asked management for a raise, and the Sociedad Alianza de Zapateros de Occidente (Western Shoemakers' Alliance) apparently negotiated standard wage rates with shopowners in Santa Ana.[34]

Martínez not only permitted this agitation, he tried to make the cause of reform his own. His speeches to the weekly Pro-Patria assemblies in early 1943 attacked the concentration of wealth in the hands of the few, while expounding on the virtues of cooperatives and Mejoramiento Social's land distribution program.[35] Newspaper articles implied that the president was responsible for the new rural credit cooperatives, and the government also made the most of the achievements of the United States–financed Servicio Cooperativo Interamericano de Salubridad Pública (Cooperative Interamerican Public Health Service).[36] On October 30, 1943, Reconstrucción Social sponsored a mass meeting "to discuss conditions of the worker and CONTRACTS . . . guarantees of the worker in accidents of work, and . . . other requirements which ought to be enacted to assure the well-being of laborers and peasants" and invited each occupational group to submit "a report regarding its present condition and future betterment. . . ."[37] In the last months of his presidency, according to some reports, Martínez even sought an alliance with the Mexican Marxist leader of the Confederación de Trabajadores de América Latina (Latin American Confederation of Workers), Vicente Lombardo Toledano.[38]

But at the same time the heavy hand of a suspicious bureaucracy, preoccupied with its own survival, alienated would-be reformers. Reconstrucción Social's mass meeting of October 30 drew some three thousand people, according to the semiofficial *Diario Neuvo,* but Massey reported that "many workers walked out when President Martínez's name was mentioned. Others hissed and murmured when the Administration's attitude toward labor was discussed." He observed shortly thereafter that "the opposition against Martínez appears to be growing among workers' groups."[39] Ainsworth concluded that members of other labor organizations resented the "intrusion" of Reconstrucción Social into their territory, as well as the fact that they themselves enjoyed "practically no freedom of action." The organizers of the rural credit cooperatives protested Martínez's efforts to identify the cooperatives with his regime and fought off efforts to bring them under Pro-Patria control.[40] *La Prensa Gráfica* complained that "reasons beyond our control" limited the scope of its editorial discussion of the problems of public education, and a few months later official censorship abruptly compelled it to suspend a literacy campaign.[41]

If Martínez's increasingly populist stance aroused no enthusiasm on the left, it sent shivers of alarm through the oligarchy. By the beginning of 1944 fears arose in some upper-class circles that the government was "inclining toward 'communism,'" "likely to adopt supposedly progressive measures—social security, a minimum wage, excess profits taxation, etc.," and might undertake "a general revision of the tax structure and particularly an overhaul of the poor tax collection system."[42] Moreover, some saw unfair competition with private business in the existing government enterprises as well as the projected Mejoramiento Social thread factory and feared a trend toward more such competition.[43]

One vociferous critic (a disgruntled North American cotton grower named Winnal Dalton, who had lost his license for refusing to join the cotton growers' cooperative) went so far as to charge that the president had a "five year plan" for a "state monopoly of electric light and power, fuel oil and gasoline, cotton spinning and weaving, distilled fermented beverages, cigarette and cigar manufacture, vegetable oil production, banking in all its branches, textile manufactures of all kinds including bags, sugar and flour mills." As evidence of the government's ambitions in the field of cotton textile manufacturing in particular, Dalton cited the cotton cooperative's control of production and marketing and Mejoramiento Social's thread factory. He also maintained that Martínez envisioned making the state, through the Compañía Salvadoreña de Café, the sole buyer and exporter of coffee, a move that in addition to bringing in "tremendous profits for the State" would give the president "an absolute control of exchange for use in purchasing equipment for his industrial schemes."[44] Although this extreme interpretation of Martínez's economic thinking is unsupported by evidence from any other source, it suggests the rumors and the fears engendered by actual and contemplated innovations in El Salvador's economy during the 1942–44 period.

A bill providing for an excess profits tax did in fact come before the National Legislative Assembly in November 1943. The assembly also imposed both a ceiling price and a tax on cotton sold to Salvadoran factories and, over "a storm of protest from the coffee growers," enacted a new system of increased export taxes on coffee.[45]

It antagonized agricultural interests still further with two laws that apparently figured in a struggle for control of the semipublic economic institutions. In June 1943 the government proposed new statutes for the Asociación Ganadera (Cattle Growers' Association), which became law in December.[46] The *Ley de Vigilancia de Asociaciones Gremiales* (Occupational Associations Oversight Law), also passed in December 1943, empowered a three-member committee named by the Ministry of Government to intervene in the affairs of a wide range of private organizations from mutual aid societies to the powerful Asociación Cafetalera. Officers of such organizations became liable to fines and/or suspension from their positions not only for fraud but also for holding onto their offices "improperly," admitting persons to membership who did not qualify under the statutes of the organization or refusing applicants who did, failing to attend general membership meetings, and failing to provide the government oversight committee with any documents it requested, including financial records, minutes, and membership lists.[47] Members of the Asociación Cafetalera complained that the state was trying to gain control of it, and Ainsworth thought the administration aimed to bring "the independent, bumptious and somewhat anti-Government Cattle Growers' Association" under government authority by classifying it "as 'an autonomous institution of public utility' . . . such as the other semi-public corporations. . . ."[48]

The Asociación Cafetalera and the Asociación Ganadera between them held 95 percent of the Banco Hipotecario's stock and appointed two of its four directors. Since the government itself named a third, control of either of these organizations would have established its hegemony over the most important credit institution in the country. Banco Hipotecario President Hector Herrera thought this was precisely what Martínez had in mind, and with some reason, for 1943 brought chronic tension between the government and the bank management. The tension may have arisen in part from questions of economic policy, for Herrera told Ainsworth in mid-1943 that certain members of the administration were pushing for "more centralized Government control" of the economy, which Herrera opposed.[49] Other contemporary reports, however, suggested more narrowly political reasons for the conflict. According to one observer, the Banco Hipotecario was

> reputedly in open conflict with the President because of his efforts to convert the economic institutions of the country, i.e., the Banco Hipotecario, Banco Central de Reserva, Cajas de Creditos [*sic*] Rural, Mejoramiento Social, etc., into a political machine which would be used to strengthen the Pro-Patria Party and to open important positions in those institutions to political appointments.[50]

Moreover, Martínez's political advisors reportedly intimated to him that Banco Hipotecario Manager Alfonso Rochac, the founder of the credit co-operatives, had become so popular as to constitute a dangerous rival, and that the mortgage bank "harbor[ed] numerous opponents . . . who should be 'cleaned out.' " Martínez persistently—and unsuccessfully—urged Herrera to dismiss certain members of the bank staff, while Rochac reportedly "refused to make political appointments even upon pressure from the President."[51] Whatever the reasons for this administrative tug-of-war, it demonstrated that Martínez was at odds not only with those who had long disliked his economic innovations but with his erstwhile collaborators in the new institutions.

The accumulated resentments, frustrations, and fears of people at every level of Salvadoran society found a focus as it became apparent that the president intended to have the constitution amended once more in order to remain in office beyond January 1945, the end of the term for which the National Legislative Assembly had elected him in 1939. From June to November 1943 a well-orchestrated campaign of tributes to Martínez, expressions of hope that he would be able to continue his work, and direct petitions that he remain in office unfolded.[52]

December brought a series of *cabildos abiertos* (open municipal council meetings) in a number of towns (but in none of the major cities) at which citizens affixed their names to a standard petition that the National Legislative Assembly then in session convoke elections for a constituent assembly.[53] Some evidence as to how this "surreptitious plebiscite" was engineered appears in Ministry of Government correspondence. The governor of the Department of San Miguel wired the minister of government that he had received instructions from the head of the Pro-Patria party to conduct a plebiscite "in order to convoke elections for a Constituent Assembly." Elsewhere the authorities called the *cabildos abiertos* in response to petitions of local citizens, probably mobilized by the Pro-Patria party. What actually went on in the *cabildos abiertos* no doubt varied. The following accounts are revealing.

The mayor of Santa Tecla apparently felt he had done his duty by permitting a Pro-Patria delegation to pass the desired resolution, leaving it open for signature by other citizens. The local chief of police reported with evident disapproval that the mayor "did not even order either his employees or the commissioners of neighborhoods and *cantones* [rural districts]" to attend the meeting. The police chief responded to an appeal for help from the instigators of the petition by dispatching "an officer and four plainclothes agents" to round up the men in the town hall and city parks and send them in to affix their signatures.

According to reports reaching Vice Consul Overton Ellis of the United States Embassy staff, other mayors displayed more energy, sending

> their "henchmen" . . . to the towns and the surrounding country informing all and sundry of the male population that they must appear in the town hall on a certain morning, vaguely threatening them with fines . . . if they did not appear. When the assembly was gathered no . . . manifestoes . . . were actually read and apparently no actual mention was made of the Constitution, the alleged necessity for revising it or anything of the kind. Brief talks were made by the mayors and others asking the peasantry if it was satisfied with conditions, pointing out all of the recent improvements in wages, roads, etc., and they were asked, rhetorically, if they did not want to see these things continued. They were told that if they did and if they wanted continued improvements in all manner of things it was their duty as citizens to come to the various desks and sign their names, or have someone sign for them. They were told that they would not be forced to sign and that if any did not wish to do so they should leave without saying anything to anyone, paying their fine as they left.[54]

On December 29, *El Diario Nuevo* (the semiofficial San Salvador newspaper of which Martínez was the principal owner) printed the report of the Legislative Assembly's Committee on Government, which announced that more than 159,562 citizens had signed petitions for the convocation of elections for a constituent assembly, thus fulfilling the requirements for the holding of such an election. United States Ambassador Walter Thurston calculated that if the figure cited really represented the constitutionally mandated two-thirds of the qualified voters, only fifteen percent of the population (1,862,980 at the end of 1942) was qualified to vote, a statistic that cast considerable doubt on the Committee on Government's conclusion.[55] Undeterred by such details, the National Assembly on December 30 set January 9, 1944, as the date for the election of a constituent assembly, and the newly elected assembly opened on January 25.

The implications of the process leading up to the seating of the constituent assembly did not escape the Salvadoran public. North American observers reported in August and September 1943 that "opposition to a fourth term, even among many persons who supported President Martínez in 1939, [was] probably considerable . . ." and was growing.[56] At the end of January 1944 the assistant United States naval attaché wrote that although none of the people with whom he had talked expected the government to be overthrown before the year ended, "it is undoubtedly true that the Government is much less popular than it was a year ago, and that the opposition is better organized and stronger."[57]

Indeed, by the time he was writing, the pockets of opposition that had developed over the years had coalesced into a broad consensus that Martínez must go. A heterogeneous collection of dissidents had forged an alliance to bring down the president.

Some active resistance to the government had long existed. Miguel Mármol recalled among his fellow political prisoners during the 1930s "a group of cavalry officers accused of plotting against Martínez . . . several young officers accused of being partisans of General Claramount, the eternal aspirant to the Presidency . . . university students. . . ."[58] As early as 1934 the minister of government, General Salvador Castaneda Castro, resigned in the face of accusations that he had played a major role in a plot to assassinate the president, and new military conspiracies followed in 1935 and 1936. At the beginning of 1939, former Undersecretary of Defense José Asencio Menéndez and some twenty-seven other officers were implicated in the biggest antigovernment conspiracy to date.[59]

Among civilians the earliest and most consistent resistance centered in the Communist party, which began to rebuild its organization immediately after the disaster of 1932, although much of its leadership spent the Martínez era in exile. Internal divisions compounded the difficulties it suffered as a result of continuing persecution, and Mármol's account of the party's activities during the 1930s indicates that it did not find any significant field for action. However, Communists undoubtedly provided some leadership in the labor movement and played a secondary role in the antifascist organizations of the World War II period.[60]

The first direct action protesting a measure of the Martínez regime came from San Salvador journalists, who waged an intensive campaign against the passage of the 1933 press law (see page 26). Following their defeat, the newspapers of the capital suspended publication for nine days of mourning.[61] Thereafter, government suppression of newspapers and sanctions against editors and owners evidenced a continuing state of war with the press. By 1944 three of the five San Salvador dailies—*El Diario Latino*, *La Prensa Gráfica*, and *El Diario de Hoy*—belonged to the ranks of the opposition.

The suspension of the autonomy of the National University in 1938 brought it into active conflict with the state. The rector resigned in protest, and the students went on strike.[62] Student dissatisfaction intensified when the state assumed authority to license professionals, and the clamor for university autonomy continued.[63] By 1944, according to one North American observer, university students "almost unanimously" opposed the Martínez government.[64] They shared the general disapproval of Martínez's perpetuation of his rule and professed a vaguely democratic ideology, although, as one activist recalled: ". . . The student sector in which we moved . . . lacked political understanding and ideological development; we did not even understand what political power was. We were a generation which from the age of reason had grown up under a ferocious dictatorship, without opportunities for political study or any political action."[65]

Student discontent found expression in *veladas*—theatrical performances poking fun at officialdom—and in a satirical magazine, *El Trompudo* (*The Thick-lipped*).[66] A series of apparently innocuous committees founded on one pretext or another served as cover for anti-Martínez activity. One, ostensibly devoted to sports, seized upon the fall of Paris in 1940 to organize the first public demonstration against the president, disguising an attack on his generally recognized fascist sympathies as a protest against Nazi aggression in Europe.[67]

Other demonstrations, whose instigators cannot be identified, were held in support of the United Nations (i.e., the anti-Axis alliance), following the entrance of the United States and El Salvador into World War II. A United States Embassy observer reported that the speakers at such gatherings "always indirectly attacked the dictatorial government of President Martínez in the name of Democracy," which no doubt explains why the National Police chief would not permit "an organization of anti-totalitarian newspaper men" to "hold a parade in honor of France" in July 1942.[68]

The war years also saw the formation of a number of anti-Axis organizations, which, like the student committees, provided a meeting ground for opponents of dictatorship in El Salvador and contributed to the diffusion of democratic ideology.

The newspaper *El Mundo Libre* (*The Free World*), founded in March 1941, survived for two years until it published in rapid succession "an 'Open Letter' . . . by a group of school teachers complaining in rather violent terms against the regime of the Sub-Secretary of Public Instruction"; the fact that Banco

Hipotecario Manager Alfonso Rochac, rather than President Martínez, was responsible for the organization of the credit cooperatives; and "another 'Open Letter,' addressed to President Roosevelt, . . . transparently alluding to local conditions by such quotations as 'Wherever there are repressive acts against those who speak under the constitutional right of freedom of speech there can be no democracy.' " Thereupon, two of its editors, Honduran émigrés, were arrested and deported.[69]

In September 1941 a group of "rich . . . young Salvador Liberals [*sic*]" organized Pro Francia Libre (For Free France), which United States Military Attaché J. H. Marsh took to be an opposition organization, and a group of young writers, headed by *La Prensa Gráfica* Editor José Quetglas, banded together in Juventud Democrática Salvadoreña (Salvadoran Democratic Youth) in order to "fight . . . for the growth of the Salvadoran democratic spirit . . . [and] to maintain . . . solidarity with all the peoples who share the same aspirations and who have resolved to face the tremendous threat to liberty." [70] A little over a year later, a group of "young intellectuals and democrats" informed the United States Embassy that they had organized the Centro Salvadoreño de Estudios (Salvadoran Study Center) for the purpose of fighting "Nazi-fascism in any of its dangerous forms" by means of cultural activity.[71]

The makeup of the short-lived Comité Nacional del Frente Juvenil Antifascista de El Salvador (National Committee of the Antifascist Youth Front of El Salvador), founded at the end of August 1943, gave some indication of the dimensions of the "antifascist" movement by that time. The organizing meeting, called by Salvadoran delegates who had returned from a Continental Youth Conference for Victory in Mexico City, attracted representatives from thirteen groups. These included two student organizations, the Comité Estudiantil Universitario (University Student Committee), an anti-Martínez front group founded in 1942 ostensibly to commemorate the centennial of the death of the Liberal caudillo, Francisco Morazán, and the Federación de Estudiantes de Secundaria (Federation of Secondary Students); an assortment of intellectual and cultural organizations, among them the Centro Salvadoreño de Estudios, a newly formed Comité de Escritores y Artistas Antifascistas (Committee of Antifascist Writers and Artists), and the Asociación de Periodistas de El Salvador (Journalists' Association of El Salvador); and four labor organizations.[72] Its president, Alfonso Morales, had been an editor of *El Mundo Libre*, and its secretary, Tony Vassiliu, was a long-time dissident who had been imprisoned for harboring "Marxist ideas" as far back as 1937.[73] The government thus had good reason to perceive this coalition as a vehicle for opposition and suppressed it within a month.[74]

By far the most enduring and significant of the opposition organizations was Acción Democrática Salvadoreña, founded on September 18, 1941, for the ostensible purpose of "cooperat[ing] with all the forces that are fighting for the triumph of democracy; [and of] incorporat[ing] the policy of American solidarity . . . into cordial relations and mutual respect between the nations of the continent."[75] Francisco A. Lima, a well-to-do retired lawyer and past president of the Asociación Cafetalera, who had served pre-Martínez governments as judge, undersecretary, and minister of government, as well as minister to Mexico, Guatemala, Honduras, and the United States, served as president. The rest of the executive committee were "by obvious design . . . nonentities." United States observers attached more significance to the presence among the founding members of former high officials in the government of Martínez: Miguel Tomás Molina (the liberal standard-bearer of the 1920s), Hermógenes Alvarado, David Rosales, and Margarito González Guerrero.[76]

The membership of the Central Committee indicated the breadth of Acción Democrática Salvadoreña's appeal. It included Vice President Juan C. Segovia, a distinguished physician; Treasurer José Luis Boza, a young commercial employee; First Secretary Salvador Merlos, a lawyer who had crusaded for a series of reformist causes since the 1920s; two respected master craftsmen-proprietors—Alberto Pérez, a jeweler, and José B. Cisneros, a printer who had helped to found the Sociedad de Obreros de El Salvador Federada (Federated Society of Workers of El Salvador); and Carlos N. Zepeda, a dentist.[77]

Acción Democrática Salvadoreña's stated dedication to international issues misled no one. Within days after its organization, agents of the government called at the legations of the other Central American countries and of the United States, charging that it had "a strong Communist and even pro-Nazi tinge." United States representatives did not take these allegations seriously, but Military Attaché Marsh concluded that the "accusation that the Acción Democrática Salvadoreña is an anti-Government party is true." Both he and Minister Robert Frazer saw in the visits to foreign legations, as well as other countermeasures that quickly followed, evidence that Salvadoran officials regarded this group as a particularly serious threat.[78] At a Pro-Patria meeting on September 23, Martínez expressed his opposition to the formation of new political parties, and a week later the law regulating public meetings was revised to require police permission for all political meetings, including "those held in private places."[79]

Acción Democrática Salvadoreña held two public meetings, at which the speakers attacked the Martínez regime. Thereafter, since the government did not respond to its application for permission to function under the new regulations, it went underground. Its members met at private dinner parties, ostensibly held to celebrate birthdays or other nonpolitical occasions.[80]

The suppression of ADS evidently turned it into the general staff of a conspiracy to frustrate Martínez's fourth-term aspirations. An anonymous document dated December 12, 1941, asserted that the "suspicion" that the president had another reelection in view became a "conviction" when he refused to permit the organization of political groups other than Pro-Patria.[81] According to Robert Elam, Acción Democrática Salvadoreña set up committees "to encourage and coordinate anti-government activities" by late October 1941.[82] Tiburcio Santos Dueñas, who apparently had some contact with the ADS activists, referred to two commissions, one of which openly published statements and undertook legal actions, while the other worked clandestinely, making contacts and producing subversive literature. In addition, ADS representatives participated with other unidentified groups in the formation of a Comité Ejecutivo de Oposición (Executive Committee of Opposition), also called Executive Committee of the Revolution and Comité Civil (Civil Committee), which sometime in 1943, if not earlier, began to prepare for an armed insurrection.[83]

The composition of these committees makes it clear that the leadership of the movement to unseat the dictator came primarily from the professions and the economic elite. Acción Democrática Salvadoreña's aboveground component included its most prominent professional men: Francisco A. Lima, Romeo Fortín Magaña, David Rosales, Hermógenes Alvarado, Manuel López Harrison, and Juan Segovia.[84]

The moving spirit of the insurrectionary conspiracy was unquestionably coffee grower Agustín Alfaro Morán, the former auditor general who had resigned from that position because he objected to Martínez's seeking a third term. Obviously a respected leader of the agricultural aristocracy, Alfaro was the principal architect of the Compañía Salvadoreña de Café. He had served as head of the Coffee Control Office, which implemented the Interamerican Coffee Agreement, and also as president of the Asociación Cafetalera.[85]

Arturo Romero, a physician in his early thirties who had belonged to the original ADS Central Committee, shared the leadership of the developing conspiracy. The son of an army captain, Romero was an archetypical young reformer whom the Salvadoran press dubbed the "symbolic man" ("*hombre símbolo*") of the 1944 revolution. As a medical student at the Sorbonne during the early 1930s, he became involved in the popular-front politics of the period and, according to some less-than-reliable sources, joined the French Communist party.[86] Following his return to El Salvador he acquired "a large following among the lower classes" for his generosity in treating poor patients without charge and became very popular with medical students, who knew him as a good teacher in the public hospital where they received their training.[87]

Romero also emerged in 1943 as an articulate champion of social reform. In addition to participating in the National Congress on the Child and the medical commission on social security, he published a series of articles in which he attacked El Salvador's "feudal system" of agricultural production and urged the government to promote the organization of campesino-owned collective farms instead of aggravating the problem by creating more minifundia. Appealing to the authority of Pope Leo XIII, he not only called for social security and a minimum wage, but defended the right of workers to organize freely and to participate in the administration of social security through representatives of their own choosing.[88]

Other key participants in the conspiracy came from the Banco Hipotecario network: Ricardo Arbizú Bosque, chief of the legal section of the mortgage bank; Francisco Guillermo Pérez, one of its directors; and Guillermo Pérez's brother-in-law, Jorge Sol Castellanos, manager of the Federación de Cajas de Crédito.[89] This lends considerable support to allegations current in late 1943 that the Banco Hipotecario served as "the center of the Opposition" and raises a question as to the role of its top officials, Alfonso Rochac and Hector Herrera.[90]

Two secondary accounts mentioned Rochac, one of the Ministry of Finance employees who had resigned in 1938, as a key conspirator, though contemporary evidence is not conclusive. He was known as a vocal critic of high-ranking government officials and army officers who had "many friends among the . . . opposition," and a short-lived, apparently unfounded, rumor that he was the opposition candidate for the presidency circulated in November 1943.[91] In December, "when it appeared imminent that he might be arrested," he left El Salvador to help organize rural credit cooperatives in the Dominican Republic. This last supports allegations that he had a part in the conspiracy, but since he was still in the Dominican Republic when the uprising occurred in April 1944, he could not have participated in the final critical phase of the planning.[92]

Bank President Herrera successfully played a double game. Contemporary observers knew that, besides being at odds with Martínez over the autonomy of the Banco Hipotecario, he opposed a fourth term for the president. In a credible reconstruction of the sources of support for the armed revolt, Overton Ellis stated that Herrera was "very reliably reported to have given money and was undoubtedly consulted on some points before the revolution, although not a member of the inner group." Yet even after the failure of that uprising sent most of the surviving participants into exile or hiding, Herrera remained among the "personal friends of and most influential economic advisers" to the president, one of the few men who could disagree with him to his face.[93]

Only fragmentary evidence exists as to the opposition leadership's links with a wider constituency. Ellis reported that the Alvarez family, which owned the world's largest coffee mill, was "undoubtedly active in preparing and swinging" the city of Santa Ana to the revolutionary cause, and Francisco Alfaro, the "most prominent and wealthy citizen of Sonsonate," probably played a similar role there.[94] Arturo Romero subsequently told United States Vice Consul Joseph Maleady that the conspirators had "cells in various labor and student organizations" in San Salvador and nearby Santa Tecla, but the only such group that has been identified is the Frente Democrático Universitario (University Democratic Front), two of whose members, according to Santos Dueñas, participated in the Comité Civil.[95] The "Workers Section of the Anti-Reelection Party," which issued a few anti-Martínez leaflets during 1943, may or may not have been a bona fide organization. Salvadoran police evidently suspected labor involvement in the burgeoning campaign, for they arrested "numerous members of the [Sociedad de Obreros] groups in Santa Ana, Sonsonate and Ahuachapán" on charges of "preparing a pamphlet against the President," as well as a few labor leaders in eastern El Salvador.[96] However, their suspicions were not necessarily well founded. One credible informant, the first president of the labor party that appeared immediately after the fall of Martínez, denied that the working class as such had any part whatever in the revolt; according to him, the few leaders of clandestine unions who participated did so as individuals.[97]

The Communist party probably played a minor role in the plot, though the only available account of its participation is that of Miguel Mármol, which on this subject is not highly reliable. According to his own testimony, Mármol did not enjoy the confidence of the party's inner circle at the time and knew nothing about the 1944 revolt until it started. Long afterward he heard that the party had prior knowledge of the conspiracy, gave advice, and helped make contacts, but decided that its members should participate "as individuals and not as communist militants."[98]

Renewed anti-Martínez plotting within the army paralleled the organization of civilian opposition. According to one report that reached United States Military Attaché Charles P. Baldwin, a group of young officers who were "organizing in all the principal cuartels (barracks)" to overthrow the president asked General Salvador Castaneda Castro to lead the movement in April 1943. Although Castaneda Castro, in retirement since his departure from the government, declined the honor, antigovernment officers reportedly continued to meet, and the Comité Civil found an army committee already in existence when it sought an alliance with military malcontents.[99]

In late 1943 or early 1944 the two committees reached an agreement, entrusting the military command of the uprising to Colonel Alfredo Aguilar, a man of liberal convictions who had left the army several years earlier, and designating a civilian-military junta to take over the government until a new president could be elected.[100] Meanwhile, in mid-1943, the civilian opposition had launched an unprecedented campaign against Martínez.

4. The Developing Crisis

The Salvadoran officers and civilians who planned and carried out the armed struggle against the tyranny of Hernández Martínez knew how to interpret and take advantage of the democratic climate in the whole world. . . . Although the tyranny won the first contest, those who triumphed were the heroes of April 2; with their self-denying and courageous action they unleashed the formidable peaceful force of all our people which crystallized in the May Strike. April 2 will always symbolize in the annals of the fatherland the struggle against despotism and sacrifice on the altar of the liberty of the people.[1]

The nonviolent campaign that unfolded even as preparations for a military insurrection went forward appears to have aimed both at pressuring Martínez into allowing the election of a successor and at winning sympathy for the planned uprising in the event that he remained obdurate. It included several lines of action: propaganda, a legal challenge to the president's continuation in power, and appeals to the other American republics, particularly the United States.

The government's attempts to counter the mobilization of its adversaries had little effect. The actions of the constituent assembly, culminating in the reelection of Martínez, intensified public hostility. The violent uprising of April 1944 failed, but ensuing repression served only to isolate Martínez still further.

The opposition campaign opened with a barrage of anonymous leaflets, which from June to September 1943 made the public aware of the existence of organized opposition to the regime, presented its program, and appealed for support. The first of these leaflets proclaimed the platform of a "Frente Democrático Salvadoreño" (Salvadoran Democratic Front), promising to reestablish the constitutional principles of 1886, with the reforms necessary to "guarantee in practice" the freedoms of thought, speech, press, assembly, travel, and property.[2]

In July, an unsigned "Manifesto to the Salvadoran People" demanded a public declaration by Martínez that he would not seek a fourth term, the dissolution of the Pro-Patria party, the scheduling of elections, and the reestablishment of freedom of the press.[3] Within a month, "reliable sources" estimated that over ten thousand copies of this manifesto had been distributed.[4] A leaflet signed "Comité Demócrata Revolucionario" (Democratic Revolutionary Committee) asserted that

> all elements distributed it: Professionals, Workers, Soldiers, Priests, old, young, men, women, children. . . . And as the number of printed copies was insufficient, typed copies are now circulating. This is the anonymous work which indicates to us that the illegal government is unanimously repudiated and that POPULAR ACTION is to come, perhaps very soon.[5]

The Comité Demócrata Revolucionario explained what it meant by "Popular Action" in two leaflets that appeared in September. "Words to the National Army" asserted that "disobedience is a right[;] the exercise of that disobedience is what is called popular action," and "Contributions for the 'Pro-Patria' " stated, "The arm is civil disobedience and passive resistance." "Words to the National Army" argued that civil servants and soldiers no longer owed obedience to Martínez because he had violated "obligations between the government and the governed," and urged officers not to make recruits who came to them for militia drills available for Pro-Patria demonstrations; "Contributions for the 'Pro-Patria' " called upon government employees to refuse to pay the Pro-Patria levy.[6]

In October reports reached the United States Embassy that an opposition party planned to petition the government for permission "to function and to present a candidate" for the presidency. Ambassador Walter Thurston surmised that this candidate "might be Dr. Francisco A. Lima."[7] The tactic Lima and his associates actually adopted to open the way for such an electoral campaign (or, as Tiburcio Santos Dueñas suggested, to test the strength of the government's position) was a petition to the Supreme Court that challenged the constitutionality of the 1941 decree restricting political organizations and asked the court to declare it null and void. It carried more than two hundred signatures, including those of David Rosales, Juan Segovia, Manuel López Harrison, Hermógenes Alvarado, Romeo Fortín Magaña, Francisco A. Lima, and Agustín Alfaro, as well as almost all the members of the initial ADS Central Committee.[8]

The publication of this petition on October 24 created a sensation in San Salvador. "For the first time in years," the United States naval attaché wrote, "citizens of influence had come out in the open and said in effect . . . that they were opposed to the Administration."[9] *El Diario Latino*, the only newspaper that dared to publish the petition, printed several thousand extra copies of the issue in which it appeared and had distributed them all by the time the police arrived to confiscate the edition about an hour after it came off the press.[10]

The Supreme Court rejected the petition on November 10

> on the grounds that no objection to the Regulation had been made by the National Legislative Assembly, which had the exclusive right to request the Supreme Court to declare an Executive Decree void; that as the country is in a state of siege, the Executive had a right to restrict meetings . . . ; and that the courts could not settle abstract questions of law raised by citizens.[11]

Nevertheless, the U.S. military attaché considered it significant that the court felt it necessary to respond at all.[12]

In the meantime, Reconstrucción Social's mass meeting of workers on October 30 (see page 35), which Ambassador Thurston interpreted as a bid for labor support of Martínez's reelection campaign, drew a strong reaction from the opposition. Thurston thought the latter tried to persuade workers to boycott the meeting and that the "flurry of police activity" that preceded it evidenced fear of hostile demonstrations or clashes between opposition groups and those who wished to attend the meeting.

Two leaflets dated October 31 and purporting to represent the views of "The Workers Section of the Anti-Reelection Party" illustrate the nature of the opposition's appeal to labor. "To All Workers" directly attacked Reconstrucción Social and urged readers not to attend its meetings, arguing that labor problems "should be discussed in the Workers' Social Centres, not in Political Centres and certainly not when the latter are headed by the HENCHMEN OF OUR GREATEST OPPRESSOR. . . ." It recalled the 1932 massacre and the continuing imprisonment and mistreatment of workers, naming several victims.[13]

The leaflet "Watch Out, Workers of the Country, Shop and Factory" criticized the government's apparently pro-worker activities, claiming that the low-cost houses it built went to soldiers and favorite employees of Martínez rather than to workers, that the parcels of land sold to campesinos were overpriced, and that the Cajas de Crédito Rurales favored a few at the expense of the proletariat as a whole by pushing up the prices of essential foods. The leaflet then focused on the administration's sins of omission:

> . . . for us there are no labor laws that guarantee us wages which would permit us to live like humans; we have no regulated working day, there is no double pay for overtime, we have no social assistance to guarantee us health and schooling, we are not allowed to organize ourselves to solve our problems[.] [N]ot even mutualist societies can act without the vigilance of the police[.] [M]utualism was permitted by the most

despotic kings of the middle ages, and today in the 20th century, when the majority of the countries of the world permit whatever form of association is desired . . . we are manacled. . . .

Finally, this leaflet accused Martínez of pinning the "Communist" label on the campesino uprising of 1932 and perpetrating the massacre to secure his own position, asserting that he was plotting another "Communist revolt" for the same purpose.[14]

On December 11 a handbill signed by the Frente Democrático Universitario invited the citizens of San Salvador to participate in a demonstration that afternoon in support of the United Nations. Police and National Guardsmen were deployed around the university building where the marchers assembled, as well as the downtown area through which they passed, but in spite of this intimidating spectacle some four hundred nervous-looking students and professional men participated. Although the demonstrators carried pro–United Nations posters, as well as United States, British, and Mexican flags, the true significance of the parade became apparent as they shouted,

"Nazism and Fascism exist where there is only one party";
"Death to Dictators";
"Death to Tyrants";
"Down with Continuismo."[15]

The student who addressed the crowd made a barely disguised attack on the Martínez regime:

. . . the Latin American countries that have subscribed to the Atlantic Charter and today support, materially and morally, the gigantic war effort that the United Nations are carrying out . . . must recognize the transcendent importance of their attitude . . . for it defines nothing less than their contribution to the coming of a world free of misery, free of fear, and fully free for the total redemption of man and of his spirit. . . . [W]e must repudiate and combat energetically, until they are destroyed completely, the poisonous transplants that fascism has made in our continent. . . . Fascism is present where the rights of man are attacked and ignored, where the people are not permitted to express their sacred will, where those pure spirits who defend popular interest are murdered and repressed. . . .

Let us fight so that governments will reflect the legitimate will of the people; only thus will we live in the democratic century which is now beginning. . . .

Free suffrage . . . is the only way of knowing the popular will.[16]

More opposition leaflets appeared in December, January, and February.[17]

Meanwhile, the press carried on a continuing "guerrilla campaign" of pinpricks at the administration.[18] Innumerable articles and brief quotations extolling liberty and condemning tyranny appeared in *La Prensa Gráfica* above the names of such worthies as Salvador de Madariaga, John Milton, Simón Bolívar, Winston Churchill, and Domingo Sarmiento. When a contestant in a radio quiz show failed to define "democracy," the editors innocently asked, "But is it possible that we don't know what democracy is?" and recommended a program of civic education. Criticism of fascist practices in Argentina subtly attacked dictatorship at home, a subtlety that *La Prensa Gráfica* refined by headlining one editorial devoted largely to Argentina "Declarations of Mr. Hull on the Coup d'Etat in Bolivia." Mr. Hull and Bolivia were forgotten after the first paragraph. *El Diario Latino*'s comment on Argentina's break with the Axis "served as the base for some observations upon the Atlantic Charter, Self-Determination, Freedom of Thought and of the Press, Freedom from Want and Fear—and led finally to some invidious comparisons with respect to Liberty. . . ."[19]

All three of the opposition dailies of San Salvador displayed their contempt for the process leading up to the revision of the constitution by declining to print a single word about it.[20]

Behind the scenes, dissidents attempted to mobilize international pressure against Martínez's continuation in power. In October 1943 Alfonso Rochac handed Ambassador Thurston an unsigned letter urging that the United States

> make known in a categoric manner that the Government of the United States trusts:
>
> 1) That El Salvador shall enjoy the benefits of the Atlantic Charter and that the Government will observe its postulates;
>
> 2) That the Electoral Law shall be respected so the people may freely elect a president;
>
> 3) That constitutional guarantees be restored; and
>
> 4) That the many political deportees be permitted to return.[21]

On December 23 a group of Salvadoran exiles in Mexico, who called their Comité Pro-Democracia en El Salvador (Committee for Democracy in El Salvador) an affiliate of Acción Democrática Salvadoreña, appealed to the Mexican government to bring the plight of political exiles from the Central American dictatorships (obviously including El Salvador) before "the governments of America," suggesting that "Martínez would not be able to resist an indication from the governments of the Continent that it is now time to give reality to the principles espoused in the Atlantic Charter. . . ."[22]

At that point the conjunction of two developments suggested a new line of action that unfolded from January to March 1944. The United States did not recognize the allegedly pro-Nazi junta that came to power in Bolivia on December 20, 1943, and on December 24 the Pan American Union's Emergency Advisory Political Defense Committee based in Montevideo

> recommended to the American governments that, for the duration of the war, they should not accord recognition to any new government established by force, without

first exchanging information and consulting among themselves to determine the circumstances surrounding the revolution and to ascertain to their satisfaction that the new government adhered to the inter-American undertakings for the defense of the continent.[23]

Although the Montevideo committee's concern did not extend beyond possible Axis penetration of the hemisphere, the opposition saw it as a possible forum in which to challenge the legality of Martínez's reelection.[24]

A Comité Revolucionario Salvadoreño stated the case in a letter to the United States ambassador:

. . . we come to ask justice of the Government of the United States. Recently all America has demonstrated by denying recognition to the new Government of Bolivia that it does not want normal relations with governments of totalitarian tendencies or born of coups d'etat. Are not the tricks used by Hernández Martínez to perpetuate himself illegally in power against the will of the whole nation real coups d'etat? Is its totalitarian form not clearly evident?

But if the will of the Salvadoran people is still in doubt, the American Nations could well require the tyrant to prove his popularity by means of a plebiscite supervised by a Commission made up of Representatives of the Nations of the whole Continent. . . . We have sent a copy of the present memorandum to all the diplomatic and consular agents accredited in this capital, so that they may notify their governments and the work of yours in the Assembly of the American Nations may thus be facilitated. . . .[25]

From January to March opposition leaders bombarded the Embassy with letters expounding on the illegality of the constituent assembly and the totalitarian character of the Martínez regime.[26]

In late January and early February the Mexico City Comité Pro-Democracia en El Salvador wired United States Secretary of State Cordell Hull and Ambassador Thurston urging that the United States not recognize Martínez's reelection. Later in February a member of this same group explored with a Salvadoran resident in San Francisco the possibility of sending a delegation to Washington to talk with the secretary of state, the president, and/or representatives of Latin American democracies. Two of its members also tried unsuccessfully to enlist the aid of the United States Embassy in Mexico City in getting space for one of their compatriots on a plane to Havana, apparently part of an elaborate plan to persuade the Cuban government to bring the Salvadoran question before the Montevideo committee.[27]

Nothing came of this effort, but when Nelson Rockefeller visited El Salvador in March 1944 Banco Hipotecario President Hector Herrera made a last quixotic appeal. Implying that Agustín Alfaro, Guillermo Pérez, Jorge Sol Castellanos, Alfonso Rochac, and Mejoramiento Social President Mario Sol, among others, shared his views, he presented Rockefeller with a proposal that the United States, Mexico, and Colombia undertake to sponsor democratic governments in Central America and specifically that they persuade Martínez to accept a new constitution and to "leave established and in perfect operation the new order before the 31st of December next."[28]

In the face of this rising tide of opposition, Martínez tried to shore up his political support while attempting—with no great success—to repress the agitation. The government cracked down on its perennial adversary, the San Salvador press; sporadically increased security measures; rounded up suspects; and tried various milder tactics of intimidation.

Martínez's overtures to labor have been described in the preceding chapter. He also promised army officers a pay raise, which materialized, along with a number of promotions, in January 1944.[29] He reportedly told some officers that "the capitalists were against him" and that "all his plans for social betterment and economic improvement—including higher pay for the Army—[were] being blocked by the selfish and uncooperative attitude of the wealthy class which disapprove[d] of his fiscal plans," while at the same time "endeavoring to frighten the wealthier classes . . . by assuring them of the existence of a well-organized Communist movement which—if elections were to be held—would ally itself with the normal opposition and thus insure victory and consequently a Communist dominated government."[30]

On October 26, 1943, two days after the publication of the Acción Democratíca Salvadoreña petition to the Supreme Court, the government imposed prior censorship on newspapers and periodicals throughout the country.[31] The director of the National Police also met with the editors of the San Salvador newspapers to ensure publication of the Supreme Court's response, though the still defiant *Diario Latino* editors refused to print it so long as they could not publish "everything regarding FREEDOM OF ELECTIONS."[32]

Restrictions on what could appear in the press multiplied until the editor of *La Prensa Gráfica* complained at the end of February 1944, ". . . we have never been subjected to the shameful and humiliating police control of the present."[33] A list of "Censorship Prohibitions," presumably furnished to the United States Embassy by one of the newspapers, included prohibitions against publishing "anything about increasing wages," "the attempt against the President of Honduras," the "organization, functioning, operations or balances of banks, the Coffee Growers' Association, Coffee Company, Federation of Rural Credit Cooperatives, Cattle Growers' Cooperative, Sugarmakers' Cooperative, Cotton Growers' Cooperative, Sugar Growers' Cooperative and other similar [organizations]," "the scarcity of nickel coins," "the scarcity of gas," "matters that for whatever reason might be misinterpreted or might give rise to disorder," "anything that might be displeasing to the Spanish government or its representative in El Salvador," "the literacy campaign that LA PRENSA GRÁFICA announced," "the balsam industry," "news with scandalous headlines," "personal or insulting attacks," "criticisms of the Ministry of Public

Instruction," "articles with a political basis or that contain veiled attacks on the constituted authorities," "criticisms of the charitable centers and that are prejudicial to the work of the government," "criticisms or jokes that ridicule functionaries of the State," and "alarming or false articles." Newspapers were also forbidden "to give importance to labor matters," "to criticize the present system of education," "to promote religious controversies" and to "publish attacks against the Catholic Church."[34] In January 1944 the government ordered the closing of the newly established Press Club in San Salvador.[35]

Opposition initiatives also gave rise to waves of intensified police activity. Along with numerous arrests in August and September 1943, the National Police issued an order requiring drivers of private cars to inform the authorities of any trips they proposed to make outside of city or town limits between 6:00 P.M. and 6:00 A.M. The number of police and plainclothesmen in some parts of San Salvador doubled as surveillance of the growing number of Martínez's opponents increased.[36]

Following the presentation of the ADS petition to the Supreme Court, security agents searched homes and automobiles for copies of the petition and detained a few individuals, though the director general of the National Police reportedly dissuaded Martínez from ordering the arrest of all the signers by telling him "it would be impossible to carry . . . out" such an order.[37] Some signers of the petition were placed under "strict surveillance," some "found themselves unable to get passports or new automobile licenses, or telephones, [and] uniformed or secret police were stationed at the entrances of lawyers' offices in order to discourage timid clients. . . ."[38] The United States Embassy also heard of one signer who lost his job with the Public Works Department.[39]

Brief detentions of more people followed the December 11 demonstration.[40] Then, at the end of the year, a general roundup of opponents of Martínez—including several leading ADS members and *Diario Latino* editor Jorge Pinto—created an atmosphere of terror.[41] David Rosales's daughter recalled that men armed with machine guns surrounded the entire block where they lived when the police arrived to take her father into custody about eleven o'clock the night of December 20. Three men in plain clothes came to Max Patricio Brannon's house without a warrant sometime after midnight the same night, and he reported the arrest of several others by similar procedures. Acting United States Military Attaché George Massey reported the imprisonment of some forty "prominent citizens" by January 11.[42] The government accused some of those arrested of involvement in a plot to assassinate the president, and their friends expressed the fear that they might be executed.[43] Both the attorney who filed a writ of habeas corpus on behalf of several of the prisoners and the representative of the court subsequently appointed to investigate their detention experienced great difficulty in seeing them.[44]

On February 1 the director general of the National Police summoned some thirty university activists to police headquarters to demand that they desist from political activities "in return for which the Government would permit them to take their examinations." He obviously failed to intimidate them: the rambunctious young men created such an uproar in his office that he finally begged them to leave.[45]

To no one's surprise, the constituent assembly that convened on January 25, 1944, amended the constitution to give itself the power to elect the president of the republic for the period March 1, 1944–December 31, 1949, and on February 29 elected Martínez. But this long-expected constitutional revision was not the only one. New shock waves spread through Salvadoran society as citizens became aware of a series of constitutional amendments and laws published in the San Salvador newspapers on February 28 and 29.

Miguel Angel Alcaine, a prominent attorney whose clients included the Banco Hipotecario, charged that the revised constitution did away with the security of citizens' rights by leaving their precise definition to secondary laws enacted (and easily changed) by the National Legislative Assembly.[46] For example, the 1944 constituent assembly not only qualified the article guaranteeing freedom of assembly with a vague prohibition of "the establishment and activities of all organizations contrary to the democratic principles set forth in this constitution, as well as meetings which have the same purpose," but added, "A secondary law will determine the manner and conditions of exercising the rights of meeting and association." Similarly, a "special law" was to "determine the cases and manner of making . . . effective" the right to seek remedies for the infringement of constitutional rights in the courts.[47] Still another new provision read, "The laws will establish the cases and the form in which the Executive Power may withdraw, definitively or temporarily, the naturalization which foreigners obtain."

Sweeping economic provisions particularly alarmed agricultural and industrial entrepreneurs. The state was authorized to establish a monopoly of any "services that may be beneficial to the community and which the laws may determine." The Legislative Assembly could give the president "extraordinary powers to resolve at his discretion economic, political, and social problems that may present themselves," and public functionaries were relieved of legal liability for their actions in "carrying out a precept, mandate, or constitutional faculty."[48]

A new press law, obviously aimed at the journalists' boycott on reporting government moves, required newspapers "to report fully on Governmental activities, making known the dispositions which issue from the public authorities. . . ."[49]

Thus Martínez began his fourth term on March 1 in an atmosphere of heightened fear and resentment. At that point, how did he stand with the general public? Contemporary evidence on this subject comes from reports over a period of months by the staff of the United States Embassy, presumably based on conversations with Salvadorans. Although both the extent and reliability of their contacts are open to question, events bore out the picture that emerges from these reports.

Most characterized the "field, mill and shop laborers," who constituted the majority of the working population, as an undifferentiated mass, increasingly discontented with its lot, but not greatly interested in who occupied the presidency. Writing in January 1944, Vice Consul H. Gardner Ainsworth interpreted the feeling of the "laboring class" toward the Martínez regime as ill-defined but negative. On the one hand, he saw it as "disorganized and divided in opinion as to who is responsible for its condition" and more hostile to "the upper class of 'capitalistas' " than to the government. On the other, he noted that "few workers have forgotten the 'massacre' " of 1932. The "lower class," he wrote, "fears and distrusts Government *per se*. . . . Much of its antipathy toward the wealthy . . . turns into political opposition to a Government which has neither done much for labor nor against the 'capitalistas.' . . . [I]t is now widely felt that the President is himself a 'capitalista' and is not personally inclined to help labor." As to Martínez's prolabor protestations, Ainsworth concluded that "evidence indicates that the lower class very widely labels them as propaganda and questions or disbelieves them. The great majority of workers . . . can see no material improvement in their prospects or way of living."[50]

In February, Vice Consul Joseph Maleady wrote, "Some people who are connected very closely with the lower class insist that this group is fed up with the President and believe that he has been in power long enough and should now step down."[51]

The feelings of citizens who stood higher on the social ladder came into clearer focus in these reports. In assessing the sources of support for the April 2 revolt, United States Vice Consul Overton Ellis had "no doubt that the great majority, probably about 80 to 90 percent of the artisans, mechanics and such skilled labor class, were thoroughly sympathetic to the revolutionists." The evidence of hostility to the government on the part of labor organizations (see pages 35, 41, 44), which probably consisted largely of skilled workers, supports this assessment.

Ellis's conclusion that "probably ninety percent of the professional class, lawyers and doctors in particular," and some "75 or 80 percent" of "the middle and white collar classes" favored the insurrection finds support in the unanimous reports of his colleagues that the strongest opposition to Martínez centered in the professions. As Ainsworth observed, these latter groups had "almost no direct economic grievances against the Government." Their hostility reflected opposition to the president's repressive policies and his manipulation of the constitution to perpetuate his rule, as well as their own reformist idealism and aspirations for political office or influence.[52]

The business community did have economic grievances, and Massey's assertion that the "middle classes . . . would benefit by less economic suppression under [a] democratic system" applied primarily to entrepreneurs, particularly would-be promoters of industry. Ainsworth heard charges from members of the "upper class" that Martínez was "personally anti-capital" and had "prevent[ed] the industrialization of the country by failing to provide an atmosphere of security for capital investment, which would involve principally the announcement of a definite industrial policy and a revision of the tax structure to assure adequate industrial profits."[53] One embassy observer thought that almost all "property owners" opposed the government because of its "socialistic tendencies" and that businessmen saw its "attitude toward 'big business'" as "one of bare tolerance," which would probably worsen once Martínez had secured another term.[54]

In addition to these general considerations, the large proportion of El Salvador's merchants and industrialists who were of foreign origin had reason to resent the discriminatory policies of the government and to fear further attacks. According to one observer, "The Chinese and Palestinian . . . colonies in particular [were] becoming alarmed." Ellis concluded that "most foreign business men . . . felt that their livelihood was threatened by the policies of the Martínez government" and sympathized with the April insurrection. Although most of those whose attitudes he specifically described remained inactive and affected neutrality, reports that he considered reliable indicated that three foreign cotton manufacturers—one Spaniard and two Palestinian families—contributed substantial sums of money to the revolutionary cause.[55]

In spite of the growing antagonism between Martínez and the top-ranking financial and landowning elite during 1943, barely two months before the insurrection Maleady thought that "the wealthy class . . . as a whole would like to see [Martínez] continue in power. The only opposition from this group is oral and probably would be centered in the city of Santa Ana."[56] He may simply have been ill informed; United States Embassy correspondence revealed very little knowledge of the developing conspiracy to overthrow the president. Embassy observers generally felt, however, that the activities of the constituent assembly, and especially the February 1944 revisions of the constitution, greatly intensified middle- and upper-class opposition to the government. "For the first time," Thurston concluded, "the business and capitalist elements felt themselves directly menaced by the Martínez regime—and in consequence, also for the first time, the . . . opposition found itself with new and strong allies and money."[57] Winnal Dalton told Maleady on February 23 that "several wealthy persons here (a Dutchman, a Spaniard, several Salvadorans and various other individuals) are ready to put up large sums of money to overthrow Martínez if the present 'Constitution' being drawn up by the Constituent Assembly is passed as it now stands."[58] It may well be that a good many hitherto apolitical citizens became aroused, and "oral" opposition turned into support for armed revolt in the month between the publication of the constitutional revisions and the outbreak of the military insurrection. At any rate, Ellis's analysis of the attitudes of twenty-four leading families at the time of the revolt revealed only two as definitely pro-Martínez and two as indifferent.[59]

Evidence regarding the attitude of the Church is inconclusive. One informant closely connected with the Martínez regime recalled that it enjoyed good relations with the Catholic hierarchy except for a few individuals of liberal political inclinations, and Military Attaché Baldwin reported in 1943 that "the close cooperation between the government and the church insures that any reasonable measure of either will receive the full support of the other. . . ."[60] However, another contemporary observer remarked, "Although the clergy apparently gets along with the President and desires a strong hand in the Government they would undoubtedly prefer a Catholic as President," and Martínez had in fact given them some cause for displeasure.[61]

In connection with a revision of the curriculum of the nation's public schools, Martínez personally wrote the program of moral education, which embodied his own theosophical beliefs. When the program appeared in the schools in 1940, the bishop of San Miguel wrote an open letter of protest to the undersecretary of public instruction, which circulated in pamphlet form until government agents seized the copies.[62] Spokesmen for the Church subsequently complained about the theosophical tendencies in printed materials that the government sent to private schools and other forms of interference in their operation, as well as Martínez's attacks on Catholic doctrine in his weekly speeches to the Pro-Patria party, the practice of theosophic rites in the presidential house, and pressure on public employees to embrace theosophism.[63] Moreover, the constitution of 1939 not only carried over the stringently anticlerical provisions of its predecessor but added a provision that "ministers of religious cults must abstain from putting their spiritual authority at the service of political interests" and brought education in private schools under the "oversight and control of the state."[64] In January 1944 the Salvadoran bishops petitioned the constituent assembly for a number of revisions in the constitution to no avail.[65]

Within the armed forces, according to Massey's analysis, the president's support came from "Army officers who were 'made' by Martínez"; the opposition included some members of this group who favored some other officer as dictator and "Army officers who owe Martínez nothing and would like to see a democratic system established, with promotions based on merit."[66] Although Robert Elam was right in concluding that the division cut across differences of age and rank, the proportion of junior and senior officers on each side differed significantly. For months before the uprising United States Embassy observers concurred in the belief that most senior officers were loyal to Martínez, while consistently reporting varying degrees of discontent among junior officers.[67] Massey heard from one of the latter that "a majority of the junior officers are against the President's continuance in office" and accepted this assessment.[68]

Thurston, reviewing the April insurrection after its defeat, noted that the conspirators had "reached an agreement with a considerable portion of the armed forces—almost exclusively, however, the younger element," a conclusion that finds support in available biographical information about the officers who became actively involved in the revolt. A high proportion of those mentioned as participants in various accounts of the insurrection and/or on lists of refugees after its failure were lieutenants. Of twenty whose ages appeared, only three were over forty; most were in their twenties. Although the National Police and National Guard remained loyal to the government (or at least passive) during the insurrection, one informant estimated that 70 to 80 percent of the army supported the revolt, and Ambassador Thurston thought it probably "involved the major portion of the officer class."[69]

The months of preparation for that insurrection came to fruition a month after the inauguration of Martínez's new term as president. On Palm Sunday, April 2, 1944, with the top officials of the administration away from the capital for the Holy Week holiday, the strategic First Infantry and Second Artillery regiments of San Salvador and the Santa Ana garrison took up arms against the government. Rebel officers took control of the air force, the state radio station (YSP), the telegraph offices of San Salvador and Santa Ana, and the Santa Ana police headquarters. The revolutionary command wired the remaining garrisons throughout the country, assuring each that all the others supported the revolt and demanding their support as well. The commander in Ahuachapán reluctantly acceded.[70] In Santa Ana, civilians responded to the revolt with a "huge demonstration" in which those assembled deposed the city council and elected a new one.[71]

In a premature proclamation of victory, the rebels at station YSP apparently named Arturo Romero as their leader and/or the new president of El Salvador, although accounts differ as to precisely what they said.[72] At any rate, the sudden prominence of the popular young physician became a significant factor in subsequent developments.

The insurrection quickly turned into a tragicomedy of overconfidence and bungling on the part of the rebels, division and distrust between various officers and between military and civilian leaders, and possibly even treachery. Martínez, who was vacationing at the port city of La Libertad when the uprising began, heard about it from the rebel radio broadcast, which provided him with the invaluable information that Fort Zapote and the police barracks in San Salvador remained loyal to the government. The detachment sent out to capture the president missed him on the road between La Libertad and San Salvador, and according to an eyewitness account, his car, accompanied by "two jeep-loads of soldiers, and a station-wagon of police," entered San Salvador and reached the police headquarters unmolested in broad daylight less than two hours later.[73] The air force, trying unsuccessfully to bomb the police barracks, started a fire that destroyed more than a square block of downtown

San Salvador.[74] The next day loyal troops from eastern El Salvador recaptured the airfield, leaving the pilots "flying around in the air with no place to land."[75] By the morning of April 4 the fighting had ended, with all of the rebel leaders captured or in flight.

The revolt might have been remembered only for the havoc it wreaked on the city of San Salvador were it not for the government's response. Martínez proclaimed martial law throughout the country and imposed a curfew on San Salvador for some weeks after the end of the revolt. The police required persons desiring to travel to other parts of the republic to obtain "safe conducts." According to Massey, shots were "heard in all parts of the city" every night, and the police killed a number of people who were on the street during the curfew.[76] Several social clubs were shut down, and labor organizations ceased to function.[77]

In a thorough and vindictive crackdown on suspected opponents of the president, the director of the Escuela Militar received orders to dismiss six cadets related to persons implicated in the insurrection.[78] The United States Embassy heard reports that "no person who signed the petition to the Supreme Court [could] obtain a permit to enter or leave San Salvador" and that Martínez had issued orders that none were "to be permitted to register deeds or issue any other legal or medical document," which, Thurston commented, would "destroy the livelihood of many of the professional classes." The police searched houses without warrants, and Banco Hipotecario President Hector Herrera told the ambassador that, for the first time, government agents were investigating withdrawals from bank accounts, "undoubtedly," Thurston observed, "to assist in checking against those suspected of having contributed funds for the uprising. . . ."[79]

A new wave of arrests resulted in the detention of several prominent citizens of Santa Ana and a leading Palestinian textile manufacturer, as well as "five lawyers connected indirectly with the [mortgage] bank."[80] Some newspaper owners and journalists were also imprisoned and others went into hiding or found asylum in foreign embassies, with the result that *La Prensa Gráfica, El Diario Latino,* and *El Diario de Hoy* all suspended publication from April 2 until the day Martínez resigned.[81]

This was not all. Only one of the military officers and civilians caught plotting against Martínez during the 1930s had been executed.[82] But the extraordinary council of war impaneled to try the insurrectionists of April 2 condemned ten officers to death within hours after it began its proceedings on April 9. The next morning San Salvadorans just returned from the Easter holiday could hear the sound of the firing squad at work in the city cemetery. In the next two weeks the council of war sentenced twenty-four more officers and ten civilians to death, most (including Agustín Alfaro and Arturo Romero) *in absentia*. Three officers and one civilian were subsequently shot, making a total of forty-four death sentences and fourteen known executions.[83]

Moreover, many believed that prisoners died at the hands of the authorities without benefit of judicial proceedings, and Thurston considered some of these allegations "credible." A Canadian journalist reported early in May that she had heard estimates (which she thought "probably high") that as many as two hundred " 'executions,' official and unofficial," had taken place.[84] Numerous tales of atrocities and general accusations of "inhuman treatment" of prisoners circulated.[85] Of these, two stories merit particular attention because of the wide publicity they received and their probable impact on Salvadoran public opinion.

The *Newsweek* account of the April insurrection claimed that "sixty-two truckloads of peasants on their way to San Salvador to demonstrate were ambushed, machine-gunned, and buried in trenches." This story undoubtedly arose from the bloody ambush at San Andrés of a rebel contingent from Santa Ana, consisting largely of armed civilians. One report of the ambush that reached Thurston claimed that some two hundred members of this group were shot and buried in ditches after they had surrendered and were en route to San Salvador as prisoners, which explains the *Newsweek* version. No mention of any such mass execution appeared in any of the many accounts of the insurrection published after the fall of Martínez, including an interview with a member of the ill-fated Santa Ana contingent. Nevertheless, Massey heard from a foreign resident of San Salvador whom he considered reliable that the Salvadoran lower class had "been affected by recent wanton killings of unarmed civilians in the fields of San Andrés."[86] Thus, although the story was untrue, in April and May 1944 many Salvadorans undoubtedly believed it.

The more credible story of the heroism of Victor Marín, the only civilian participant in the revolt to die before the firing squad, originated with the priest who gave him the last rites. According to the report of an anonymous Salvadoran:

> One of the heroes of this revolt was tortured the whole night—from six in the evening until ten the following morning, when he was shot. When he was brought out to be shot, both his arms had been broken, one knee smashed to splinters, his right hand was a bloody pulp. His finger-nails and toe-nails had been pulled out—wood splinters had been driven into the tips of his fingers, and they had filed his teeth. They had fractured his collar-bone; there was only a bloody, gaping hole where an eye had once been.
>
> The priest who was attending him during the last moments noticed his trembling and asked, "My son, are you afraid to die?" This boy who the day before was filled with life, whose body had been smashed and twisted beyond repair, answered, "No, father. It is only my body which trembles. Not my spirit."[87]

The violence of the repression inspired widespread fear, but it also solidified opposition to Martínez. Of particular significance, some observers believed it had aroused lower-class Salvadorans, the group that had appeared least committed to the opposition before the insurrection. At the end of April, Massey reported that "market people, shopkeepers and civilians on the street are openly decrying the executions and tortures. . . ." [88] Members of the clergy joined in the general effort to save fugitives, and citizens of all ranks, from market vendors to the archbishop of San Salvador, pleaded for an end to the executions.

From beyond the borders of El Salvador, the Venezuelan Chamber of Deputies, Latin American labor leader Vicente Lombardo Toledano, and a group of Latin American physicians resident in Baltimore, Maryland, sent similar petitions. Editorials attacking the "blood bath" appeared in Panamanian, Venezuelan, and Ecuadoran newspapers, and no less a celebrity than the Chilean poet Pablo Neruda raised his voice in protest.[89]

Confidence in the president's ability to govern began to erode. U.S. Ambassador Thurston reported on April 10:

> . . . it may be difficult for Martínez to maintain his regime and there are reports that it may be urged upon him that he deposit the Presidency with a member of the government (under guarantees as to his person and property) and retire. This procedure has been mentioned to me by [Hector] Herrera . . . and I believe he may have submitted it to Martínez.[90]

Indeed, Herrera subsequently reported that he had called upon Martínez on April 12 with a view to making such a suggestion but gave up the idea when the president asserted truculently, "Whether people like it or not, I am going to stay." [91]

5. The Civic Strike

> . . . Perhaps never have Salvadorans been able to raise their heads with greater right and justice, boasting of their citizenship with legitimate pride before the eyes of the civilized world, of this poor world shaken by war and hatred, which turns its excited eyes toward this little bit of American territory to contemplate with sympathy and admiration the heroic act of a brave and determined people which has risen up as a single man to defend its rights and reconquer its lost liberty.
>
> The most beautiful and admirable thing about this civic and patriotic movement was the participation of all the people of El Salvador, spontaneously and unanimously, without distinctions of any kind: rich and poor, professional and student, industrialist and worker, landowner and peasant, merchant and clerk, man and woman, youth and child. . . . All together—including the foreigner who now feels Salvadoran—have given a demonstration of what a brave and united people can do.[1]

Contemporary observers had no doubt that Martínez's opponents would soon make another attempt to unseat him, but no one anticipated the form the new insurrection would take. The rumors and speculation that flourished during April 1944 focused on the possibility of renewed fighting or the assassination of the president.[2]

What, then, accounts for the civic strike? Where did the idea originate and how was the strike organized? Who supported it and why? Following an examination of these questions, this chapter concludes with an account of how the strike developed. The following two chapters will examine the response of the Martínez government to the new insurrection, the process by which that regime came to an end, and finally, the question of foreign intervention. To follow these diverse threads in relation to each other, the reader may wish to consult the appended chronology for the period April 17–May 11.

Ironically, an exiled Salvadoran journalist, Joaquín Castro Canizales, had suggested a civic strike (though he did not call it that) to overthrow Martínez some months earlier. When José Luís Boza, one of the Acción Democrática Salvadoreña group, brought a copy of the "Manifesto to the Salvadoran People" to Castro Canizales in Costa Rica, probably in July 1943, the latter took the opportunity to expound the idea of a general withdrawal of cooperation from the government and gave Boza a written proposal to take back to El Salvador.

"Toward Civil Disobedience: My Message to the Salvadoran People" began with the assertion that other dictators—Manuel Estrada Cabrera of Guatemala, Gerardo Machado of Cuba, and Benito Mussolini of Italy—had fallen before the collective resistance of their subjects. It continued:

> There is a decent way to achieve the overthrow of the government of Martínez, without the country's suffering any damage to its international credit. This solution is that which has come to be called PASSIVE RESISTANCE or CIVIL DISOBEDIENCE. In what does this consist? In that every citizen who at present is a piece of the administrative and economic gearing of the country ceases by his own will to be one. This was how the "ABC" of Cuba brought down, in 1933, the dictatorship of Machado, and the creator of this policy, Mahatma Ghandi [*sic*], has achieved great conquests, in this form, for his people. With this system organized workers of the world are obtaining economic advantages. And when this system has been extended to all human activities, then useless bloodshed will have been avoided.

Castro Canizales then proposed the "secret organization" of the army, the police, and the National Guard so that they would not obey any orders "that would tend to disorganize the popular movement" once the strike began; of public employees, with a view to shutting down the university, the schools, the postal system, the telegraph and wireless services, the ministries, and municipal governments; and of commercial employees, drivers, railroad operators, and other workers, in order to bring about a "complete paralysis of all activities." The plan further envisaged the creation of a finance committee to raise the necessary funds and "Popular Brigades" to prevent strikebreaking. (Castro Canizales did not say how strikebreaking, often a cause of violence in other strike situations, could be prevented without bloodshed.) Finally, he suggested that workers prepare for the strike by saving enough money to live on for one or two months if necessary and that each household stockpile everything essential for survival.

Boza objected that this strategy would take too long "and that 'they' planned to use more rapid methods," a reference to the planned military insurrection.[3] The proposal evidently reached the anti-Martínez conspirators in El Salvador, however, for the leaflets "Salvadoran People" and "Contributions for the Pro-Patria" echoed certain of its key concepts.[4] This raises a question as to whether the idea of a civic strike figured in the strategy of the opposition leaders.

A few fragments of contemporary evidence suggest that it did. After the strike began, some participants in the April 2 uprising claimed they had expected all along that the armed revolt "would be but the spark that would set off the powder train" of civilian action.[5] The Federal Bureau of Investigation agent attached to the United States Embassy heard from two unidentified individuals whom he considered reliable that Agustín Alfaro, Francisco Guillermo Pérez, Jorge Sol Castellanos, and other unknown persons might have planned the general strike

> before they became aware of the fact that they would be able to obtain the cooperation of the army in staging a revolution against MARTÍNEZ. According to these sources, the plans for the strike . . . were dropped when it became evident that the military men would assist in staging an armed rebellion . . . [but] held in reserve in the event that the military men should fail the civilians.[6]

United States Vice Consuls Overton Ellis and Joseph Maleady believed, possibly on the basis of the same information, that Alfaro had "left behind" an organization "which was the major directive force in the . . . general strike and civilian passive resistance movement" and identified Carlos Aviles, who had replaced Alfonso Rochac as manager of the Banco Hipotecario, as "one of . . . the guiding spirits behind the strike."[7] If there was such an organization, however, it was the best-kept secret of the entire anti-Martínez movement and has remained one for over forty years.

The weight of the evidence supports the contention of one participant in the events of May 1944 "that the strike . . . definitely *was not organized in advance by any group* and that it had no particular leaders until its later stages."[8] No opposition propaganda that appeared between September 1943 and late April 1944 mentioned the subject of passive resistance, and no evidence exists of any attempt to organize or prepare for it during that period. Carlos Aviles himself told Maleady that "the strike was organized solely by students," and some participants interviewed in 1976–78 indicated that the students had stimulated a multifarious effort in which a number of groups worked independently.[9]

Two developments gave impetus to the new insurrectionary movement. On April 17 the university reopened after a week-long extension of the Easter vacation.[10] Also on that day, word reached San Salvador that Arturo Romero, already under a sentence of death, had been captured at the Honduran frontier. He was severely wounded in the process and remained in the hospital in San Miguel.[11]

The news of Romero's capture produced an immediate reaction. A "delegation of young ladies who claimed to speak for the 'society of San Salvador' " appeared at the United States Embassy on April 17, presumably to ask for the ambassador's intercession. The diplomatic corps, which was meeting at the embassy, responded by calling upon the president in a body that evening, urging once again that he adopt a policy of clemency toward the rebels.[12]

At the university on April 18 or 19, according to one contemporary account, "all of the medical students arrived . . . wearing black ties to signify that they were in mourning because of the capture and wounding of Dr. ARTURO ROMERO and also because of the executions carried out by the government." A minor confrontation between policemen and a group of students on Wednesday, April 19, caused the rector to suspend classes for the rest of the week "in order that things might quiet down a little bit." [13]

An unidentified group called for a demonstration on Sunday, April 23, variously reported as being against the execution of Romero and in favor of clemency for all civilians imprisoned as a result of the April 2 insurrection. Official sources announced that no demonstration would be permitted, and no contemporary evidence that it took place has come to light. However, one person interviewed in 1978 recalled hearing that the police had prevented people who gathered for that purpose from marching.[14] The following vivid personal recollection may have referred to the April 23 event, though the writer was uncertain of the date.

> There was a large demonstration of women and children for the release of political prisoners . . . [which marched] from the Central Penitentiary . . . to Independence Avenue. You could shake hands with several prisoners who extended theirs from several windows of the Penitentiary, but very few [prisoners] were seen, for the others were on a side in which the windows were very high. But it was in vain; it was not a success because although at first they were allowed to walk without hindrance there were [then] several shots to disperse the demonstration. Many women whose sons or husbands had been killed or were prisoners marched in it.[15]

During the week between April 17 and April 23, students took the first steps toward the organization of the civic strike. The process by which they did so remains somewhat unclear, for the evidence consists almost entirely of the recollections of participants interviewed more than thirty years after the events, and no two told the same story.

Fabio Castillo, then a medical student, recalled that the idea of a strike first came up in informal discussions among students who knew each other through previous opposition activities and came together with the intention of organizing an effort to rescue Arturo Romero. The first concrete action originated in the law school, probably on April 17. According to Reynaldo Galindo Pohl, then a seventh-year law student, the sixth-year students assembled on the day the university reopened and called a meeting of delegates from each class to consider the question of a university strike. These delegates reached no agreement—Galindo Pohl remembered his class as being less enthusiastic than the sixth-year students—but they did call a further meeting of representatives from all the university faculties. Apparently they also sent representatives to the other schools, for Jorge Bustamante remembered attending a meeting of two delegates from each class in the medical school, at which Galindo Pohl and another law student spoke.

The next step was the election of either a small central committee to lay plans for the strike or of some forty delegates—two from each class in each faculty (except that of dentistry, which for some reason did not participate in this phase of the organizing)—which then chose the central committee. Reports as to the precise composition of the latter vary. Bustamante remembered it as having four members: himself representing the medical students, Jorge Mazzini of the law school, Raúl Castellanos of the engineering school, and Mario Colorado of the school of pharmacy, each of whom then named a subcommittee of students within his own faculty known only to each other. Other accounts, however, indicated that the central committee itself was secret and established Castillo and Galindo Pohl as members of the inner circle.

The date the central committee began work also remains in some doubt. Castillo remembered it as having been selected only after the university student body voted to strike on April 24. According to Bustamante, however, the central committee called the student body meeting, as well as meetings of each individual faculty, on that day, by which time it had already begun to make contacts outside the university. A leaflet that he identified as the central committee's first publication bore the date of April 19.[16] "Let us do something," it urged,

> but something effective, so as not to permit the blood of loved ones . . . to continue to be spilled with the aid of our passivity.
>
> . . . Let us unite in a single purpose[,] . . . the shaking off of the yoke of oppression and of treason that we have borne patiently for the space of twelve bitter years. Let us look for the means necessary to destroy to its foundations the bloody and destructive work of the jackal, Martínez. We are not in a position to provoke a revolution, nor is it fitting that more innocent blood be shed. But there are methods, which however unlawful they may be, could be considered honorable and praiseworthy. . . . We are fighting with an astute and sagacious man[;] . . . then to this astuteness and sagacity let us oppose ours, which because it is that of an entire people which demands vengeance and which in other epochs has demonstrated virility in similar situations, will now take by force that which has been usurped, ITS LIBERTIES. . . .
>
> . . . Conduct yourself like a man and not an animal, do not allow the yoke of the TYRANT to be placed on you. OUR WATCHWORD IS: EVERYTHING [NECESSARY] TO THROW OUT THE TYRANT.[17]

Some evidence exists for simultaneous organizing outside this structure. José Colorado, a law student who stayed away from his own school that week for fear of being apprehended in connection with the April 2 insurrection, thought the idea of the civic strike originated with a group consisting of both students and nonstudents that met at the engineering school to consider protest action against the executions. He remembered a number of people independently organizing their own committees to promote the strike.[18]

April 24 brought the last round of executions. On that day perhaps half the

San Salvador, abril 19, de 1944.

SALVADOREÑOS:

El sad de sangre que devora al Tirano Martínez no está saciada todavía con la inmolación de tantos héroes de la joventud salvadoreña. Hagamos algo, pero algo efectivo, que no permita que la sangre de seres quéridos, esposos, hijos, padres o amigos se siga derramando al amparo de nuestra pasividad. Todos sabemos que la tranquilidad aparente del país es ficticia. El pueblo entero de El Salvador se encuentra de duelo, son contados los hogares en donde no se ha derramado sangre, en todas las clases sociales se regleja el odio, la protesta absoluta por la abominable sangría que está siendo objeto nuestro indefenso pueblo.-

Es resible que pretendamos en un país libre, que hayamos declarado la guerra a los Dictadores de Europa y que nos contemos entre los Demócratas. Donde está nuestra Democracia? En la prensa libre? No. Los salvadoreños solo podemos leer los diarios que el Tirano paga y mantiene para que adulen y que pretenden tenernos engañados y aislados de la realidad, pero todos sabemos cual es la disgraciada realidad. No tenemos libertad de pensamiento, ni libertad de palabra. No podemos leer siquiera lo que los otros países comentan acerca de nuestra ridicula y triste situación, porque confiscan en el correo todo lo que no le conviene al dictador. Y estamos en un país demócrata, en el cual el pueblo eleje a su presidente cada cuatro años.-

Todo esto y otros hechos má exijen un castigo ejemplar para el presidente Martínez y sanciones fuertes para sus esbirros-Unanomos en un solo propósito y que esta sea el sacudirnos con hombría el yugo de la opresión y de la traición que por espacio de doce amargos años hemos llevado con paciencia. Busquemos los medios necesarios para destruir hasta cimientos la obra destructora y sangrienta del chacal Martinéz. No estamos en condiciones de probocar una revolución ni conviene que se derrame más sangre inocente. Pero hay medios que por ilícitos que sean, podrían clificarse de honrados y cables si con ellos se trata de destruir la casta opresora de los Martínez. Estamos luchando con un hombre astuto y sagáz (como todo mal curcucho) pues bien, a esta astucia y sagacidad la nuestra que por ser la de un pueblo entero que clama venganza y que en otra épocas ha demostrado virilidad en situaciones semejantes, ahora tomará por la fuerza lo que le ha sido usurpado, SUS LIBERTADES.-

No pretendemos impresionar al público con una obra de literatura, sino solamente dar a conocer lo que sentimos en estos momentos aciagos que atravezamos.

LOS HIJOS DEL PUEBLOS

Nota: Sea Vd. compatriota, un hombre limpio de conciencia, copie este escrito y hagalo circular profundamente. Portese como hombre y no como animal, no se deje poner el yugo del TIRANO.-NUESTRA CONSIGNA ES: TODO HASTA BOTAR AL TIRANO.-

First Leaflet Issued by the Student Strike Committee

student body returned to the university, in the words of one of their number, "no longer as slaves but as free citizens conscious of the imperious and urgent duty which we had to the soil that saw us come into the world free; and we decided in a great and solemn Assembly to declare ourselves on STRIKE as a protest and homage to all those victims of April 2. . . ."[19]

An anonymous leaflet informed the public of that decision in these words:

We, the Salvadoran university students, on Monday, April 24, have decreed a suspension of all student activities in view of the present national events, which are cause for profound grief for every Salvadoran citizen. . . . This suspension of activities extends to the hospital work of medical students, attendance in the courthouse by students of jurisprudence, the employment of engineering students in Development, Public Works and Mejoramiento Social, and attendance at the Dental Clinic by students of Dentistry.

Here is our watchword:

TO THE UNIVERSITY STRIKE FOR THE DIGNITY OF THE FATHERLAND.[20]

The forty-odd representatives of the various faculties—who evidently continued to function as a cadre, sharing organizing responsibilities with the central committee—also met that day or the next and "swore . . . by the Constitution of 1886, by the memory of the founding fathers, and by that which each one most honored, to maintain the strike, extend it, and not to return to the University until our country should recover the liberties that had been trodden under foot."

These words suggest that some students already envisioned a more far-reaching movement than a university strike in protest against the executions. Galindo Pohl recalled that the unsuccessful university strike of 1938–39 had convinced him, as well as other students, that "strikes of intellectuals were merely symbolic, that they could serve to initiate wider movements, but that by themselves they were not sufficient to win political battles."[21]

As Bustamante and Castillo remembered it, however, the idea of a national general strike to compel Martínez to resign evolved in meetings of the central committee after April 24. Bustamante had heard of Castro Canizales's proposal, though he did not see it. He attributed the idea of closing down San Salvador to Castillo, who he thought had heard or read something about the civic strikes against Machado and President Carlos Ibáñez of Chile (1931).[22] According to Castillo:

. . . Within the student strike committee . . . I proposed the idea of the general strike, which naturally was rejected at first because they thought it was too great a task for students. Nevertheless, because of the national conditions, I maintained that it was possible. . . .

. . . The fundamental thesis was the following: General Martínez dominated the Salvadoran scene militarily and by force. . . . General Martínez, I maintained, was an individual who was capable of waging war without moderation. If he confronted a group or one confronted him, he would fire on all, and he was capable of defeating anyone militarily. Therefore it was necessary to organize a popular movement that did not confront Martínez, so that he would not have anyone to shoot. This led to the conclusion that the movement should be a movement not of the streets, but of hiding. And the *huelga de brazos caídos* emerged. Nobody do anything. Simply stay in his house without going into the streets, so that there would not be possibilities for repression.[23]

The students thus chose a nonviolent strategy for purely pragmatic reasons: they lacked the means to do anything else. Nevertheless it was a clear and conscious choice. Their thinking, Bustamante said, was that "the use of nonviolence would attract more supporters than if violence were used, and besides, we knew that if things became violent then the army would take a hand in the matter, would dissolve the strike by pure force." When one of the group suggested sniping at the police, the others squelched the idea.[24] Explicit contemporary evidence on this point came from a member of the United States Embassy staff whom the "Comité Estudiantil" (Student Committee) asked to tell the ambassador that "their revolt is a pacifist one. They plan to paralyze the country and thus force the President to relinquish power. They do not wish to see more blood shed."[25]

The following excerpts from an undated compilation of material, which evidently circulated as a leaflet or leaflets, shed light on the students' thinking about nonviolent resistance (as well as the sentiments to which they appealed), probably at an early stage in the organization of the civic strike.

> By means of a GENERAL PASSIVE resistance, a systematic and massive ORGANIZED PASSIVE OPPOSITION, and by means of STRIKES, great tyrants of the stature of Machado and Ibáñez fell. The Salvadoran people can and MUST do likewise, supporting in every way the students and our honorable and valiant soldiers, . . . in order to hasten the fall of the despot and thief. . . . Moreover it is our great duty to do so to show solidarity and demonstrate our sympathy and GRATITUDE [to] so many mothers, widows, children, brothers and sisters etc. of the many *patriots* who have already been shot. . . .
>
> . . . LET NO ONE GIVE THE GOVERNMENT ANY COOPERATION. In this way the TYRANT will fall as others fell, for without the cooperation of Salvadorans Max. H. Martínez will be unable to continue governing. Let us show the tyrant that there is a great abyss between him and the people, let us make him feel alone, as isolated as possible. . . .
>
> Let *no one* go to the *movies* . . . ; all the theaters of the country are operated by Max. H. Martínez.
>
> LET NO ONE buy more LOTTERY TICKETS (not one more). . . .
>
> LET NO ONE pay one's MUNICIPAL TAXES (or at least may each one delay as much as one can). . . .
>
> LET US PRAY daily for the soul[s] of the fallen, whose heroism and composure should serve as encouragement and example for us. . . . Let us also pray for our humble, holy and beloved archbishop, who has now been humiliated several times by the tyrant, for Max. H. Martínez (the Theosophist) does not believe in God and is a crafty persecutor of our beloved Catholic Religion.
>
> . . . This call to this SACRED NATIONAL CRUSADE is directed to all the great Salvadoran family in the whole country: STUDENT[S]—NURSES—DOCTORS—LAWYERS—ENGINEERS—DRIVERS—EMPLOYEES—etc. . . . and to the *patriotic* and *brave* MARKET WOMEN *of all the markets of the country*.
>
> RISE ALL GOOD SALVADORANS, if we want to be free we must each put our grain of sand in the struggle.

> Let us all unite in a GREAT PASSIVE RESISTANCE. . . .
> May we carry on a constant and TENACIOUS OPPOSITION TO THE GOVERNMENT[.]
> May we carry out the greatest *sabotage* possible in all that which can affect the government directly or indirectly. . . .
> Let powerful public employees resign from their positions as soon as possible, let NO ONE accept the vacancies at any price.
> Let no one buy either Diario Nuevo or Gran Diario [the progovernment newspapers]. . . .
> Let us all wear for a long time some SIGN OF MOURNING . . . and of course—NO MORE PARTIES OR DANCES, because we are in mourning and in struggle with the tyrant. . . .[26]

The writers obviously saw noncooperation as the principal means of bringing down Martínez, though it is unclear what they meant by "sabotage," and they also called for symbolic protest. The concept of noncooperation put forward embraced several lines of action in addition to going on strike: boycotts, tax resistance, and resignations from government office.

There is little evidence, however, of any organized effort to promote these other forms of resistance. North American news magazines, whose coverage of events in El Salvador was not altogether trustworthy, reported that "women wore mourning in the streets" and that people refused to buy lottery tickets or progovernment newspapers or to frequent the movie theaters. José Quetglas also reported the boycott of progovernment newspapers and noted that some women stationed themselves in front of the theaters to keep people from entering them.[27] One reporter also observed a spontaneous boycott of an army band concert in the central plaza of San Salvador, "the swarms of hawkers and loiterers who usually infest the place ostentatiously packing up and leaving when the band struck up."[28] Only a handful of resignations from government positions were reported, and nothing was done about tax refusal.[29]

The student strike committee may have thought these were all good ideas, but it focused its energy on bringing about a simultaneous general shutdown in San Salvador, originally scheduled for May 1 but later postponed to May 5 to allow more time for organizing.[30] It gave priority to closing the banks and paralyzing transportation, which it viewed as "the Achilles heel of the Salvadoran economy." If they could achieve this, the students thought, other sectors of the economy would also support the strike. Moreover, since the committee had no means of communication outside San Salvador, it counted on the failure of the trains to appear on schedule to carry the message of the strike throughout the country. It also attached major importance to the psychological impact of closing commerce and of a strike by physicians, who enjoyed great public respect. In particular, the students felt that the loss of medical services and the closing of drugstores would push the general public to take a stand, either declaring for Martínez or demanding his resignation.[31]

Evidence as to what the committee intended to do about the most essential services is mixed. Galindo Pohl told the writer it never considered cutting off electricity, water, or food supplies. In an interview published two years after the strike, he explained that "it was natural: the people could not struggle for a long time without the essentials of life." Indeed, according to one account the strike leaders "had difficulty persuading some of the smaller food stores to keep open to provide the population with essentials."

Bustamante, however, recalled that the bakers and the proprietors of the small grocery stores had agreed to strike as a last resort, in the event that the other strikes did not bring down Martínez. A leaflet that evidently appeared after some shops had closed listed both the bakers and the employees of the electric light company among the groups that were "about to strike and whose cooperation is almost indispensable to the movement," although the bakeries apparently did not close and electric power was not interrupted.[32]

The strategy of this insurrection excluded street demonstrations so as not to provoke confrontations with government forces. However, student organizers did collaborate with the widows of some of the executed officers in planning a mass for the martyrs of the April uprising in the downtown Church of the Rosary on May 5, which served to rally the public behind the movement.[33]

As the organization of the strike went forward, a steady stream of leaflets spread news of the developing revolt and called for support. Although Bustamante remembered mimeographing some of these in an attic, and the students eventually found a printer, the leaflets that have survived are almost all typewritten (usually carbon copies), bearing a request to the reader to make and circulate additional copies.[34] Secretaries in offices—even of government departments—and girls in secretarial schools joined in this effort.[35] "Pamphlets by the hundreds now snow nightly on the city," a contemporary journalist observed. "Typewritten, mimeographed, or even scrawled by hand on coarse paper, they are pushed through window gratings, left in automobiles, tacked on walls."[36]

The strike effort provided a rallying point for the remnants of Acción Democrática Salvadoreña and other adult opposition groups. One contemporary Salvadoran writer claimed that members of ADS met almost daily to decide how they could contribute to the effectiveness of the movement and assign tasks, and Galindo Pohl remembered assistance from Carlos Aviles and other people associated with the Banco Hipotecario. Another account attributed the success of the strike "in large part" to the physicians Arturo Romero had recruited to the opposition cause in earlier years.[37]

Bustamante remembered an active strike committee in Santa Ana, as well as groups that came from Ahuachapán and San Miguel to consult with the strike organizers, though he said the students never knew what came of their efforts.[38]

The organization of the strike unquestionably involved a substantial outlay of money, though it is impossible to estimate the amounts spent for maintenance of striking workers, paper, printing, and transportation of people on strike business. Like all other facets of the movement, the collection and disbursement of funds became quite decentralized. The central committee's initial cash came from the treasury of the Comité Estudiantil Universitario, reimbursed from contributions that subsequently poured in. Castillo, the strike committee's treasurer, remembered receiving some donations as large as five thousand colones (two thousand U.S. dollars).[39] Some of these large contributions no doubt reflected the efforts of the Comité Económico (Finance Committee), formed early in May, which included Banco Hipotecario President Hector Herrera and Roberto Alvarez, a Santa Ana coffee grower who was also connected with one of the San Salvador banks. Bustamante heard that someone collected fifty thousand colones in half an hour in the prestigious Club Salvadoreño.[40] Another informant remembered groups of young women distributing money they had collected to striking workers, and a member of one of these informal fundraising committees described delivering a contribution to a meeting of railroad workers.[41]

The most essential organizing task, however, was clearly to persuade key groups to strike. This depended almost entirely on personal contact, which reinforced the predominantly middle- and upper-class character of the active opposition to Martínez. The student organizers initially divided up the work as far as possible along the lines of their natural associations: medical students approached physicians; law students, lawyers and employees of the courts; engineering students, engineers and employees of the Ministry of Public Works; pharmacy students, the drugstore employees. Other committees concentrated on commercial employees, railroad workers, and Palestinian proprietors. Individuals within various *gremios* (occupational groups) then took on the task of winning over their colleagues.

Spontaneous little committees, consisting largely of women, went from door to door talking with shopkeepers, who generally responded positively, although some, especially Palestinian and Chinese proprietors, evidenced fear of retaliation from the authorities if they closed their doors. José Colorado remembered throwing stones at a few stores so the owners could say they had closed under duress; others kept the shops open but declined to wait on customers. Most paid their employees for the time lost from work, and some contributed to the strike fund.[42]

Indeed, one Salvadoran closely connected with working people maintained that what happened in May 1944 was really not a labor strike at all, but a shutdown by management.[43] Evidence from several sources indicates that the movement inspired less-than-unanimous enthusiasm in the working class.

Castillo, one of the students who dealt with the railroad engineers, found that "neither sufficient political consciousness nor political objectives that could interest them existed." They evidently feared reprisals even more than the shopkeepers, for in addition to demanding their full salaries in advance they agreed to absent themselves from work only on condition that the strike committee find houses where they and their families could take refuge.[44] Bus and taxi drivers were also slow to join the strike, and some remained on the job the day after almost all commercial establishments had closed.

A meeting of the progovernment workers' organization, Reconstrucción Social, that night (May 6) drew "perhaps 1,300 persons."[45] There may have been many who shared the sentiments a member of the United States Embassy staff overheard being expressed by "three independent groups of the poorer class peons gathered in the plazas" the day after Martínez resigned:

> . . . What difference does it make what crowd gets in. We will gain nothing by it. To hell with both of them. I wonder when we will be able to raid the houses of the rich. I have no money. Never had any. Just enough to buy a little food from day to day. Damn them all. I have had no money since the strike began.[46]

One anonymous leaflet writer scolded the students for neglecting to win worker support, charging that the strike had "been translated into unemployment for them," a situation that Martínez could readily exploit.[47] Some awareness of this problem is evident in the organization of food distribution during and immediately after the strike.[48]

Nevertheless, working people did become involved in the strike, though the means by which they were reached remain unclear. Bustamante recalled that the organizers consulted Salvador Merlos, the Acción Democrática Salvadoreña activist who had collaborated with the labor movement of the 1920s, about making contact with workers' societies. A lawyer for the "motormen" claimed to have "talked with numerous groups of employees [and] with labor unions" to enlist their support.[49] However, the only available evidence for the relationship of any particular labor organization to the strike is the fact that an officer of the Unión de Empleados de Comercio (hardly a proletarian group, as evidenced by the fact that he was then assistant manager of one of the banks) served on the committee that represented the strikers in negotiations with Martínez.[50]

The Communist party probably served as a channel of communication with some clandestine unions, but the extent of its influence is unclear. A Communist party commission appointed in the wake of the April insurrection to organize a mass political party included one of the student strike leaders. Miguel Mármol, who also served on this commission, recalled that it encouraged workers to support the general strike.[51] Arnoldo Ferreto, a Costa Rican Communist organizer who visited El Salvador shortly after the fall of Martínez, claimed that Salvadoran Communists "were the agents who worked most to lead the proletariat to strike."[52] However, since neither Mármol nor any participant interviewed in 1976–78 credited the party with a major role in the movement, Ferreto (or his Salvadoran informants) probably exaggerated its importance.

The testimony of a taxi organizer illustrated the way many workers must have become involved. He recalled that a representative of Benjamin Bloom, one of the leading bankers, approached him to ask whether the taxi drivers would be willing to join the strike and offered to provide a daily stipend to those who did. The informant then undertook to persuade the men at his stand and a number of others to keep their cars off the streets, and made daily rounds to distribute the allowances provided by Bloom and other wealthy citizens.[53]

A former meatcutter remembered that the natural leaders of his *gremio,* which had no formal organization, went to the university to offer the students their support, and a number of meatcutters subsequently stayed home from work. He thought the shoemakers, textile workers, graphic arts workers (*obreros gráficos*), and bakers had also joined the strike.[54] Two strike organizers paid tribute to the active efforts of the market women (*señoras del mercado*), whom United States Ambassador Walter Thurston described as "a formidable factor in the less polite strata of Salvadoran politics." In addition to abandoning their own business, they played an important role in persuading others to join the strike.[55]

The Church took no position on the civic strike, but the attitude of many clergymen probably encouraged it. After the president's resignation, the archbishop of San Salvador went so far as to tell one member of the United States Embassy staff of "his dislike of the oppression and cruelties of the MARTÍNEZ regime and his gratification when MARTÍNEZ abdicated and departed from the country."[56] Catholic schools closed, and churches were used for the distribution of food, with the Jesuit fathers taking charge in one instance.[57]

In spite of the exceptions noted earlier, all contemporary commentators outside the Martínez government and the official press saw the civic strike as an expression of overwhelming national unity, and most Salvadorans interviewed in 1976–78 agreed. Even the pro-Martínez account by Alberto Peña Kampy conceded that "a great majority of the [nation] at first adhered to the Strike, voluntarily abandoning its work. . . ."[58] Two participants in the movement remembered it as the product of a "very emotional force," something "mystical." They thought it even affected the criminal population, for crime ceased as though "even the thieves were on strike."[59]

Although all the grievances that had motivated earlier opposition to the Martínez regime undoubtedly contributed to this highly contagious state of mind, accounts of the civic strike unanimously emphasized the impact of the death sentences and executions that followed the April insurrection. The imminent threat to Arturo Romero's life moved not only his students and colleagues but the taxi drivers and other working-class citizens as well.[60] Ana Pérez de Sol, whose brother and husband were among the exiles (the former sentenced to death *in absentia*), recalled the desperation with which she and her friends asked each other, "What can we do?"[61] A contemporary journalist captured that desperation in these words:

> . . . People felt that the shootings were simply the beginning of a new nightmare. They feared Martínez' revenge.
>
> "It was this collective fear," a coffee plantation owner told me, "which gave us courage. We were deathly afraid of Martínez because we knew him to be a brave and decided man. Fear drove the students to strike. Fear forced the merchants to close their shops. Fear made the banks suspend operations."[62]

Certainly the organizers of the strike did not take the threat of government retaliation lightly. The central committee kept its membership secret and rarely met all together in the same place—Galindo Pohl recalled that on one occasion word was passed from one member to another as they came and went in a swimming pool. He himself did not sleep at home. Bustamante remembered committing to memory every bit of information he had to carry with him rather than leave his house with any incriminating pieces of paper.

Yet fear coexisted with bravado. William Krehm, a journalist who was in El Salvador during the strike, wrote of children waving strike leaflets at policemen, "dar[ing] them to make an arrest," and of people who came to the mass on May 5 "defiantly spell[ing] out their names to the informers" posted at the doors of the church. Although the taxi organizer said he and his fellows did not talk much about the strike for fear of the police ("They would have killed us if they'd known!"), he nevertheless went his rounds, coolly telling the policemen who asked him his business that he was trying to persuade the drivers to go back to work. It was a joke among the students that the emotions of one of their number who drove his car, "*el automóvil de la huelga*" (the strike automobile), all over town loaded with leaflets and organizers were revealed so plainly on his face that the police need only have watched him to gauge how the movement was going. "Of course we were scared!" Bustamante asserted, but then he added, "We didn't believe in the possibility that they would kill us, just as young soldiers going to the front believe they will come back to their homes alive." And, he recalled, the students never worried about the consequences of failure, for the possibility that the strike might fail literally "never crossed our minds."[63]

The strike gathered momentum gradually over a period of two weeks. By April 26 the interns at the principal public hospital, Hospital Rosales, as well as the private Hospital Bloom, had left their posts; most of the engineering students employed by the Ministry of Development, Mejoramiento Social, and other government agencies had resigned; and "law students who were assigned cases in the Justice of the Peace Courts no longer attended the sessions."[64]

A report reached Joseph Maleady on April 27 that some schoolteachers had gone on strike after police broke up a novena that one of their number, the widow of an executed officer, attempted to hold for him.[65] The next day brought the walkout of secondary students at the public Instituto Nacional (national high school) and some private schools, as well as a rumor that parents might take their children out of school "as part of the '*huelga pacifista*' [peaceful strike]."[66] Indeed, teachers, students, and parents were of one mind, and on May 3 Thurston reported the continuing spread of the strike in the secondary schools, as well as among "the younger professional employees" of the government.[67]

Meanwhile, on May 2 the newly appointed director of Hospital Rosales, Luís A. Macías, called a meeting with the physicians on his staff, who seized the opportunity to draft a memorandum to Martínez outlining the following conditions for their continuing "full collaboration in behalf of those needing it":

1) That all death sentences be commuted and that general amnesty be extended to all persons charged with political offenses;

2) That all doctors who have been removed from their posts because of political activities be returned to them; and

3) That democratic principles be respected and fulfilled, especially that concerning freedom of suffrage.[68]

Macías reportedly objected to the implicit strike threat on humanitarian grounds, to which one of the physicians retorted that "it was just as humanitarian to consider the great number of people . . . being executed."[69]

Theater employees walked out on May 3, and by May 4 the market vendors had announced their intention to absent themselves from their stands on May 5 and 6.[70] On the night of May 4, the engineers and technicians of the Servicio Cooperativo Interamericano de Salubridad Pública (Cooperative Interamerican Public Health Service) met and voted to join the strike. At eight in the morning on May 5 the dentists of San Salvador followed suit.[71]

In the meantime, Martínez had rudely rebuffed Macías and his predecessor as director of Hospital Rosales when they presented the physicians' statement to him, burning it before their eyes. Macías promptly resigned. At nine-thirty in the morning on May 5, sixty doctors signed a new and stronger statement in which they agreed both to leave their posts in public institutions and to close their private clinics and offices pending a "change in the system of government of the country," which, they stated, "implies the immediate necessity that the presidency be handed over to any designate, in order that he may call the People to free elections." Only a handful of clinics remained open to provide emergency service, contributing fees received to the strike fund.[72]

Pharmacists, lawyers, and justices of the peace also went on strike on May

5, along with "virtually all employees of all banking institutions."[73] Office employees of the International Railways of Central America and the British-owned Salvador Railway Company, the electric light company, Mejoramiento Social, and the credit cooperatives walked out, as did "hundreds [of] government employees."[74]

One woman recalled that when she came to her school on May 5, adults on the scene announced that there would be no classes, and some of the students pelted classmates who persisted in trying to enter the building with a "rain of tomatoes." In the end, the school was closed because "nobody arrived, neither students nor teachers."[75]

At the Church of the Rosary an overflow crowd waited in vain for the arrival of a priest to say mass, which the authorities had evidently forbidden.[76] Finally the assembled worshippers dispersed throughout the city to "close everything."[77] A member of the United States Embassy staff in downtown San Salvador that morning observed that "stores closed gradually as the strikers went from store to store requesting the owners to lock their doors and asking the employees to return to their homes."[78]

At eleven o'clock in the morning the sanitation department became the first government agency to declare itself on strike "by order of its chiefs," though the daily analysis of the water supply and the "demographic service" continued.[79] May 5 may also have been the day one of the train dispatchers came to the university to tell the jubilant students that his co-workers stood ready to strike, for the Salvador Railway Company suspended operations the next day.[80] Students went on strike in Santa Ana and San Miguel. In Santa Ana physicians joined them.[81]

With the strike underway, someone had to be authorized to negotiate on behalf of the strikers. This problem was greatly complicated by the fact that the various participating groups had not yet talked to each other.[82] Two committees claiming to speak for the strikers emerged, but the one that maintained ties with the student organizers and received general recognition bore the imprint of the Acción Democrática Salvadoreña–Banco Hipotecario network.

On the night of May 5 in the home of ADS stalwart Hermógenes Alvarado, representatives of the Banco Hipotecario, the credit cooperatives, Mejoramiento Social, the Banco Central de Reserva, three private banks, an insurance company, physicians, lawyers, dentists, pharmacists, students, commercial employees, market women, day laborers, and bus and taxi drivers met to elect a national strike committee that came to be known as the Comité de Reconstrucción Nacional (National Reconstruction Committee). Jorge Bustamante represented the students on this committee, which also included the physicians' elected representative, Luís V. Velasco; Luís Escalante of the Unión de Empleados de Comercio; Banco Hipotecario attorney Miguel Angel Alcaine; and General Salvador Castaneda Castro, evidently the favorite of anti-Martínez elements in the armed forces.[83] Hector Herrera also played a key role in the activities of this committee, though his name never appeared publicly in connection with it.[84]

Alcaine called the committee together on May 6 to agree on its final demands. On the same day it delivered to the United States Embassy a manifesto, which asserted that "passive resistance" would continue until Martínez resigned and offered "Martínez, his associates and partisans" guarantees against reprisals, while "recommend[ing]" that the president leave the country.[85]

This visit to the United States Embassy evidently figured in an effort to obtain assistance of some sort from the ambassador and representatives of other foreign governments as well, for Escalante remembered visiting other embassies. Thurston reported on May 5 that his embassy was "being subjected to pressure to intervene," and on May 6, "despite insistent pressure I have not called a meeting of the diplomatic corps."[86]

The strike continued to spread. On May 6 employees of the Subsecretariat of Development walked out "in a body." Municipal employees and "subordinate personnel in several ministries including the Foreign Office" joined them.[87] The meatcutters and some artisans had probably stopped working by May 6, though it is impossible to say with certainty. Some unspecified groups in Sonsonate and Ahuachapán also went on strike.[88]

By this time the central committee, realizing that the strike could not be sustained indefinitely, had begun to consider the possibility of bringing people into the streets to intensify the pressure on Martínez.[89] Tragedy provided the occasion and brought the drama to its final climax.

On Sunday, May 7, an apparently nervous or trigger-happy policeman fired without warning at a group of boys on the street, instantly killing seventeen-year-old José Wright, a member of a prominent San Salvador family. Indignation banished fear as San Salvadorans poured into the streets. Literally thousands of people arrived at the Wright home that evening and attended the funeral the next morning.

According to Castillo, the student strike committee saw its opportunity and called upon supporters to gather in Plaza Barrios (the square opposite the Palacio Nacional [National Palace] where the National Assembly met and national government offices were located) after the funeral, though Bustamante thought the proposal to proceed to Plaza Barrios arose spontaneously from someone else in the crowd at the cemetery. He remembered that the strike leaders worried about the possibility of violence following Wright's death, with talk of killing policemen and other acts of revenge in the air. At that point they set up a peacekeeping force of some fifty students charged with the task of calming public feeling. Members of this group spoke in various parts of the city on the night of May 7, at the funeral, and at Plaza Barrios. They also had to dissuade people at the Plaza from lynching army chief of staff Francisco Ponce, who, according to a contemporary account, "drove among the crowds . . . while under the influence of alcohol[,] urging them to disband and abandon their strike and apparently threatening them as well."[90]

Inside the Palacio Nacional on the morning of May 8, five employees of the Corte de Cuentas (comptroller general's office) presented their resignations and appealed to their fellow workers to join them, with the result that the latter left the offices in a body. When the students outside broadcast the news with loudspeakers, all the other employees in the building joined the walkout.[91] The crowds that invaded the Palacio Nacional later that morning cheering liberty, the Salvadoran people, and the four freedoms found it almost empty.[92] Busses disappeared from the streets that day, and late in the afternoon the International Railways of Central America suspended all service except the delivery of gasoline from North American oil companies to Guatemala.[93]

In Santa Ana on the night of May 7, the department heads of the municipal government informed the mayor that the city's employees had decided to join the strike, suspending all services except those of the waterworks and the gravediggers as of the next day. The mayor accepted the news amiably, asking only that the civil register be included in the services that would continue. The next morning the city council passed a resolution supporting the employees' right to exercise their "political convictions" and promising that their jobs would be waiting for them at the conclusion of the strike.[94] On May 8 "the majority of the business firms" in Santa Ana shut down, the governor of San Miguel wired the minister of government that banks there had closed, and in San Vicente schoolteachers went on strike.[95]

As Galindo Pohl recalled, it was as though a small stone rolling down a mountain had loosed an avalanche.[96]

6. The Fall of Martínez

In the first days of April, I defeated the insurrectionists with arms, but finally they provoked a strike. Then I no longer wanted to fight. At whom was I going to fire? At children and youths who did not completely realize what they were doing? Women also were enlisted in the movement, and thus there was no longer a target at which to fire.[1]

The Martínez government proved unable to deal with the new insurrection. Its ineffectual response reflected divisions within the administration and a general collapse of morale stemming from the April uprising.

That event had demonstrated the unreliability of the army. Although no one doubted the loyalty of the minister and undersecretary of defense or the army chief of staff to Martínez, "disunity, mistrust and fear pervaded the whole officer corps."[2] Soldiers disappeared from the streets, leaving law enforcement in the hands of the police and National Guard.[3]

Information "from two or three reliable sources" convinced Overton Ellis of the United States Embassy staff that members of Martínez's cabinet saw the president's retirement as the only way to salvage the situation. By April 17, Minister of Government Rudolfo Morales, Foreign Minister Arturo Ramón Avila, and Finance Minister Hector Escobar Serrano were "known to be thinking along these lines" but afraid to mention the subject to Martínez. Escobar Serrano had "spoken up in informal meetings of Government men against the . . . 'reign of terror,' counseling moderation and the cessation of killings and persecution," and Morales was "reported to be entirely out of sympathy with [the] present course of affairs and particularly anxious to get out of his present position. . . ." Ellis concluded:

. . . there is little doubt that a feeling of apprehension, doubt and fear is developing among the ranks of the President's followers . . . not only because they feel the President's position is ill-advised, vengeful and likely to prove ruinous to all interests, but also because these men, and certainly a large number of minor officials, are beginning to think of their own personal and economic safety in the event that the Government is . . . overturned. . . . It seems that the desire to be noncommittal, to hedge and to express no opinion and play safe, is becoming almost more marked among the followers of the President than among sympathizers of the revolution.[4]

According to a high official of the Martínez government, the civic strike took everyone in the administration by surprise. The cabinet opposed repressive measures and favored a strategy of waiting out the strike, on the theory that the funds necessary to maintain it would eventually run out.[5]

Several actions of the government evidenced a desire to placate its adversaries and avoid confrontations. The authorities lifted the curfew on April 25 and at some point withdrew National Guardsmen from the streets of San Salvador.[6] On May 4—too late to stem the rising tide of revolt—the government announced the release of civilians still held in connection with the April 2 uprising, though an opposition leaflet attacked the announcement as fraudulent.[7]

In the meantime, the semiofficial newspaper *El Diario Nuevo* launched a propaganda campaign designed to identify the government with the interests of the masses and link the opposition with the wealthy. On April 27 it commented on the hospital interns' strike: "To abandon a center of charity where there are hundreds of people who suffer is an action that can only be taken by impassioned or selfish people." The next day a leaflet signed by a number of private citizens (though Thurston attributed it to the government) pointed out that the student strike affected precisely those public agencies that served the poor, suggesting that their fate was of no concern to the students because the latter came from wealthy families.[8]

On April 29, *El Diario Nuevo* asserted that of El Salvador's two million people the "capitalists: agriculturalists, industrialists, merchants and professionals" constituted a mere ten thousand, with whom the campesinos and workers could not join "in any social movement." Two days later, the newspaper published a defense of the Martínez government that emphasized its economic and social achievements and attacked opponents of the government as ambitious egotists who, "having had the opportunity to do much for the country," had done nothing.[9]

On the night of May 5 Martínez himself went on the air, lavishly praising the honest workers who remained on the job and labeling the propaganda for the general strike a Nazi tactic "to develop a war of nerves, to sow panic in the different social classes."[10]

At some point Martínez issued an order for the dismissal of certain physicians at Hospital Rosales, which only antagonized the hospital director. In fact, although rumors circulated that employees of banks and other enterprises who failed to appear for work would lose their jobs, the anti-Martínez press reported the dismissal of only one government employee for promoting the strike.[11]

Government pressure on the church presumably prevented the saying of the memorial mass on May 5, and a few merchants reportedly opened their shops under threats that they would lose their licenses or be expelled from the country.[12] These threats probably came from Martínez himself, who on May 6, according to Thurston, "summoned . . . the heads of many business establishments . . . and . . . strongly urged them to open their business . . . even though they were without employees for their proper management." [13]

Police repression, however, was minimal. This probably reflected the reluctance of the cabinet—in particular Rudolfo Morales, whose ministry controlled the National Police—to sanction harsh measures. Moreover, the policemen themselves were not unanimously interested in suppressing the strike. The taxi organizer interviewed in 1978 heard from a friend on the police force that some in fact sympathized with the strike, and agents who captured one group of organizers sent them off in another direction where no police were stationed.[14]

Word of an order for the arrest of "a number of University students" reached the United States Embassy on May 1, but actual arrests did not go beyond the brief detention of a few people for possession of strike leaflets.[15] Ambassador Thurston stated categorically on May 6 that there had been "no arrests or other repressive action." [16]

Policemen did go to the homes of some strikers to compel them to return to work, although, according to Miguel Mármol, their efforts to round up absent public servants in their homes met with little success because the latter had prudently taken refuge elsewhere.[17] The police also offered protection to strikebreakers, and one anonymous informant told a member of the United States Embassy staff that he had seen "the names of various people entered in the police records, charged with not complying with the duties of strikebreaking assigned to them by the 'Reconstrucción Social' organization." [18]

May 6 brought a series of incidents that at the time suggested an effort to mobilize government supporters in Reconstrucción Social and/or Pro-Patria to use violence against participants in the strike. A leaflet announced the formation of a "Workers Anti-Revolutionary Committee"

> which is already acting, demanding the return to normality of the drugstores of this capital; and likewise of all stores who refuse to attend our request[,] which is the request of the PEOPLE.
>
> The C.O.A. [presumably "Comité Obrero Antirevolucionario"] also has the purpose to collaborate with the authorities, inasmuch as the authorities—as we are well aware—are serving the people's cause. . . .
>
> The revolutionaries . . . ask . . . the resignation of General Martínez, whose crime we already know: that of being a democratic ruler for the exclusive benefit of the

people. We also know the fate awaiting the country should it fall in[to the] hands of these revolutionaries, secret Nazis, who act on [*sic*] the service of foreign forces and who pretend to restore economic and financial privileges cut at the root by General Martínez and which have given to the people such prosperity[,] because this measure has benefited the middle class, the laborers[,] and rural workers. . . .

Our voice is as yet prudent. We trust you will hear us when [*sic*] there is still time.[19]

Reports reached the United States Embassy that "groups of men had forced open the doors of at least two drug stores . . . in an effort to force the proprietors to open for business" and that workers who attended the regular Reconstrucción Social meeting that evening "would be directed to commit various acts of violence and to break open various stores throughout the city." The anti-Martínez *Diario de Hoy* charged that at the meeting "it was agreed to organize a demonstration to demand in the streets that stores be opened, to fire shots over the houses of strikers, and to commit other excesses."

According to other reports, "some doctors who were participating in the general strike . . . received anonymous threats of violence to their persons or property," and one of a group of men who tried unsuccessfully to lure a leader of the striking physicians out of his home "was heard to say to another, 'Let's see, who is next on the list.' " A list of persons to be beaten or threatened subsequently appeared in *La Prensa Gráfica*, which interpreted it as instructions given to Pro-Patria *orejas* ("ears," hence, spies).[20]

The most alarming rumors of May 6 concerned the arrival of some hundreds of campesinos, reportedly armed with machetes, in San Salvador. Fear spread that they had been brought in to sack the city and provide the army with an occasion to intervene.[21]

In fact, however, no progovernment demonstration, concerted campaign of intimidation, or serious violence developed. The United States Embassy staff member who attended the May 6 Reconstrucción Social meeting at the request of its director, Manuel Escalante Rubio, reported that the latter, while attacking the strike, urged his hearers to refrain from violence. This supports Escalante Rubio's subsequent testimony that Martínez instructed him "to avoid trouble with the strikers."[22] *El Diario de Hoy*'s assertion that "platoons of provocateurs" appeared in the streets on May 7 and that Martínez withdrew them after the shooting of José Wright is unsupported by any other source.[23] In all probability the perpetrators of the few incidents cited above acted on their own, without official sanction.

As the strike spread, disaffection within the president's entourage intensified. On the afternoon of May 5, according to one report that Thurston described as authoritative, the president of the National Legislative Assembly, supported by "the entire Cabinet with the exception of the newly appointed Minister of Public Instruction," advised the president to resign. Martínez at first seemed to be impressed by this advice, but finally rejected it.

A member of the administration who was in a position to know denied that members of the cabinet ever suggested to the president that he should step down, but they may well have discussed their own withdrawal from the government as early as May 5, for rumors of the imminent resignations of high officials began to circulate that day. According to this informant, opposition leaders persuaded cabinet members who offered to resign to stay on because the opposition saw the cabinet as the best guarantee that the government would not take "violent measures."[24] This may explain the report Thurston received that a second meeting of the cabinet with the president of the Legislative Assembly "and perhaps the Chief Justice" on the evening of May 6 was interrupted by reports of the menacing presence of armed campesinos in "various military establishments" in San Salvador, and "those who had pledged themselves to resign if Martínez again refused to abandon the Presidency decided to remain in office in order to protect the city."[25]

The shooting of José Wright on May 7 precipitated a crisis. The son of a North American father, Wright was a United States citizen. At about six o'clock in the evening, Ambassador Thurston called on Martínez to ask him "what action the Salvadoran Government intended to take in order to bring to justice the persons responsible for the shooting."[26] This visit probably gave rise to the rumor of imminent United States intervention that rapidly spread through San Salvador.[27]

Accounts of developments within the government during the night of May 7 vary. The police were speedily concentrated in their barracks, presumably on the authority of either Minister of Government Morales or President Martínez, but National Guardsmen had replaced them on patrol by the early hours of May 8. Civilians at the Palacio Nacional reportedly cheered the Guardsmen, who made no attempt to interfere with the crowd—not even when angry demonstrators threatened General Ponce.[28]

According to Roberto Molina y Morales, a nephew of the minister of government then employed in the Ministry of Foreign Relations, his uncle went to Martínez with the archbishop of San Salvador and the president of the Legislative Assembly after the shooting of José Wright and advised the president to resign. Rebuffed by Martínez, Morales then dictated his own resignation from the cabinet. No other record of the meeting Molina y Morales described has come to light, although word of Morales's immediate resignation did reach the United States Embassy.[29]

Later that night all or most members of the cabinet met and reached the decision to present their collective resignation. Massey felt that Wright's death "tipped the balance and shocked the cabinet into its decision to act," but the informant closest to the events implied that what alarmed the cabinet was the appearance of crowds in the streets, which gave rise to the possibility of bloody repression. He made no mention of the rumors of United States intervention, though he saw Martínez immediately after the latter's interview with Thurston and found the president "perturbed."[30]

The same informant recalled that Martínez received the ministers at nine o'clock on the morning of May 8. Chief of Staff Ponce appeared during that meeting to assure the president that the army supported him 100 percent and only wanted an order from him to disperse the crowds in the streets. When the spokesman for the cabinet told the president, "We cannot join you in any violent measure," Martínez interrupted him with the assertion that he did not favor violent measures either. He added that he had shown he was no coward in putting down the April 2 insurrection and would not hesitate to put the army in its place if it should rebel again. "But against the people," he reiterated, "I will not take any violent measure. If the people now want me to retire, I am willing to do it without difficulty."[31]

Word that the Comité de Reconstrucción Nacional wanted him on hand for negotiations reached Bustamante during José Wright's funeral. About ten o'clock in the morning, the five members of the CRN sat down with the ministers to discuss the terms of the president's retirement. Two issues prolonged the deliberation: Martínez's proposal that he continue in office until the end of the month and the selection of his successor. On the first point the CRN refused to yield, insisting that the strike would continue until Martínez left office.

On the second, the evidence is unclear as to exactly what was at stake. Martínez, according to the account of his meeting with the cabinet cited above, insisted that the transfer of power follow legal procedures. Under the Constitution of 1939 the Legislative Assembly annually elected three "designates" ("*designados*") from whom it would choose an interim chief executive in the event that the presidency should become vacant during the year. It had elected as designates for the year 1944 Minister of War Andrés I. Menéndez, Minister of Government Morales, and Supreme Court President Alberto Gómez Zarate. Given the subservient character of the Legislative Assembly, the opposition could expect that it would follow Martínez's dictates as to who should succeed him. Bustamante recalled that the CRN at its first meeting on May 6 was prepared to negotiate the selection of one of the designates.

According to a contemporary press report, however, the opposition negotiators went to a meeting with the cabinet in the afternoon of May 8 with a list of four persons from whom Martínez might choose his successor: Minister of Government Morales, Hermógenes Alvarado, and two of its own members, General Salvador Castaneda Castro and Luís Velasco.

This list undoubtedly was the result of political haggling among the rebels. A large group of opposition notables met at midday to discuss the negotiations, and as Bustamante recalled, "Everybody wanted to be minister or president." The students pressed for an interim president entirely unconnected with the Martínez regime, supporting the candidacies of Alvarado and Velasco. Bustamante thought other elements wanted Castaneda Castro; they may have presented his name in a bid for military support. The assembly reached no agreement and apparently left the power of decision in the hands of the Comité de Reconstrucción Nacional.[32]

After an hour-long discussion with the cabinet, the CRN finally agreed to add General Menéndez's name to the list. The cabinet probably knew that Martínez wanted Menéndez to succeed him.[33] The minister of defense had served as acting president for six months between Martínez's first and second terms, although he declined to play the same role in 1944. He demonstrated his unswerving loyalty to Martínez during the April 2 uprising when he took charge of the wavering Sonsonate garrison just in time to hold it for the government. In the troubled days following the insurrection, Ellis observed that Menéndez was

> reported to be very calm and self-possessed, very moderate in his views and uninfluenced by the general lack of moderation and very emotional state of the other men around the President. It is believed that General Menéndez is one of the few, probably the only one, who still enjoys the President's complete confidence and respect, and that he would be the only one to assume the President's responsibilities if the latter decided to step out.[34]

On the other hand, the CRN may have felt that its constituency would accept Menéndez because he was entirely lacking in political ambition and universally respected for his integrity. According to Bustamante, the CRN agreed to the naming of Menéndez in return for a promise that he would lift the state of siege, decree a general amnesty, and permit the return of political exiles.[35]

The cabinet took the agreed-upon list of candidates to Martínez at four o'clock and returned an hour later with the report that he still wanted to delay his departure until the end of May.[36]

In the meantime tension mounted. The appearance of truckloads of soldiers early in the afternoon gave rise to a flurry of alarm. The people in the streets relaxed when the soldiers made it clear that "they did not come as fighters but were bearers of a message of peace, and that their presence was only to protect the demonstrators themselves."[37] Others, however, did not wait to find out what the army would do. Hector Herrera and Mejoramiento Social President Mario Sol arrived at Thurston's house about one o'clock "in deepest distress," for they interpreted the reappearance of troops in the streets as evidence that "the President [had] violated his word and [would] dominate the situation by the armed forces." One informant remembered that most of a group assembled in the office of Miguel Angel Alcaine went into hiding upon hearing that Martínez was about to bring out the police and disperse the crowds, and when Bustamante went to consult other student strike leaders about Martínez's last offer late in the day, almost all had disappeared.[38] Moreover, the crowds jamming the streets were growing impatient, and although they remained entirely peaceful, the possibility existed that some incident would touch off a bloody clash with the security forces. The authorities announced an eleven o'clock curfew, and between five and six o'clock Ambassador Thurston "received delegations of Committee [of National Reconstruction] members and private citizens who expressed grave concern that the crowd . . . would not disperse before curfew [and] . . . that Martinez . . . would direct the army to shoot down the crowds and hold himself in power by pure force."[39]

According to one report, a member of the second committee claiming to represent the groups on strike obtained an audience with Martínez himself in the late afternoon after the cabinet left the president's house. He insisted that Martínez resign immediately, asserting that "if MARTINEZ . . . persisted in remaining in office[,] there would be a great deal of bloodshed and trouble through-out the country for which MARTINEZ would be directly responsible."[40]

At five-thirty, on the urging of Velasco, two members of the cabinet returned to the president's house to make one last try and emerged with Martínez's solemn promise to relinquish the presidency the next morning to whichever of the legal designates the National Assembly should elect. At seven o'clock that evening, Martínez himself announced his resignation in a brief radio address.[41]

The transfer of power was accomplished smoothly on the morning of May 9. The cabinet met with the president of the National Legislative Assembly and the president of the Supreme Court, and after deliberating for two hours and ten minutes submitted the name of Menéndez to the Legislative Assembly, which had reconvened to receive the resignation of Martínez.[42]

The new president moved quickly to win the confidence of the opposition. In his first meeting with the Comité de Reconstrucción Nacional, he promised that the constitution would be reformed and elections convoked as soon as possible. "Authorized sources" also told the press that martial law would continue "for the shortest possible time."[43] Late in the afternoon of May 9 the Legislative Assembly approved a decree of "full and unconditional amnesty to all those soldiers or civilians" implicated in acts of rebellion, sedition, or other political crimes prior to passage of the law.[44]

The strike continued, however, for two issues remained unresolved. The composition of Menéndez's cabinet became the focus of extended negotiations, and other citizens joined the student strike leaders in demanding Martínez's departure from the country. The dentists voted on May 10 to continue their strike until he left; women demonstrated for the same objective; and striking bank workers and groups calling themselves the Frente Obrero Salvadoreño (Salvadoran Workers' Front), Women of El Salvador, and Salvadorans on Strike (the last of which reportedly mustered more than three thousand signatures) wired the ex-president urging him to leave.[45]

According to Bustamante, Menéndez had agreed to serve as interim president on May 8 on the condition that he name his entire cabinet. Nevertheless the Comité de Reconstrucción Nacional gave him a list of nominees, which consisted largely of ADS stalwarts and other prominent opponents of Martínez, telling him "he was free to accept or reject any name." The cabinet appointments announced on May 10 included one of this group, Hermógenes Alvarado, named minister of public instruction. The more politically sensitive posts of minister and undersecretary of government went to two members of the rival strike committee, Joaquín Parada Aparicio and Napoleón Rodríguez Ruiz. The new foreign minister, Julio Enrique Avila, in Bustamante's opinion, represented anti-Martínez elements of the oligarchy. Three members of Martínez's cabinet remained: Minister of Finance Hector Escobar Serrano continued in the same post, Undersecretary of Defense Fidel Garay became minister of defense, and former Undersecretary of Government Carlos Alberto Liévano became undersecretary of finance.[46]

This obvious compromise did not please the students. Three of them told a member of the United States Embassy staff on the morning of May 10 that "their committee had rejected the Cabinate [*sic*] proposed by Menéndez . . . , that it was a reshuffle [of] old loyal Martínez' [*sic*] supporters" and predicted that the strike would continue if the government did not make more concessions to the opposition.[47] But, as Bustamante recalled, the student leaders could see that the general public felt the fight had been won with the removal of Martínez, and they themselves were exhausted. When Menéndez promised the Comité de Reconstrucción Nacional on May 10 that Martínez would leave El Salvador the next day, both the CRN and the students agreed to end the strike.[48]

The transition period was a tense one. With demonstrations to celebrate Martínez's resignation and to press other demands erupting all over San Salvador, and in other cities as well, Thurston reported "danger of a clash between patrolling troops and the populace or of a seizure of government by the military."[49] But El Salvador was spared the bloody rioting that followed successful civic strikes in some other countries. Opposition leaders made strenuous and largely successful efforts to maintain discipline in their ranks. A leaflet signed "Comité Ejecutivo Est." (Student Executive Committee) warned that "premature excesses of enthusiasm can spoil our ends." Orators, leaflets, and the press repeatedly urged the public to keep calm. The student peacekeeping committee proved its worth. A group of students told a member of the United States Embassy staff how it had blocked the efforts of eight men to incite a group of over a hundred "poor peons" to break into stores in downtown San Salvador:

> . . . One of the "orejas" for the students immediately went and brought back with him fifty more of his cohorts. They grabbed the eight men and discovered that they were armed with pistols and disclosed identification as being Martínez' private police. The students disclosed this fact to the peons along with speeches to the effect that they should beware of any attempt on the part of Martínez or his supporters to instigate riots, robbery, ect. [*sic*][50]

La Prensa Gráfica acknowledged that some "irresponsible individuals" under the influence of alcohol created "spectacles," but contemporary observers reported only two cases of bloodshed between May 8 and May 11, namely, a clash between strikers and other workers in Santa Ana in which two people were injured, and one murder in San Salvador unconnected with the political developments.[51]

Life in San Salvador returned to normal on May 11. Busses reappeared, and government offices, the markets, and most stores and factories reopened. The doctors and dentists voted to return to work. The Ministry of Government, noting that the reasons for the suspension of railroad service had "disappeared," asked the director of the International Railway to resume service immediately.[52]

Martínez crossed the border into Guatemala shortly before noon. *El Diario Latino* sounded its siren, which had "been used to announce . . . great events," to notify San Salvadorans of his departure from Salvadoran soil, and a group of students proclaimed this final triumph with an enormous sign, which read simply, "He's Gone."[53]

7. The Question of Intervention

I have been endeavoring since my arrival at this post to demonstrate by my actions that the United States Government and its diplomatic mission in San Salvador have no desire or intention to become involved in the political affairs of the country. . . .[1]

Some accounts of the end of the Martínez regime mention intervention in the crisis by members of the diplomatic corps, and almost all assert that United States Ambassador Walter Thurston played some role in Martínez's resignation.[2] What is the evidence on these points?

Reports of intervention by the diplomatic corps after José Wright's death can probably be discounted. The files of the United States Embassy and State Department show no action whatever by the diplomatic corps between its visit to Martínez on April 17 and his resignation, and Luís Escalante of the Comité de Reconstrucción Nacional confirmed that it played no role in the developments of May 7–9.[3]

The question of Thurston's role requires more extended consideration. As the conflict developed in the critical months of 1943 and 1944, the embassy staff was involved in complex interaction with the Salvadoran government, the opposition, and the State Department in Washington. Both the Martínez government and its opponents saw North American influence as a factor in the conflict and tried to turn it to their advantage.

In the course of Martínez's reelection campaign in 1943, the government cited United States pressure for "the liquidation of Axis properties in El Salvador [as] an excuse to revise the Constitution." Reports even reached the Embassy that Martínez had "started a rumor and whispering campaign . . . to the effect that the administration has sounded out the American Embassy and has its support as the United States does not wish to see any change of administration or political disturbances in El Salvador so long as the war lasts."[4]

Members of the opposition complained that Martínez was "permanently entrenched as dictator because the United States will not countenance a change of the status quo." In their view, the arms El Salvador received through the wartime lend-lease program and even humanitarian assistance, such as sanitation and public health programs, served to maintain the government in power.[5]

The small North American business community, which felt threatened by the Martínez regime's increasing economic nationalism as well as by the constitutional amendments of February 1944, echoed these charges by the opposition.[6]

On the other hand, United States Military Attaché George B. Massey heard reports that the chief of police had told Martínez the United States Ambassador approved of the Acción Democrática Salvadoreña petition to the Supreme Court, that "several military men" believed Thurston had a hand in the December 11 demonstration, and that the Pro-Patria party thought the diplomatic corps favored the opposition.[7] Similarly, members of the opposition insisted upon believing that the ambassador intervened to save the lives of the men arrested in late December 1943.[8]

The record of what the State Department and its representatives in El Salvador actually said and did does not support charges of United States intervention on either side, but it does show that the "noninterference" policy came under increasing strain as the conflict intensified. The voluminous reports and memoranda of United States Embassy staff members indicate that most were competent, conscientious professionals, neither naive nor deliberately biased in their observations. Nevertheless, they inevitably looked at Salvadoran politics through the spectacles of North American political traditions, New Deal liberalism, and the ideological polarization of World War II, and disapproved of much of what they saw. They obviously maintained extensive and friendly contacts with leading opponents of Martínez and listened sympathetically to the questions Salvadorans raised about the sincerity of the United States' commitment to the democratic principles it professed.

Early in January 1944 Thurston apprised the State Department of the dilemma in which he found himself:

> Our pronouncements such as the Atlantic Charter and the Declaration of the Four Freedoms (the latter blazoned by us throughout El Salvador in the form of posters) are accepted literally by the Salvadorans as endorsement of the basic democratic principles we desire to have prevail currently and universally. . . . It is difficult for them to reconcile these pronouncements with the fact that the United States tolerates and apparently is gratified to enter into association with governments in America which cannot be described as other than totalitarian. . . .
>
> The principal defect of a policy of nonintervention accompanied by propaganda on behalf of democratic doctrines is that it simultaneously stimulates dictatorships

and popular opposition to them. Moreover, by according dictators who seize or retain power unconstitutionally the same consideration extended to honestly elected presidents we not only impair our moral leadership but foment the belief that our democratic professions are empty propaganda and that we are in fact simply guided by expediency.

It is of course unthinkable that we should revert to the folly of intervention—but it seems to be evident that our present policy is not satisfactory, especially in the Caribbean and Central American areas.[9]

A State Department communication to its representatives throughout Central America a month later reiterated the noninterference policy in terms that failed to address the dilemma:

The Department has noted an increase in the scope and intensity of political activities in Central America in recent months. There appears to be a possibility that this may, in certain instances, lead to political turmoil. Domestic strife in any of the United Nations would, of course, be disquieting under the present circumstances, and our enemies would doubtless seek to derive advantage from it. In the course of these political activities many efforts have been made both by the Administration forces and the opposition to secure from the United States Embassy accredited to the country some sign of favor which might be effectively used for political propaganda. . . .

The Department has noted the many ingenious devices by which the contending political factions have sought to draw United States officials into local politics. It has been much gratified to observe the skill and tact with which the officers of the respective missions have sought to escape from committing themselves. . . .

In view of the particularly delicate situation existing at the moment, the Department wishes to reiterate its injunctions against any avoidable act of omission or commission which might be interpreted as reflecting on the local political situation. Excessive public friendliness toward the Administration in power or the participation of United States officials in pro-administration meetings of a political nature would be almost as undesirable as the identification of the Embassy with opposition to the existing Administration. It is to be remembered that there is bitter open or covert opposition to virtually all of the administrations in power; that it is almost inevitable that this opposition will eventually come to power in some countries and that the rule of non-interference in internal politics applies even to those regimes which, in seeking to perpetuate themselves in power, have gone out of their way to emphasize their friendship for the United States. . . .[10]

Thurston conscientiously tried to adhere to the policy of noninterference. He declined an invitation to a luncheon that he understood would open the president's reelection campaign. Upon learning that the government had invoked the United States' interest in the liquidation of Axis property in support of amending the Salvadoran constitution, he made it "very clear that the United States could in no way be a party to such a revision of the Constitution. . . ."[11] In July 1943 he responded to an inquiry from the secretary of state as to why the Salvadoran government sought to purchase one thousand submachine guns from the United States with the suggestion that it might want them to repress "civil disorders" in the event that opposition to Martínez's reelection plan developed. After further inquiries, the State Department recommended against the sale, which apparently never materialized, although six lend-lease tanks did arrive in El Salvador in August 1943.[12]

On the other hand, when representatives of the Frente Democrático Universitario called upon the ambassador to discuss their plan for a gathering at the United States Embassy to commemorate the attack on Pearl Harbor, he recognized the antigovernment import of the proposal and emphatically discouraged any demonstration in front of the embassy, with the result that the students postponed the action and chose another location.[13]

When the diplomatic corps received invitations to the inauguration of Martínez's new term in office, the Mexican ambassador asked Thurston what he planned to do. Thurston reported:

> I informed the Ambassador that I had decided to attend the ceremony since to do otherwise would be an affront to the Government to which I was accredited. I stated that according to my conception of things, an Ambassador is an agent not a maker of policy, save under very extraordinary conditions, and that when his Government has issued no particular instructions to guide him in a given situation he should follow customary procedure and not place his Government in the position of having initiated a new policy. . . .[14]

The April 2 insurrection required more difficult decisions. On April 3 the Mexican ambassador telephoned his colleagues in the diplomatic corps with the proposal that they "make representations to President Martínez to prevent the loss of life and property damage that would follow bombardment of the police barracks." Thurston suspected the ambassador had acted at the request of the revolutionary junta whose purpose was "probably . . . to secure the safety of the opposition prisoners also in the barracks and to inspire the belief that the revolutionary movement is about to be successful." Thurston declined to participate, thereby scuttling the project.[15]

However, the diplomatic corps convened at the United States Embassy that afternoon to consider a request for its intervention from the junta. By that time the tide was beginning to turn against the insurrection, and the diplomats finally decided "to limit themselves to sending a message to the two sides offering their good offices if desired." It was never sent, probably because Martínez's counterattack decided the issue within hours, but another development at that meeting became a *cause célèbre*.[16]

Colonel Tito Calvo, military commander of the insurgents at the First Infantry barracks, appeared at the embassy with a companion, asking for asylum. Thurston explained to them that United States policy forbade giving anyone asylum in the embassy, and the other diplomats present also, on one pretext or another, declined to take them in. However, when government soldiers came looking for the two men, Thurston refused to surrender them, saying that he would "report their presence to General Martínez, unless they should elect, as they were at liberty to do, to leave the Embassy before I had done so." He waited until evening to discuss the matter with Martínez, and "after failing to receive assurances that they would if surrendered be treated with clemency I said I would relinquish them under an assurance that they would be given the benefits of the processes of the laws of El Salvador. This . . . was given." [17]

Thurston subsequently called upon Martínez, inquired about Calvo, and appealed to him to exercise clemency toward the prisoners. He also asked the minister and undersecretary of foreign affairs to "contribute their influence insofar as possible toward a policy of clemency." [18] Nevertheless, both men were executed on April 10.

This incident probably accounts for reports of opposition bitterness toward the United States that frequently reached the embassy after the insurrection.[19] On the other hand, officials of the government reportedly thought the United States Embassy had supported the rebels, and Thurston observed that the inevitable rumors about the embassy's attitude were "about equally divided between assertions that I fomented and directed the uprising and that I destroyed the uprising by detaining and turning over . . . Colonel Calvo," with "the preponderance of the reports" representing the United States mission "as having been anti-Martínez and pro-revolution." He noted that the demeanor of President Martínez and other government officials with whom he talked after the insurrection remained as cordial as ever.[20]

Late April brought rumors that the expected new insurrection would be accompanied by an attack on North American residents of San Salvador for the purpose of provoking United States intervention to remove Martínez. Both Vice Consul Joseph Maleady and Thurston suspected that the rumors had been planted by the government to discredit its opponents and give the authorities a pretext for " 'protecting' us against unruly hoardes [*sic*]." [21]

On April 25, without consulting Thurston, Massey sent the following cable to the War Department in Washington:

> Insistent reports indicate possibility recurrence revolution younger military and armed civilian groups at any time. . . . Considerable confusion and irresponsible shooting expected. . . . Assistance US military police may be requested. Protect American lives and property, if law enforcement breaks down. . . .[22]

Massey's initiative gave rise to the following exchange of correspondence between John M. Cabot, chief of the State Department Division of Caribbean and Central American Affairs, and Ambassador Thurston:

May 9, 1944

Dear Walter:

We note that in his cable no. 12364 of April 25, the Assistant Military Attaché in San Salvador indicated to the War Department that the assistance of United States Military

Police might be requested, in order to protect the lives and property of American citizens, in the event that law enforcement in El Salvador should break down. It may have been that his message was badly paraphrased before reaching me and in any case, I feel sure that anything of this nature would be brought to your attention before actions were taken. Nonetheless, I thought you might be interested, in as much as our established policy and commitments would hardly permit such use of American forces.

May 12, 1944

My dear Jack:

I have read with considerable interest your note of May 9 about the cable sent by the Assistant Military Attaché to the War Department regarding the use of United States Military Police in maintaining order here. I have long held a kindred feeling toward the man who said "God save me from my friends—I can take care of my enemies myself," and would amplify it by saying, "God save Chiefs of Missions from their Military Attachés!" . . .

I am sure I need not tell you that I had no more intention of calling for U.S. Military Police than I did of calling in the Waves—although now that I think of it that latter idea has its attractions! You may know that I had some part myself in the shaping of the policy and commitments to which you refer.

P.S. What the Military Attaché was probably trying to work out in his own way and without consulting me was an approach to the problem which I have . . . reported . . . : there were persistent stories here of a deliberate attack on Americans in the event of new troubles in San Salvador (including the tossing of hand grenades into a residence hotel occupied by many Americans)[,] and in order not to dignify such stuff by bringing it to the attention of the Martínez regime I decided to build a backfire against it by pointing out that any premeditated and deliberate outrage upon the American colony certainly would bring very serious consequences—and you may be sure Jack that it would have done so.[23]

Thurston's reports did not say to whom he directed these remarks, or what his audience might have understood by "very serious consequences," but his warning very likely figured in the significance Salvadorans attached to José Wright's death. (Massey's telegram would doubtless have sounded even more menacing, but since it was sent in code it is highly unlikely that Salvadorans had any knowledge of its contents.)

On April 26 the ambassador squelched a proposal from the United States military air attaché in Guatemala to help reorganize the Salvadoran Air Force. Noting that the offer of such assistance would be construed as support for Martínez, Thurston reported that he had told the assistant military attaché in Guatemala "that no action of the kind should be undertaken or discussed with the Salvadoran authorities without my prior approval."[24]

In Washington the State Department had begun to perceive United States relations with the government of El Salvador as a delicate problem, as evidenced by the seemingly trivial matter of a response to Martínez's letter to President Roosevelt announcing the inauguration of his new term in office. Officials in Washington apparently conferred at some length about the text of a covering letter for Roosevelt's reply. The first draft that appears in the State Department files bears the following note dated April 13 and signed by William P. Cochran, assistant chief of the Division of Caribbean and Central American Affairs:

> Both Mr. [John M.] Cabot [chief, Division of Caribbean and Central American Affairs] and I suggest that the . . . clause marked on the draft, . . . referring to Martínez' "continuance in office . . . in accordance with the terms of the Political Constitution in force" . . . should be deleted, lest an attempt be made to use it to convince the Salvadorans of the Department's approval of the so-called "constitutional" procedure by which Martínez was continued in office[,] and for other reasons.

The final text, without the paragraph to which Cochran referred, was sent to the embassy in San Salvador for transmittal to the Salvadoran government on April 26.[25]

Thurston wired the secretary of state on May 1: "Despite their routine nature, the delivery of your letter and that of the President . . . would probably be deliberately misconstrued by the Government and innocently by the opposition. I should like to be authorized to withhold them for the time being."

The State Department's reply went through three drafts:

> [undated]
>
> You are authorized in your discretion to withhold delivery of the letters . . . for a few days, but it is desired that they be delivered sometime during the month of May. . . . It is the Department's purpose to continue relations with the Government of El Salvador, and it does not wish comment to develop with respect to its attitude as a result of withholding delivery of the letter.

> May 4, 1944
>
> You are authorized in your discretion to withhold delivery of the letters . . . for the present. It is hoped that you will feel warranted in delivering them within the next month.

> May 8, 1944
>
> Please withhold delivery of the letters mentioned in your telegram no. 129 of May 1, 4 p.m. until the present political crisis has passed.[26]

The increasing caution in Washington undoubtedly reflected the pressure on the embassy in San Salvador, which mounted as the civic strike got underway.

On May 4 it came to Thurston's attention that a Colonel van Hovenberg of the U.S.-financed Servicio Cooperativa Interamericano de Salubridad had threatened to fire any of the organization's Salvadoran engineers who joined the strike and had said that they would not be eligible to work for any other U.S. agency in El Salvador. Thurston also heard that "the students were under the impression that the Embassy was in favor of this attitude." He promptly called in van Hovenberg, who claimed "that his words had been incorrectly translated" and promised "to make it clear that the SCISP would maintain an absolutely neutral position toward the strike."[27]

In reporting the developments of May 5 to the State Department, Thurston concluded:

> The Embassy is being subjected to pressure to intervene . . . accompanied by the suggestion that if the Embassy and the Government of the United States again stand by . . . the prestige of the United States will be irreparably damaged.
>
> I would appreciate any suggestions the Department may care to make for my guidance.[28]

A telegram dispatched at nine in the evening on May 6 contained the State Department's last unequivocal word on the subject:

> The Department authorizes you with respect to the question raised in your 137 of May 5, 11 p.m. strictly informally to indicate in your discretion the Department's policy as follows:
>
> In 1933 the United States solemnly pledged itself to a policy of non-intervention in the internal political affairs of the other American Republics. . . . This policy was adopted after long and careful consideration to allay the complaints which had frequently been voiced in the other American Republics to policies theretofore pursued by the United States. . . .
>
> The United States has sincerely endeavored to fulfil the obligations which it thereby assumed. The fact that it has not voiced disapproval of domestic political developments in various of the other Republics does not necessarily mean that it approves all of those developments. It merely means that the United States feels itself bound not to express either approval or disapproval.

This instruction probably crossed Thurston's report of the same date, which reflected rising tension in San Salvador: "Despite insistent pressure I have not called a meeting of the diplomatic corps and of course I have taken no independent action. I fear, however, that events will soon make it impossible for me to escape action as dean of the diplomatic corps, or more important, as the agent of American policy."[29]

Then came the death of José Wright. Alberto Peña Kampy (a generally unreliable informant who may, however, have heard the story of Thurston's visit to Martínez on May 7 from Martínez or someone close to him) asserted that the ambassador made a formal protest of the "murder" of Wright,

> adding menacingly "that he would let the Government of the United States know what was now happening in El Salvador so that it might take the immediate necessary measures which his government believed most appropriate. Among them, possibly military intervention to impose peace and tranquility and guarantee the lives and security of the many resident North Americans."[30]

The only first-hand account of that meeting is the following telegram dispatched by Thurston at eight in the evening on May 7:

I called on President Martínez this evening accompanied by Secretary Gade and the Military Attaché with respect to the murder of young Wright. The Minister for Foreign Affairs was present.

The President stated that both the policemen involved had been captured and that a representative of the Embassy would be permitted to attend the hearings. He did not appear to be particularly concerned over the incident and neither he nor the Minister for Foreign Affairs made any expression of regret although I pointedly afforded them an opportunity to do so. As I reached the head of the stairs when leaving[,] however[,] the President lamely made some reference to the effect that of course the Government lamented the occurrence. I replied to this belated and perfunctory remark by stating that I had made my representations on the case without prejudice to such further representations as my Government might decide upon.[31]

Later that evening Thurston had two more conversations which bore significantly on the crisis. The ambassador recorded on May 8:

Mr. Llanos, Manager of the Pan American Airways[,] called last evening and informed me that he had virtually decided to cancel Pan American Airways planes landing at San Salvador today [May 8] and desired to know my opinion with respect to this procedure. I replied that I suspected that if he took such action he would find himself summoned to the presidential palace early this morning for an explanation[,] and I asked him what explanation he would be able to give. He said that it was general knowledge that grave disorders such as rioting and looting or even worse were widespread and generall[y] believed [*sic*]. . . . The greater part of my staff was in my office during this conversation and upon checking with them as to their opinion of the possibility of serious disturbances today it was ascertained that there was unanimous agreement that such danger was real. I thereupon authorized Mr. Llanos to say that he had consulted me with respect to canceling plane service and that I had approved.

The flights were canceled "for several days" beginning May 8, and a North American journalist picked up the rumor that the president decided to step down immediately after Thurston informed him that he (the ambassador) had ordered the suspension of service.[32]

Finally, Thurston also wrote on May 8:

Shortly before midnight last night Mr. W. A. Dalton called and said that he had just participated in a conversation with ex-President Jorge Meléndez and General Trabanino, the Salvadoran Minister at Tegucigalpa. He said that Meléndez had pointed out the gravity of the general strike situation to General Trabanino[,] who had suddenly declared that he had made up his mind and that[,] while he was a friend of General Martínez[,] he would go at once to the Presidential palace and describe the facts of the situation to him and urge him to relinquish the Presidency. Mr. Dalton said that Trabanino had expressed a desire to see me after this interview and to inquire if I would receive him. I replied that of course I would.

While Dalton was still in my office General Trabanino was announced and Dalton withdrew. General Trabanino, who appeared to be quite nervous[,] stated that he had heard of the murder of young Wright and the serious situation that had arisen as a result thereof and that as a patriotic Salvadoran he desired to do all possible to spare his country the humiliation of armed intervention by the Government of the United States and that if I would tell him what the situation was in this respect he would immediately go and see President Martínez. It was thus apparent that Trabanino had not seen the President on any such errand as Dalton had described but that he probably had come to the Embassy from President Martínez to gain a clearer understanding of the implications of my visit to the presidential palace earlier in the evening.

As I considered it highly inadvisable to leave uncorrected any impression that I had threatened or contemplated armed intervention in El Salvador as a consequence of the murder of Wright I informed General Trabanino of the exact nature of my visit to General Martínez and my statements in connection therewith and assured him that no thought or mention of intervention had taken place insofar as I was concerned with respect to the Wright case.[33]

What can be concluded from this record?

Washington policymakers had no interest in the removal of Martínez—indeed, they would probably have preferred to maintain the status quo in Central America for the duration of the war. Their concern throughout the developing conflict in El Salvador was to keep the United States from becoming implicated in it in any way.

If Thurston at any time failed to abide by his repeated and emphatic instructions on this point, he had good reason not to report or leave any record of the fact. The documents indicate, however, that he fundamentally agreed with the State Department's policy, his awareness of its ambiguities notwithstanding. He tried consistently to implement it, even going so far as to resist mediation that other foreign diplomats wanted during the April revolt because he felt that such seemingly neutral intervention would favor the insurrection.

It is certainly safe to conclude that Thurston did not at any point threaten Martínez with military action by the United States. Even if he had wanted to do so, he would have been rash indeed to do it, knowing that the State Department would not back him up. The record of his conversation with General Trabanino shows that he explicitly disclaimed any thought of such intervention, and that disclaimer should have reached the president before his meeting with the cabinet on the morning of May 8.

On the other hand, Thurston probably found it difficult to maintain his accustomed detachment in the face of recriminations against the United States following the failure of the April insurrection, as well as the personal distress that the execution of the two men he had handed over to the government must have caused him. Developments during the last two weeks of the Martínez regime suggest that he was anxious to avoid giving the opposition any further cause for complaint, and the weight of the embassy's influence subtly shifted into the balance against the government.

8. The May Strike in Perspective

What came to be known in El Salvador as *The huelga de brazos caídos* or the *huelga de mayo* (May Strike) followed a long period of growing disaffection with President Martínez's autocratic rule. This discontent united people in all segments of the urban population, though active resistance came principally from members of the landowning and financial elite, professional men, and students. The campesino majority was notably *not* involved. There is no way to know how the people of the countryside felt about the president; after the tragedy of 1932 it is unlikely that anyone would have risked trying to mobilize them.

Martínez could perhaps have finished out his third term as president, scheduled to end in 1945, but his grab for a fourth term, in violation of a long-standing Salvadoran political norm, galvanized his enemies. The insurrection of April 2, 1944, was the predictable outcome of mounting opposition within the armed forces as well as the civilian elites. Martínez survived it by good luck, but his vengeful reaction precipitated a far larger uprising.

Salvadorans who lived through the civic strike invariably attributed the outpouring of popular support for it to the fear and revulsion aroused by the execution of participants in the April 2 revolt. But the far larger number of executions following the 1932 insurrection met with no such response. Other factors entered into the picture: the sentences were imposed and carried out in the capital city and were well publicized by the government itself; people already hostile to the regime perceived the armed revolt of 1944 as a just cause; and the imposition of death sentences on participants in an upper- and middle-sector movement threatened groups that had hitherto enjoyed relative immunity to the more violent forms of repression.

The civic strike was more than a spontaneous surge of public indignation. It reflected the evolution of a sophisticated strategy and three weeks of intensive organizing. The clandestine character of the organizing, without benefit of mass media, public meetings, or an extensive network of voluntary organizations, presented no serious obstacle to enlisting the cooperation of the relatively small white-collar, professional, business, and landowning groups, linked to the student organizers and to each other by their work, family ties, and friendships. The strike leaders lacked such ties to people in the lower sector of Salvadoran society, and this, along with the latter's less intense interest in the ouster of Martínez, explains why the lower classes became involved later and less unanimously.

Why did Martínez resign? His own statement quoted at the beginning of Chapter 6, as well as the testimony of one of his close associates, implied that he made the choice on moral grounds, a dubious claim in light of the 1932 massacre. In May 1944, however, Martínez faced a very different situation. The entirely nonviolent character of the resistance would have made it far more difficult to justify harsh repression either to himself, to his civilian associates, who were already alienated by the April executions, or to the world at large. Although his top military commanders would undoubtedly have tried to carry out any measures he asked of them—indeed some evidence exists to support the United States ambassador's belief that "some of these officials would have welcomed the opportunity to overcome the movement by force" —they could not rely on their subordinates.[1] Perhaps most important, the insurrection enjoyed the nearly unanimous support of the urban population, including economically powerful elements whose cooperation was essential to the functioning of the country.

The influence of the United States on Martínez's decision remains somewhat problematic. He was a tough, determined man who had survived in office for two years without United States recognition and pursued a relatively independent course throughout his rule. Some of his associates evidently perceived the United States Embassy as less than friendly to his administration by the end of 1943, but this did not deter him from putting through constitutional amendments that threatened North American business interests (as well as those of others), spurning the entire diplomatic corps' pleas for clemency toward the captured rebels of April 2, and remaining in office in the face of mounting pressure to step down.

On the other hand, Thurston's attitude following the April 2 insurrection probably did contribute to the erosion of Martínez's support and the constriction of his options. In particular, the ambassador's veiled warning about the "very serious consequences" that would follow any attack on United States citizens may well have influenced the Salvadoran government's policy of avoiding violence during the strike. Although Thurston knew perfectly well that the use of military force in El Salvador was not an option the United States would even consider in 1944, Salvadorans did not. The United States' record of armed intervention elsewhere in Latin America was evidently enough to stimulate the belief in some quarters that the shooting of José Wright could bring on such intervention.

Martínez surely knew better, but the crisis precipitated by Wright's death brought him face to face with his nearly total isolation. The option of brute force remained, but he was an astute enough man to realize that he could not govern on that basis alone.

With the removal of Martínez, the proponents of free elections confronted the military elite that he had established in control of the government. A full analysis of the ensuing struggle between the armed forces and the liberal coalition, once again headed by Agustín Alfaro and Arturo Romero, must await another study. The evidence indicates, however, that the aspirations of this coalition implied divesting the military establishment of the political power that had accrued to it during the Martínez era, whereas the officers were determined to hold on to that power.

The showdown came with a military coup that ousted Provisional President Andrés I. Menéndez on October 21, 1944. The determined nonviolent resistance, including two civic strikes, that extended over the next month created serious problems for the new rulers. However, the civilian leadership relied primarily on an armed revolt, which was launched from Guatemala in December 1944. Challenged on the terrain where its greatest strength lay, the military establishment swiftly and decisively defeated the insurgents.

The fight was not over. One participant in the anti-Martínez conspiracy compared the movement of 1944 with the overture to an opera.[2] What he called the opera was the revolution of 1948, in which the generation of young officers whom the liberals had wooed in 1944 took over the government and initiated an era of modest reform. The government they established perpetuated military control, however, and at this distance it is clear that although the 1948 revolution brought to power a new ruling group with new policies, it did not lead to democracy in El Salvador.

The insurrection of 1944 thus failed to achieve its larger objective. Nevertheless, the downfall of Martínez marked a turning point of historic significance. It ended the era of government by individual strongmen, making El Salvador the first country in the hemisphere to replace personal dictatorship with rule by the military as an institution. At the same time it set in motion forces that would increasingly challenge military control.

The *huelga de mayo* revived and gave powerful impetus to the tradition of popular mobilization that had begun to take shape in the years before Martínez. That tradition flowered in the popular organizations of the 1970s and survived the unprecedented repression of the early 1980s. It lives on, and the last word on its significance for the nation's history is still to be written.

Reference Material

Chronology

1931

December 2	President Arturo Araujo ousted by military coup.
December 5	Vice President and Minister of War Maximiliano Hernández Martínez assumes presidency.

1932

January 21	State of siege decreed.
January 22	Campesino uprising begins in western El Salvador.
January 24	Campesino uprising crushed. Mass executions of campesinos continue.
February 5	Martínez elected by National Legislative Assembly to fill out Araujo's term.
March	Government promulgates moratorium on foreclosure of mortgages on land.
July	Government establishes Fondo de Mejoramiento Social. Promotion of ideas "contrary to political, social, or economic order" made a crime.
October	Promulgation of law authorizing creation of Junta de Defensa Social.

1933

April	Criticism of government officials by the press made a punishable offense. San Salvador newspapers suspend publication for nine days in protest.

1934

January	Minister of Government Salvador Castaneda Castro resigns in the face of accusations that he was involved in a plot to assassinate the president.
	United States recognizes Martínez government.
June	Legislation provides for creation of Banco Central de Reserva.
August	Minister of Defense General Andrés Ignacio Menéndez takes over presidency while Martínez campaigns for second term.
December	Legislation provides for creation of Banco Hipotecario.

1935

March 1	Martínez begins second term.
October	Military conspiracy against government uncovered.
November	Amendments to the military penal code increase penalties for rebellion and conspiracy to overthrow the government.

1936

November	Another coup plot discovered. One implicated officer executed.

1938

Uncertain	Government suppresses autonomy of university.
Uncertain	University students go on strike.
August	Undersecretary of defense dismissed, apparently because of his opposition to third term for the president.
September	Several Treasury officials resign.
October	Three members of cabinet and several other government officials resign over third term issue.

1939

January	Former Undersecretary of Defense José Asencio Menéndez and twenty-seven other officers implicated in an antigovernment conspiracy.
	New constitution promulgated.
	Legislative Assembly elects Martínez to third term.
March 1	Martínez begins third term as president.

1940

June	Students mark the fall of Paris with first antigovernment demonstration.
October	Martínez removes a number of pro-Nazi government officials.

1941

March	*El Mundo Libre* begins publishing.
September	Pro Francia Libre, Juventud Democrática Salvadoreña, and Acción Democrática Salvadoreña founded.
	Law regulating public meetings amended to require police permission for all political activities, including private meetings.
October	Acción Democrática Salvadoreña sets up committees to carry on antigovernment activities.
December 8	El Salvador declares war on Axis powers.

1943

February	Federación de Cajas de Crédito organized.
March	*El Mundo Libre* suppressed.
June	Campaign for a new term for Martínez begins.
	First opposition leaflet appears.
July 14	Opposition "Manifesto to the Salvadoran People" appears.
August	Opposition leaflet "Al pueblo salvadoreño" appears.
	Comité Nacional del Frente Juvenil Antifascista de El Salvador organized.
	Police arrest various presumed opponents of the government.
September	Government suppresses Comité Nacional del Frente Juvenil Antifascista de El Salvador.
	Drivers of private cars required to notify police of any proposed travel outside city or town limits at night.
	Opposition leaflets "Palabras para el ejecíto nacional" and "Las contribuciones para el Pro-Patria" circulate.
	Members of workers' societies arrested for antigovernment activity.
October 24	Petition to Supreme Court challenging constitutionality of 1941 restrictions on political activity published.
October 26	Government imposes prior censorship on all newspapers and periodicals.
October 30	Progovernment organization, Reconstrucción Nacional, holds mass meeting to discuss labor conditions.
October 31	Two opposition leaflets addressed to workers appear.
November 11	Supreme Court rejects petition on political activity.

December	Legislative Assembly approves *Ley de Vigilancia de Asociaciones Gremiales* and new statutes for Asociación Ganadera.
	Cabildos abiertos held in a number of towns to collect signatures on petition for a constituent assembly.
December 11	Students hold antigovernment demonstration.
December 20–21	Government begins roundup of prominent opponents. Some are accused of involvement in an assassination plot.
December 30	Legislative Assembly votes to call a constituent assembly.

1944

January	Government orders closing of Press Club.
January 9	Constituent Assembly elected.
January 25	Constituent Assembly opens.
February	Director of National Police calls in group of student antigovernment activists to order them to desist from political activity.
	More labor leaders arrested on suspicion of antigovernment activity.
February 24	Constituent assembly decrees a series of controversial amendments to the constitution.
February 29	Constituent assembly elects Martínez to new six-year term as president.
March 1	Martínez begins fourth term.
April 2	Air force and large part of army rise in revolt against Martínez.
April 3–May 7	Antigovernment newspapers *El Diario de Hoy*, *El Diario Latino*, and *El Gráfico* do not appear.
April 4	Loyal troops defeat insurgents.
April 9	Military court condemns ten officers to death for participating in revolt.
April 10	The ten officers are executed.
	10:00 P.M.–5:00 A.M. curfew imposed on San Salvador.
April 11	Nine officers and six civilians (most *in absentia*) condemned to death for involvement in the insurrectionary conspiracy.
	One civilian executed.
April 17	News of the capture of Arturo Romero reaches San Salvador.
	Group of women asks diplomatic corps to intercede with Martínez.
	Diplomatic corps calls upon Martínez to urge clemency for captured rebels.
	University reopened after extended Easter recess.
	Students begin to lay groundwork for university strike.
April 19	Minor confrontation between students and policemen leads to suspension of classes at university.
	Students promoting strike issue first leaflet.
April 23	Police stop march on behalf of political prisoners.
April 24	Fifteen officers and four civilians implicated in April 2 revolt

	sentenced to death (most *in absentia*). Three of the officers are executed.
	University student body declares strike in protest against executions.
April 25	Government lifts curfew.
	United States military attaché cables War Department that U.S. military police may be needed to protect North Americans in the event of a new uprising.
April 26	Students employed in public agencies stop working.
	United States ambassador squelches proposal for United States assistance in reorganizing Salvadoran air force.
April 27	Progovernment newspaper attacks strike of hospital interns.
	Police break up a novena for an executed officer.
	Officer's widow and some other schoolteachers go on strike.
April 28	Leaflet attacking student strike appears.
	Secondary school students and teachers in San Salvador begin to absent themselves from school.
April 29	Progovernment newspaper attacks strike as the work of a well-to-do minority.
May 1	Government issues order for arrest of some university students.
	United States ambassador asks for authorization to hold up delivery of a routine letter from the president of the United States acknowledging the inauguration of Martínez's new term in office.
May 2	Physicians at Hospital Rosales draft memorandum to Martínez demanding an amnesty for "persons charged with political offenses," the reinstatement of doctors who had been fired for political reasons, and respect for "democratic principles."
May 3	Theater employees walk out.
May 4	San Salvador market vendors announce intention to strike beginning May 5.
	Employees of the Servicio Cooperativo Interamericano de Salubridad announce intention to join the strike on May 5.
	Government releases civilians still held in connection with April 2 uprising.
May 5	Announced mass for the martyrs of April 2 attracts enormous crowd, but no priest arrives to conduct it.
	San Salvador physicians and dentists vote to strike.
	Pharmacists, lawyers, and justices of the peace go on strike.
	All banks and most stores close.
	Office employees of one railroad company, many government agencies, and the electric company walk out.
	Sanitation department declared on strike "by order of its chiefs."
	Santa Ana students and physicians go on strike.
	Students strike in San Miguel.
	Cabinet and president of National Legislative Assembly meet with Martínez and reportedly advise him to resign. Rumors of

imminent resignations of high officials of the government begin to circulate.
Martínez makes radio address attacking strike.
Representatives of striking groups name Comité de Reconstrucción Nacional to represent them.

May 6 Comité de Reconstrucción Nacional draws up manifesto demanding Martínez's resignation.
One railroad suspends operations.
San Salvador municipal employees and more national government employees stop working.
Strike spreads to Ahuachapán and Sonsonate.
Martínez urges many business owners to reopen their establishments.
Leaflet demanding reopening of stores appears.
Doors of two stores forced open and a few threats against people on strike are reported.
Rumors spread that government has brought armed campesinos into San Salvador.
Meeting of Reconstrucción Nacional attracts about three thousand people.

May 7 San Salvador police fire at group of boys in street, killing one, a U.S. citizen.
Angry crowds pour into streets.
Students set up a peacekeeping force.
United States ambassador calls upon Martínez, giving rise to rumors of United States intervention. In subsequent interview with Salvadoran government official, ambassador disclaims any threat of intervention.
Police withdrawn to their barracks.
President's cabinet decides to resign.
Santa Ana municipal employees announce intention to strike.

May 8 Pan American Airlines suspends landings in El Salvador.
Huge crowd gathers before Palacio Nacional.
Remaining government employees walk out.
Busses disappear from streets of San Salvador.
Service on second railroad ends.
Most businesses in Santa Ana close.
Banks close in San Miguel.
Schoolteachers in San Vicente declare themselves on strike.
After all-day negotiations, Martínez agrees to resign immediately.

May 9 National Assembly receives Martínez's resignation and names General Andrés I. Menéndez to replace him.
Amnesty declared.

May 10 Menéndez names his cabinet.

May 11 Martínez leaves country.
Strike ends.

Notes

Introduction

1. Clamp, "Overthrow of Jorge Ubico," p. 60; Bell, *Crisis in Costa Rica*, p. 102.

2. Virgilio Padilla Vega, "Manifiesto al pueblo hondureño" (San Salvador, May 1944), enclosed with John D. Erwin (United States ambassador to Honduras) to secretary of state, despatch 1108, June 5, 1944, Decimal File 800.20210 Krehm, William/5, General Records of the Department of State, Record Group 59, United States National Archives, Washington, D. C. (hereinafter abbreviated as RG 59, NA). Cuscatlán is an Indian name frequently used for El Salvador.

Except as otherwise indicated, all translations are by the author.

3. On the influence of the Salvadoran insurrection in Guatemala, see Petersen, "Students in Guatemala," pp. 72–73; Clamp, "Overthrow of Jorge Ubico," pp. 60–61.

4. James B. Stewart (United States ambassador to Nicaragua) to secretary of state, despatch 2364, July 3, 1944, Decimal File 817.00/7-344, RG 59, NA.

5. For contemporary reports and documents on the attempt to overthrow Carías, see Erwin to secretary of state, despatch 1144, June 20, telegrams 207, July 3, 208, July 4, 209, July 5, 210, July 6, despatch 1183, July 7, 1944; Francis C. Jordan (American vice consul, Puerto Cortes) to Erwin, July 15, 1944; Lee M. Hunsaker (American vice consul, Puerto Cortes), Voluntary Report no. 43, July 15, 1944; Concha R. de López, Mercedes A. de Collier, Maria A. de Gonzalez, Irma C. de Ocano, Leonor de Gómez Robelo, Eva de Peraza, E. de Guerrero, and Blanca Bonilla Reina to Hunsaker, July 20, 1944, enclosed with Hunsaker, Voluntary Report no. 50, July 29, 1944, Decimal File 815.00/4993, 7-344, 7-444, 7-544, 7-644, 7-744, 7-1544, 7-2944, RG 59, NA.

A brief pro-Carías account appears in González y Contreras, *Último caudillo*; pp. 191–97.

On the parallel movement to unseat Somoza García, see Stewart to secretary of state, despatch 2364 and telegram 409, July 3, telegram 417, July 4, despatch 2368, July 5, telegrams 425, July 6, 431, July 7, 1944, Decimal File 817.00/7-344, 7-444, 7-544, 7-644, 7-744, RG 59, NA.

6. Bell, *Crisis in Costa Rica*, pp. 100–103.

7. See, for example, Berardo García, *Explosión de mayo*, p. 88: "The civic front never intended to grasp deadly arms, but rather to maintain itself in inactivity, in *brazos caídos,* in simple inaction. . . ." The Spanish anarchist writer, Diego Abad de Santillán, made a similar distinction: "General strikes may be of *brazos caídos* and of fights and sabotage." *F.O.R.A.*, p. 291. The earliest use of the term I have seen in print occurs in Ochoa Mena, *Revolución de julio*, p. 103.

8. The term *civic strike* (*paro cívico*) was used to describe a general strike called by opposition political parties in Uruguay in 1984. "Uruguay," *Latin America Regional Report/Southern Cone*, p. 3. Cf. use of the term "*paro civil*" to describe the civic strike against Colombian President Rojas Pinilla. Londoño Marín, *Soldados sin coraza*, p. 73. *Jornadas de mayo*, p. 170.

9. Office of Strategic Services, Research and Analysis Branch, "President Somoza's Relations with Labor in Nicaragua," R&A no. 2970C, October 10, 1944. RG 59, NA; Bell, *Crisis in Costa Rica*, p. 102.

10. For a comparative study of fifteen such strikes between 1931 and 1961 see "The General Strike as an Unarmed Insurrection" in Parkman, "Insurrection Without Arms," pp. 5–42.

Chapter 1. Preparation

1. "Discurso pronunciado por Br. Reinaldo [Reynaldo] Galindo Pohl a nombre de la Asociación General de Estudiantes Universitarios (A.G.E.U.S.)," June 6, 1944, *La Universidad* (San Salvador), p. 19.

2. Woodward, *Central America*, pp. 38–39, 48, 54–55, 67–70. The quotation is from p. 70. The Kingdom of Guatemala included the present nations Costa Rica, Nicaragua, Honduras, El Salvador, and Guatemala, plus the present Mexican state of Chiapas. The intendency was an administrative division introduced in the Spanish colonies in the eighteenth century, roughly comparable to the earlier province.

3. Woodward, *Central America*, pp. 45–46; Olmedo, *Apuntes de historia*, p. 140; Luna, *Historia económica*, p. 136; Luna, "Bayonetas," p. 10.

4. Woodward, *Central America*, p. 70.

5. "José María Peinado, quoted in Guardado, "Ideas económico-políticas," p. 41.

6. Woodward, *Central America*, p. 90; C. Anderson, "El Salvador," pp. 56–57.

7. Woodward, *Central America*, p. 152.

8. Luna, *Historia económica*, pp. 205–6; Guardado, "Ideas económico-políticas," pp. 85–91; White, *El Salvador*, p. 93.

9. White, *El Salvador*, pp. 86–87; Rodriguez, *Central America*, p. 93. The quotation is from Rodriguez.

10. T. Anderson, *Matanza*, p. 7; Wilson, "Crisis," pp. 102–4.

11. Munro, *Five Republics*, pp. 107–8.

12. White, *El Salvador*, pp. 86–88.

13. Hermógenes Alvarado h., "Prólogo" in Fortín Magaña, *Inquietudes*, p. vii. (The "h." is an abbreviation for "hijo"—"child" or "son." It is the equivalent of "Jr." in English.)

14. White, *El Salvador*, p. 90; Vidal, *Nociones*, pp. 319–22, 334, 346–47; Luna, *Historia económica*, pp. 217–18; Luna, "Análisis," pp. 44, 124.

15. White, *El Salvador*, p. 104.

16. Browning, *El Salvador*, pp. 162, 167–72, 203, 205–16.

17. Browning, *El Salvador*, pp. 170–71; Durham, *Scarcity and Survival*, p. 22.

18. Munro, *Five Republics*, p. 114.

19. Wilson, "Crisis," pp. 30, 36–37, 34, 39, 84, 116–32. The quotations are from pp. 30 and 127.

Cf. opinion of José Salvador Guandique that both world wars impoverished the middle class. "Clase media en El Salvador," p. 117. The phenomenon to which he referred may have reflected in part the squeezing out of smaller landowners during the 1920s, as well as the displacement of Salvadoran manufactured products by imports in the same period. Wilson, "Crisis," p. 48.

20. Wilson, "Crisis," pp. 96–99, 111–12, 143–44, 509–11. The quotations are from p. 143.

21. Jones, *Caribbean*, p. 441.

22. G[eorge] B. Massey, acting United States military attaché, El Salvador, Report 207, February 24, 1944, Army Intelligence Project Decimal File, 1941–45, El Salvador 091.4, Records of the Office of the Assistant Chief of Staff, G-2, Intelligence, Records of the Army Chief of Staff, Record Group 319, United States National Archives, Washington National Records Center, Suitland, Maryland (hereinafter abbreviated as RG 319, WNRC). Cf. Marroquín, "Crisis de los años treinta," p. 116. Marroquín estimated, on the basis of an occupational analysis of the 1930 census, that only 0.2 percent of the *economically active* population could be described as upper class.

23. Wilson, "Crisis," pp. 132–33.

24. Browning, *El Salvador*, pp. 146–47.

25. White, *El Salvador*, p. 85 n. 90.

26. Luna, *Historia económica*, pp. 210–11; Munro, *Five Republics*, pp. 101, 99.

27. Vidal, *Nociones*, pp. 362, 359; Luna, "Análisis," p. 45; Macaulay, *Sandino Affair*, pp. 148–49.

28. Wilson, "Crisis," pp. 142–45. Although Wilson said he "[drew] upon the middle-sector thesis advanced by Professor John J. Johnson," he appears to include skilled workers in the "middle groups" as Johnson does not (pp. 142, 145). Cf. Johnson, *Political Change*, pp. 1–2.

Skilled workers did figure in all descriptions of the "middle class[es]" of El Salvador that the writer reviewed. Massey identified the "lower middle class" with "tradesmen, craftsmen, farm and shop mechanics [and] government office workers" and the "upper middle class" with "a small group of professional men and junior executives." He estimated in 1944 that these groups together comprised about 20 percent of the population. Report 207, February 24, 1944 (see n. 22 above). (Cf. Marroquín, "Crisis de los años treinta," p. 116, who placed 4.4 percent of the economically active population as of 1930 in the middle class.) Massey's contemporary colleague in the United States Embassy, Vice Consul H. Gardner Ainsworth, described the "middle class" as consisting "of a well-developed professional group and an important small-business and property-owning group which extends well down into the 'lower middle' artisan class." "The Interaction of Economic and Political Forces in El Salvador" (no. 10/American Embassy, San Salvador, El Salvador, January 13, 1944), Decimal File 816.00/1182, General Records of the Department of State, RG 59, NA.

These descriptions agree with those of T. Anderson, *Matanza*, p. 11, and Guandique, "Clase media en El Salvador," pp. 115–17. Guandique estimated that the middle class constituted 30 percent of the population, which seems like an inflated figure. It may have reflected changes brought about by World War II and the 1948 revolution.

None of these observers drew lines between employees and self-employed small proprietors or between manual and intellectual workers, and as noted hereafter, groups that they included in the middle classes—artisans, white collar employees, and teachers—figured prominently in the Salvadoran labor movement. This may help to explain the relative solidarity of the urban population in 1944.

29. Parada, *Etapas políticas*, pp. 62–65, 104–5; García, *Recopilación*, pp. 9–10, 120, 188–92; Luna, "Historia de la Universidad," pp. 5–6; Vidal, *Nociones*, pp. 420–22.

30. Arias Gómez, "Reforma universitaria," pp. 3–4.

31. Wilson, "Crisis," p. 147; Arias Gómez, "Reforma universitaria," p. 4; Magaña Menéndez, *Estudios*, pp. 126–29.

32. López Vallecillos, "Reflexiones," p. 20 n. 19; Elam, "Appeal to Arms," pp. 7–8; White, *El Salvador*, p. 86.

33. Wilson, "Crisis," p. 164; Elam, "Appeal to Arms," p. 9; Munro, *Five Republics*, p. 108.

34. Elam, "Appeal to Arms," pp. 9–10. The quotations are from p. 9.

35. Wilson, "Crisis," p. 168; Luna, "Bayonetas," p. 10; López Vallecillos, "Reflexiones," p. 21. Cf. Monteforte Toledo, "Liberalismo en Mesoamérica," p. 15, in which Toledo stated that in El Salvador—in contrast to other Central American countries—"strong nuclei of career officers from the conservative upper class exist." Munro observed that the Escuela Politécnica attracted "many young men of the better classes." *Five Republics*, p. 108. The meaning of the term "better classes" is unclear, however, and in any case he knew the pre-1922 officer corps. According to Elam, many of the senior officers retired between the closing of the Escuela Politécnica and the opening of the Escuela Militar. This suggests that the latter created an essentially new military establishment. "Appeal to Arms," pp. 14–15.

36. Wilson, "Crisis," pp. 164–66, 168; Elam, "Appeal to Arms," pp. 16, 23–25. The quotations are from Wilson, pp. 165 and 168.

37. Menjívar, *Formación y lucha*, pp. 25, 32, 26–27; Morales Pleitez de Gómez et al., "Federación unitario sindical," p. 34; Wilson, "Crisis," pp. 50–53, 149; White, *El Salvador*, p. 91.

38. Menjívar, *Formación y lucha*, pp. 43–47; Larín, "Historia del movimiento sindical," pp. 136–37; Wilson, "Crisis," pp. 144, 81; Luna, *Historia económica*, p. 230.

39. Dalton, *Miguel Mármol*, pp. 73, 150; White, *El Salvador*, p. 94; Wilson, "Crisis," pp. 54, 146.

40. Larín, "Historia del movimiento sindical," pp. 138–39; Wilson, "Crisis," p. 148; Dalton, *Miguel Mármol*, p. 144; Menjívar, *Formación y lucha*, p. 49.

41. Dalton, *Miguel Mármol*, p. 143–44, 150–51, 155; White, *El Salvador*, p. 97. Cf. T. Anderson, who maintained that "there was a small Communist party working underground in El Salvador from about 1925. . . . founded by organizers from Guatemala and Mexico" and gave the date of the showdown between Communists and anarchosyndicalists in the FRTS as January 1930. *Matanza*, pp. 24, 27.

42. Luna, "Análisis," pp. 101–2; Wilson, "Crisis," pp. 156–57, 92–93, 191. For a detailed explanation of the 1922 loan, see Astilla, "Martínez Era," pp. 23–27.

43. Wilson, "Crisis," pp. 170–75, 96, 178; Munro, *Five Republics*, p. 114.

44. Wilson, "Crisis," pp. 140–43.

45. Arias Gómez, "Reforma universitaria," p. 4; Luna, "Historia de la Universidad," p. 6; T. Anderson, *Matanza*, pp. 32–36; 71–74.

46. López, "¿Masferrer socialista utópico, reformista o revolucionario?" p. 103.

47. Wilson, "Crisis," pp. 42–46, 85, 88–90, 120–21, 81, 84, 153–56; Larín, "Historia del movimiento sindical," p. 138.

48. Menjívar, *Formación y lucha*, p. 44; Dalton, *Miguel Mármol*, pp. 96–97, 93–94, 84; Wilson, "Crisis," p. 102. Mármol remembered the market women's protest as occurring in 1921.

49. Luna, "Historia de la Universidad," p. 6; Wilson, "Crisis," pp. 180, 175–176.

50. Larín, "Historia del movimiento sindical," pp. 137–38; Wilson, "Crisis," pp. 152–53.

51. López Vallecillos, *Periodismo*, p. 135; White, *El Salvador*, p. 91.

52. Larín, "Historia del movimiento sindical," p. 141; Luna, "Análisis," p. 96. Cf. Wilson, "Crisis," p. 146, which calls the "Ligas Rojas" "workers' associations" organized by the Meléndez-Quiñónez candidates.

53. T. Anderson, *Matanza*, pp. 42, 44; Wilson, "Crisis," pp. 205–6. The quotation is from Anderson.

54. Wilson, "Crisis," pp. 206, 200–203.

Chapter 2. The Martínez Regime

1. Dalton, "El general Martínez," in *Poemas*, p. 91.

2. Luna, "Análisis," p. 99; G[eorge] B. Massey, acting United States military attaché, El Salvador, Report 176, December 24, 1943, Army Intelligence Project Decimal File 1941–45, El Salvador 201.3, RG 319, WNRC; Wilson, "Crisis," pp. 165, 242–43. The quotations are from Wilson, pp. 165 and 243.

3. Luna, "Análisis," pp. 98–105, 94; Wilson, "Crisis," p. 257; author's interviews with David Luna, San José, Costa Rica, October 1976, and Rafael Carranza Anaya, San Salvador, September 23, 1976. Carranza Anaya was an army officer in the time of Martínez.

4. White, *El Salvador*, p. 99; T. Anderson, *Matanza*, pp. 60–63; Grieb, "Rise of Martínez," pp. 157–58.

According to Joaquín Castro Canizales, who served as secretary of the military directorate, the insurgents asked Martínez to serve as provisional president at the suggestion of the diplomatic corps (in the course of its mediation between the directorate and forces loyal to Araujo) only after General Salvador Castaneda Castro had declined the honor and the rebels had failed to locate their second choice, General Claramount Lucero, who had been a candidate in the 1931 election. Author's interview with Castro Canizales, San Salvador, December 13, 1976.

5. Elam, "Appeal to Arms," pp. 21–23, 25.

6. T. Anderson, *Matanza*, pp. 8, 12, 27, 40–41; Luna, "Heróico y trágico suceso," p. 55.

7. López Vallecillos, "Insurrección popular," p. 7.

8. Marroquín, "Crisis de los años treinta," p. 152; Luna, "Bayonetas," p. 10; Wilson, "Crisis," p. 210; López Vallecillos, "Insurrección popular," p. 8.

9. Elam, "Appeal to Arms," pp. 20–21.

10. Dalton, *Miguel Mármol*, pp. 244–46; López Vallecillos, "Insurrección popular," pp. 7–8; Wilson, "Crisis," pp. 214–15, 208, 217.

11. T. Anderson, *Matanza*, pp. 86–87, 91–92; Dalton, *Miguel Mármol*, pp. 267–70.

12. T. Anderson, *Matanza*, pp. 92–136. The quotation is from p. 135.

13. Luna, "Análisis"; Marroquín, "Crisis de los años treinta," pp. 143–45, 170–71; Salazar Valiente, "El Salvador," p. 98; Guidos Vejar, *Ascenso del militarismo*, pp. 7–8, 152; Elam, "Appeal to Arms," p. 109.

14. López Vallecillos, "Reflexiones," p. 28.

15. Luna, "Análisis," p. 98.

16. Elam, "Appeal to Arms," pp. 40, 46–47; White, *El Salvador*, pp. 102–3. The quotation is from White.

17. H. Gardner Ainsworth, United States vice consul, El Salvador, "The Interaction of Economic and Political Forces in El Salvador" (no. 10/American Embassy, San Salvador, El Salvador, January 13, 1944), Decimal File 816.00/1182, RG 59, NA.

18. T. Anderson, *Matanza*, p. 130; Luna, "Análisis," p. 95.

19. Wilson, "Crisis," pp. 264, 236; Astilla, "Martínez Era," pp. 61, 99–132, 184–87.

20. Poder Legislativo, Decreto no. 49, May 15, 1936, and Decreto no. 39, July 22, 1941, El Salvador, *Diario Oficial*, vol. 120, no. 111 (May 20, 1936), and vol. 131, no. 174 (August 9, 1941).

21. Assistant United States naval attaché, El Salvador, Intelligence Report, Serial 7-44-R, January 31, 1944, G-2 Regional File 1933-44, El Salvador, file 3000-3020, Box 817, Records of the Office of the Director of Intelligence, Records of the War Department General and Special Staffs, Record Group 165 (RG 165), WNRC; J[oseph] E. Maleady, United States vice consul, El Salvador, memorandum, July 17, 1943, enclosure to despatch 577, July 20, 1943, Decimal File 711.16/55, RG 59, NA.

22. Wilson, "Crisis," pp. 256, 264.

23. Baloyra, *El Salvador in Transition*, p. 11.

24. Articles 56, 55. Cf. 1886 Constitution, Art. 34.

25. Ainsworth, "Government Measures," p. 235; Browning, *El Salvador*, pp. 273–74.

26. Articles 32, 55, 62. The quotation is from Article 62.

27. Luna, "Análisis," p. 62.

28. Wallich et al., *Public Finance*, p. 201.

29. Banco Hipotecario [de El Salvador], Junta Directiva, *Lo ocurrido en el Banco Hipotecario de El Salvador*, p. 9; José Antonio Monterrosa, "El Dr. Menéndez Castro y el hambre del pueblo," *La Prensa Gráfica* (San Salvador), October 3, 1944; Ainsworth, "Government Measures," pp. 234, 236.

30. *La Prensa Gráfica*, December 11, 14, 18, 1943, January 15, 1944.

31. *El Diario Nuevo* (San Salvador), January 20, 1944.

32. Mario Sol, letters to *El Diario Latino* (San Salvador), June 5 and 21 1944; *La Prensa Gráfica*, November 13, 1943.

33. Reynolds, *Rapid Development*, p. 71; C[harles] P. Baldwin, United States military attaché, El Salvador, Report 100, May 3, 1943, G-2 Regional File 1933-44, El Salvador, file 3020, Box 817, RG 165, WNRC; Ainsworth, "Interaction" (see n. 17 above).

34. Guidos Vejar, *Ascenso del militarismo*, p. 139; Baloyra, *El Salvador in Transition*, pp. 13–14.

35. Wilson, "Crisis," pp. 233–34.

36. Ainsworth, "Government Measures," p. 235.

37. Browning, *El Salvador*, p. 275.

38. Elam, "Appeal to Arms," p. 109 n. 32.

39. [Julio C. Calderón], Gobernador Deptal., Ahuachapán, to Ministro de Gobernación, November 22, 1943, and attached leaflet beginning "Los Dueños de Taller, Tiendas y Almacenes de Calzado Al Público en General (Ahuachapán, November 1943)," (attached to Calderón, November 22, 1943). File 210; Calderón to Ministro de Gobernación, November 23, 1943, and Rudolfo V. Morales, Ministro de Gobernación, to Gobernador, Ahuachapán, November 24, 1943, both in file 083, El Salvador, Ministerio de Gobernación, file known as "Antecedentes," 1943, Sección de Archivos, Ministerio del Interior, San Salvador (abbreviated hereinafter as MG, "Antecedentes," with year).

40. Salvador Peña Trejo, Gobernador, Santa Ana, to Ministro de Gobernación, December 11, 1943, file 210.; Rudecindo Monterrosa, Director General de Policía, to Ministro de Gobernación, December 19, 1942, file 313.1, MG, "Antecedentes," 1943; "Dirección General de Policía," número de orden 726, July 3, 1943; "Gobernación Política de Santa Ana," número de orden 2296, November 30, 1943; El Salvador, Ministerio de Gobernación, *Entrada de correspondencia, 1943*, Sección de Archivos, Ministerio del Interior, San Salvador (abbreviated hereinafter as MG, *Entrada* with year of volume).

41. Wilson, "Crisis," p. 241; Ainsworth, memorandum, November 3, 1943, enclosure to despatch 929, November 4, 1943, Decimal File 816.00/1153, RG 59, NA.

42. See, in particular, [Manuel] Escalante Rubio, "Aclaración a capitalistas y trabajadores," *El Diario Latino*, May 20, 1944. Escalante Rubio was Reconstrucción Social's *jefe de organización*.

43. Ainsworth, November 3, 1943 (see n. 41 above); Massey to Walter Thurston, United States Ambassador to El Salvador, January 10, 1944, G-2 Regional File 1933-44, El Salvador, file 3600-3610, Box 818, RG 165, WNRC.

44. *La Prensa Gráfica*, March 20, 1940; Massey, Report 259, April 27, 1944, Army Intelligence Project Decimal File, 1941-45, El Salvador 004.06, RG 319, WNRC; Luna, "Análisis," p. 65.

45. *La Prensa Gráfica*, January 3, 6, February 4, 1940, January 22, February 2, 1944; *El Diario Nuevo*, March 23, April 1, 14, 1944; author's interview with Ernesto Mauricio Magaña, San Salvador, March 1978; Larín, "Historia del movimiento sindical," p. 143.

46. Elam, "Appeal to Arms," p. 41; Luna, "Análisis," p. 121; Maleady, memorandum, February 2, 1944, enclosure to despatch 1235, February 3, 1944, Decimal

File 816.00/1190, RG 59, NA.; Poder Legislativo, Decreto no. 134, November 16, 1935, *Diario Oficial*, vol. 119, no. 252 (November 16, 1935).

47. Baldwin, Report 142, July 30, 1943, G-2 Regional File 1933-44, El Salvador, file 3020, Box 817, RG 165, WNRC; Maleady, February 2, 1944 (see n. 46 above); Elam, "Appeal to Arms," p. 60.

48. Peña Kampy, "*General Martínez*," p. 69.

49. Remarks attributed to a Salvadoran attorney in an anonymous memorandum by a member of the United States Embassy staff, El Salvador, enclosure no. 1 to despatch 1156, January 8, 1944, Decimal File 816.00/1172, RG 59, NA.

50. W. J. McCafferty, United States chargé d'affaires ad interim, El Salvador, to Secretary of State, despatch 394, January 20, 1934, Decimal File 816.00/938; Robert Frazer, United States minister to El Salvador, to Secretary of State, despatch 48, January 25, 1938, Decimal File 816.00/1019; both in RG 59, NA.

51. Gallardo, *Constituciones*, vol. 2, p. 96; Wilson, "Crisis," p. 258.

52. Poder Ejecutivo, Secretaría de Gobernación, Acuerdo no. 324, February 26, 1944, and Acuerdo no. 348, February 29, 1944, *Diario Oficial*, vol. 136, no. 54 (March 4, 1944) and no. 56 (March 7, 1944); "Presidencia de la República," número del orden 13374, September 28, 1943, El Salvador, Ministerio de Gobernación, *Salida de correspondencia, 1943*, Sección de Archivos, Ministerio del Interior, San Salvador (abbreviated hereinafter as MG, *Salida* with year of volume).

53. Frazer to Secretary of State, despatch 1786, October 20, 1941, Decimal File 816.00/1088; Robert L. Brown, legal advisor, United States Embassy, El Salvador, memorandum, April 29, 1943, enclosure to despatch 430, June 4, 1944, Decimal File 816.00/1120, RG 59, NA; author's interview with Marina Rosales, San Salvador, October 4, 1976. The quotations are from Frazer.

Monthly lists of employees in various agencies who had—and had not—contributed to Pro-Patria appear in file 120.0, "Contribuciones Para el Partido Nacional Pro Patria," El Salvador, MG, "Antecedentes," 1943.

54. Elam, "Appeal to Arms," p. 44.

55. Poder Legislativo, Decreto no. 143, July 21, 1932, *Diario Oficial*, vol. 113, no. 169 (July 25, 1932); *Constitución Política de la República de El Salvador, decretada por la Asamblea Nacional Constituyente el 20 de enero de 1939*, Article 124.

56. Ortiz Mancia, "Memorial general," p. 25; Luna, "Análisis," pp. 50, 73, 123.

57. J. Humberto Huezo, letter headed "Debemos tener leyes democráticas," *El Diario Latino*, May 12, 1944.

58. Author's interview with Jorge Bustamante, San Salvador, March 22, 1978; Salvador Cañas, "La juventud en marcha," *La Prensa Gráfica*, July 26, 1944.

59. Romeo Fortín Magaña to Thurston, Ahuachapán, January 1, 1944, enclosure no. 3 to despatch 1156, January 8, 1944 (see n. 49 above).

60. McCafferty to secretary of state, despatch 282, April 7, 1933, Decimal File 816.911/33, RG 59, NA.

61. Figeac, *Libertad de imprenta*, p. 254; Gerhard Gade, United States chargé d'affaires ad interim, El Salvador, to secretary of state, despatch 3100, December 7, 1942, Decimal File 813.00/1320, RG 59, NA.

62. Figeac, *Libertad de imprenta*, pp. 252–53; "Setenta horas de ayuno," pp. 9, 26; interview with Castro Canizales, December 13, 1976.

63. Salvador Peña Trejo, Gobernador, Santa Ana, to Ministro de Gobernación,

November 27, 1943, file 210., El Salvador, MG, "Antecedentes," 1943; Baldwin, Report 100, May 3, 1943 (see n. 47 above).

64. Elam, "Appeal to Arms," p. 55; Larín, "Historia del movimiento sindical," pp. 143, 145. The quotation is from Elam.

65. *El Nacionalista* (San Salvador), June 6, 1935; Dalton, *Miguel Mármol*, pp. 420–21; Frazer to secretary of state, despatch 1786, October 20, 1941. On prison conditions and torture, see Dalton, *Miguel Mármol*, pp. 406–8; Rogelio Moreno M., letter in *La Prensa Gráfica*, July 13, 1944.

66. Elam, "Appeal to Arms," p. 55.

67. Author's interview with Marina Rosales, October 4, 1976. Marina Rosales is David Rosales's daughter.

68. Elam, "Appeal to Arms," pp. 51–52, 54; [Romeo Fortín Magaña et al.], "Opinión jurídica sobre convocatoria a una asamblea nacional constituyente," *El Diario Latino*, June 29, 1944. Reprinted as Anexo IX in Fortín Magaña, *Inquietudes*, pp. 239–44.

69. Grieb, "Rise of Martínez," pp. 151, 155–70; Astilla, "Martínez Era," pp. 12–13, 50–86.

70. Stanisfer, "Tobar Doctrine," pp. 269–70.

71. Wood, *Good Neighbor Policy*, pp. 137–51. The quotations are from pp. 137 and 151.

72. Luna, "Análisis," p. 95; Elam, "Appeal to Arms," p. 48; Astilla, "Martínez Era," pp. 150–52, 155–58.

73. Alas, "Comercio exterior," pp. 71, 73–77; Astilla, "Martínez Era," pp. 133–35.

74. Elam, "Appeal to Arms," p. 50; Frazer to secretary of state, despatches 1797 and 1884, October 22 and December 5, 1941, Decimal File 816.00/1089 and 1091, RG 59, NA. The Germans who served as head of the Escuela Militar and manager of the Banco Hipotecario had been replaced in September 1939. Astilla, "Martínez Era," p. 168.

75. Baldwin, Report 135, July 10, 1943, G-2 Regional File 1933–44, El Salvador, file 3020, Box 817, RG 165, WNRC; Thurston to secretary of state, despatch 624, July 29, 1943, Decimal File 816.00/1131, RG 59, NA. William Renwick was the North American fiscal agent responsible for collection of the 1922 loan.

The United States Legation in El Salvador was upgraded to an embassy in January 1943; hence Thurston's title changed to "Ambassador."

Chapter 3. The Opposition

1. Comité Revolucionario Salvadoreño to "Muy señor nuestro" [United States consul], n.p., n.d., typed carbon copy in an album entitled "Apuntes de política patria[:] Dic 1941/44[,] Dic 1954/Feb. 1955," Biblioteca Dr. Manuel Gallardo, Santa Tecla (abbreviated hereinafter as "Apuntes").

2. Romeo Fortín Magaña to Maximiliano Hernández Martínez, September 17, 1938, as published in *La Prensa Gráfica*, May 12, 1944; Luna, "Análisis," pp. 120, 122.

3. Walter W. Hoffmann, United States chargé d'affaires ad interim, El Salvador, to

secretary of state, despatches 281, 308 and 327, August 24, September 14 and October 7, 1938; O[verton] G. Ellis [Jr.], United States vice consul, El Salvador, memorandum, March 14, 1944, Decimal File 816.00/1031, 1036, 1038, and 1277, RG 59, NA. The quotation is from despatch 327.

Colonel José Asencio Menéndez is not to be confused with General Andrés I. Menéndez, the loyal *martinista* who served as minister of defense in 1944. The former, one of the few political liberals in the officer corps, was a son of former President Francisco Menéndez, and upheld the principles of the 1886 constitution as a matter of family honor and tradition. Luna, "Análisis," p. 122.

4. Fortín Magaña to Martínez, September 17, 1938, as published in *La Prensa Gráfica*, May 12, 1944; Figeac, *Libertad de imprenta*, pp. 255–58. Fortín Magaña listed his previous positions in a letter to U.S. Ambassador Walter Thurston, Ahuachapán, January 1, 1944, enclosure no. 3 to despatch 1156, Decimal File 816.00/1172, RG 59, NA.

5. A[rcher] B. Hannah, assistant United States military attaché, Guatemala, Report 1155, April 18, 1944, G-2 Regional File 1933-44, El Salvador, file 3000-3020, Box 817, RG 165, WNRC; Robert Frazer, United States minister to El Salvador, to secretary of state, despatch 1786, October 20, 1941, Decimal File 816.00/1088, RG 59, NA.

6. Elam, "Appeal to Arms," pp. 107–9. Cf. Rufus A. Byers, chief, United States Military Mission to El Salvador, to chief, Military Intelligence Service, War Department, April 10, 1944, which listed among causes of the April 1944 armed revolt "the feeling that General Martínez has been in power too long; changes his high public officials too infrequently, and keeps some who are thoroly [*sic*] bad; . . ." G-2 Regional File 1933-44, El Salvador, file 3000-3020, Box 817, RG 165, WNRC.

7. G[eorge] B. Massey, acting United States military attaché, El Salvador, Report 162, November 9, 1943, G-2 Regional File 1933-44, El Salvador, file 3020, Box 817, RG 165, WNRC; Fausto Salvador Crespo Sánchez, interview with author, San José, Costa Rica, October 1976.

8. C[harles] P. Baldwin, United States military attaché, El Salvador, Report 117, July 3, 1943, file 2600; United States naval attaché, Guatemala, Intelligence Report, serial 234-43-R, August 10, 1943, files 3000-4000 and 3020 (continuation), both in Box 817, G-2 Regional File 1933-44, El Salvador, RG 165, WNRC.

9. Elam, "Appeal to Arms," pp. 175–76.

10. Paul A. Goodin, assistant United States naval attaché, El Salvador, Intelligence Report, serial 1-43, September 24, 1943, G-2 Regional File 1933-44, El Salvador, file 3020, Box 817, RG 165, WNRC; H. Gardner Ainsworth, United States vice consul, El Salvador, "The Interaction of Economic and Political Forces in El Salvador," (no. 10/American Embassy, San Salvador, El Salvador, January 13, 1944), and memorandum, November 3, 1943, enclosure to despatch 929, November 4, 1943, Decimal File 816.00/1182 and 1153, RG 59, NA; José Angel Zepeda, interview with author, San Salvador, December 17, 1976.

La Prensa Gráfica reported on December 25, 1943, that some three hundred persons left for the United States every month.

11. Ramón Pleites, "Importancia del Convenio Interamericano del Café en la economía de la nación salvadoreña," *La Prensa Gráfica*, October 21, 1943.

12. *La Prensa Gráfica*, September 22, 1943; assistant United States naval attaché,

El Salvador, Intelligence Report, serial 7-44-R, January 31, 1944, G-2 Regional File 1933-44, El Salvador, file 3000-3020, Box 817, RG 165, WNRC.

13. Assistant United States naval attaché, El Salvador, January 31, 1944 (see n. 12 above); *La Prensa Gráfica*, September 21, 29, October 7, November 26, 1943; January 15, 1944.

14. Massey, Report 201, February 14, 1944, G-2 Regional File 1933-44, El Salvador, file 3020, Box 817, RG 165, WNRC; Ainsworth, "Interaction" (see n. 10 above); *La Prensa Gráfica*, February 1, 1944.

15. Assistant United States naval attaché, El Salvador, January 31, 1944 (see n. 12 above); Elam, "Appeal to Arms," p. 57.

16. Goodin, September 24, 1943 (see n. 10 above); interview with Zepeda, December 17, 1976. Zepeda, a barber (not a "worker" in his own view, since he owned his barbershop), was the first president of the Unión Nacional de Trabajadores, a labor party that emerged immediately after the fall of Martínez.

17. Assistant United States naval attaché, El Salvador, January 31, 1944 (see n. 12 above); Ainsworth, "Interaction" (see n. 10 above).

18. Byers, April 10, 1944 (see n. 6 above).

19. Alexander, *Organized Labor*, p. 202; United States naval attaché, Guatemala, August 10, 1943 (see n. 8 above).

20. Baldwin, Report 111, June 12, 1943, G-2 Regional File 1933-44, El Salvador, file 3020, Box 817, RG 165, WNRC.

21. Baldwin, Report 29, October 7, 1942, G-2 Regional File 1933-44, El Salvador, file 2930, Box 817, RG 165, WNRC.

22. Astilla, "Martínez Era," p. 181; Baldwin, Report 117, July 3, 1943 (see n. 8 above); interview with Fausto Salvador Crespo Sánchez, October 1976.

23. Castro Ramírez, "Camino de la esperanza," pp. 13–14.

24. Frazer to secretary of state, despatch 1810, October 30, 1941, Decimal File 816.00/1090, RG 59, NA.

25. See, for example, September 22, October 23, November 3, 18, 1943, January 3, 29, February 2, 1944.

26. *La Prensa Gráfica*, September 23, 1943; November 13, 1943; January 28, 1944; November 6, 13, 26, 1943; October 21, 18, 1943; January 2, 1944.

27. Dalton, *Miguel Mármol*, pp. 454–64. Neither the date of the shoemakers' meeting nor the date of the founding of the Alianza Nacional de Zapateros are given.

28. *El Diario Latino*, June 29, 1944.

29. Walter Thurston, United States ambassador to El Salvador, to secretary of state, despatch 1560, May 12, 1944, Decimal File 816.504/42, RG 59, NA.

30. Sociedad de Ayuda Mutua de los Ferrocarrileros (Larín, "Historia del movimiento sindical," p. 145); Unión Magisterial Salvadoreña, Sociedad de Empleados y Obreros "5 de Noviembre" (Cojutepeque), Unión de Empleados de Comercio, Sociedad de Artesanos "Esfuerzo y Cultura," and Unión de Carpinteros Salvadoreños (San Miguel) (*La Prensa Gráfica*, September 21, 22, 23, November 3, 26, 1943, February 3, 1944); Centro Social de Obreros (Jiquilisco), ("Varios," número de orden 1408, July 3, 1943, El Salvador, MG, *Entrada, 1943*); Sociedad de Amigos Impulso Obrero (La Unión) (Carlos Alberto Liévano, subsecretario de gobernación, to Gobernador Político, La Unión, December 9, 1943, El Salvador, Ministerio de Gobernación, *Correspondencia despachada*, 1943 (hereinafter abbreviated as MG, *Correspondencia*

despachada with year), Sección de Archivos, Ministerio del Interior, San Salvador). A thorough check of available sources would no doubt reveal more.

31. *La Prensa Gráfica*, November 26, 1943; March 25, 1944.

32. Interview with José Angel Zepeda, December 17, 1976; J. C[ordes] Dalworth, legal attaché, United States Embassy, El Salvador, "Strike of Dockworkers at La Libertad, El Salvador," August 20, 1943, Records of the Foreign Service Posts of the Department of State, Record Group 84 (RG 84), San Salvador, 1943, 850.4, WNRC.

33. *La Prensa Gráfica*, September 23, October 1, November 10, 21, 1943; Ainsworth, November 3, 1943 (see n. 10 above).

34. *La Prensa Gráfica*, November 26, 12, 19, 1943.

35. See, for example, texts of talks on January 5, 19, and March 2, 1943, in file 180.0, "Asuntos Políticos: Pláticas del Sr. Presidente," El Salvador, MG, "Antecedentes," 1943.

36. J[oseph] E. M[aleady], United States vice consul, El Salvador, memorandum, March 19, 1943, RG 84, San Salvador, 1943, 800, WNRC; Ainsworth, "Interaction" (see n. 10 above).

37. Thurston to secretary of state, despatch 929, November 4, 1943, and enclosure no. 1, "Formal Invitation to Workers of Every Class, Laborers and Peasants" (translation; n.p., n.d.), Decimal File 816.00/1153, RG 59, NA.

38. Massey, Report 284, May 30, 1944, G-2 Regional File 1933-44, El Salvador, file 3020-3410, Box 818, RG 165, WNRC; Thurston to secretary of state, despatch 1653, May 31, 1944, Decimal File 816.00/1436, RG 59, NA.

39. *El Diario Nuevo*, November 3, 1943, cited in Thurston, despatch 929, November 4, 1943 (see n. 37 above); Massey, Report 166, November 16, 1943, G-2 Regional File 1933-44, El Salvador, file 3020, Box 817, RG 165, WNRC.

40. Ainsworth, "Interaction" (see n. 10 above); Maleady, memoranda, March 19 and June 29, 1943, RG 84, San Salvador, 1943, 800, WNRC.

41. *La Prensa Gráfica*, December 30, 1943, February 12, 16, 1944; "Prohibiciones de la censura (hasta el 28 de febrero de 1944)," RG 84, El Salvador, 1944, 891, WNRC.

42. Ainsworth, "Interaction" (see n. 10 above).

43. Santos Dueñas, *Aurora*, pp. 8, 10; Dalton, *Miguel Mármol*, p. 485. See also the barrage of attacks on the thread factory after the fall of Martínez (*El Diario Latino*, May 30, 31, June 10, 14, 15, 17, 21, 28, 1944).

44. Winnall A. Dalton to Thurston, San Salvador, February 24, 1944, enclosed with despatch 1346, March 1, 1944, Decimal File 816.00/1214, RG 59, NA. Dalton has been identified on the basis of a handwritten note on Baldwin, Report 100, May 3, 1943, G-2 Regional File 1933-44, El Salvador, file 3020, Box 817, RG 165, WNRC.

The Salvadoran government in 1942 declared "the control of the planting, ginning and selling of cotton . . . a public utility" and made the Cooperativa Algodonera Salvadoreña Limitada, founded in 1940, the sole supplier of cotton used in textile manufacturing in El Salvador. Feltham, *Textile Industry*, pp. 4–5. For fuller descriptions of the functions of the Cooperativa Algodonera see Feltham, *Textile Industry*, p. 7; Reynolds, *Rapid Development*, p. 17; Browning, *El Salvador*, pp. 230–31. It is not clear from any of these descriptions, however, which powers other than those mentioned above were acquired during the Martínez era or to what extent the government controlled the Cooperativa Algodonera, another of the private agencies carrying on governmental functions that characterized El Salvador in the 1940s.

45. *El Diario Nuevo*, November 11, 1943; Massey, Report 167, November 23, 1943, G-2 Regional File, 1933-44, El Salvador, file 3020, Box 817, RG 165, WNRC, and Report 162, November 9, 1943; Ainsworth, "Interaction" (see n. 10 above). The quotation is from Massey, Report 162.

46. Ainsworth, memorandum, June 23, 1943, misfiled in RG 84, San Salvador, 1944, 800, WNRC. *El Diario Latino*, June 7, 1944.

47. *La Prensa Gráfica*, December 29, 1943.

48. Massey, Report 179, December 28, 1943, G-2 Regional File, 1933-44, El Salvador, file 4000-4130, Box 819, RG 165, WNRC; Ainsworth, June 23, 1943 (see n. 46 above).

49. Ainsworth, "Interaction" (see n. 10 above) and memorandum, June 23, 1943 (see n. 46 above).

50. H. L. Wightman, acting United States military attaché, El Salvador, Report 156, September 17, 1943, G-2 Regional File, 1933-44, El Salvador, file 3020, Box 817, RG 165, WNRC. Cf. Ainsworth, June 23, 1943 (see n. 46 above), citing reports that reached him through Maleady that the government "would like to take over the Cajas de Credito Rurales [*sic*] . . . and make use of them as political organizations during the coming elections."

51. Ainsworth, "Interaction" (see n. 10 above); assistant United States naval attaché, El Salvador, Intelligence Report, serial 6-43, November 8, 1943, G-2 Regional File, 1933-44, El Salvador, file 3020, Box 817, RG 165, WNRC.

52. Thurston to secretary of state, despatch 430, June 4, airgram 204, June 10, despatches 458, June 12, 582, July 20, 602, July 24, 611, July 28, 618, July 28, 630, July 31, 786, September 23, 936, November 8, 1009, November 24, 1943, Decimal File 816.00/1120, 1122, 1123, 1125, 1126, 1129, 1130, 1132, 1140, 1154, 1157, RG 59, NA. For additional light on the means by which this campaign was organized see Baldwin, Report 141, July 24, 1943, file 3020, and "Re: Current Political Activity" (San Salvador, n.d.), p. 2, file 3000-3020, both in G-2 Regional File 1933-44, El Salvador, Box 817, RG 165, WNRC. For official reports from mayors and governors on demonstrations and petitions, see file 180.0 "Asuntos Políticos: Pláticas del señor Presidente de la Repub [*sic*] (1943), "El Salvador, MG, "Antecedentes," 1943.

53. Thurston to secretary of state, despatch 1098, December 18, 1943, Decimal File 816.00/1163, RG 59, NA; "Re: Current Political Activity," n.d. (see n. 52 above), pp. 3–4.

Incidentally, the standard resolution made no mention of another term for President Martínez. The stated purposes of the proposed constituent assembly were "among others: legalization of the status of property belonging to foreigners whose countries are at war with ours; facilitating participation by the State with National funds in private and stock companies dependent from [*sic*] Mejoramiento Social; contributing to the formation of Banks o[r] Companies which shall develop social security, medical attention, and other problems which will present themselves in the post war [*sic*] period and whose solution is essential." "Re: Current Political Activity," n.d. (see n. 52 above), p. 4.

54. J. Somoza, h., Gobr. Depmtl. (San Miguel), to Ministro de Gobernación,

December 10, 1943; [signature illegible] Gobernador Departamental (San Vincente) to Ministro de Gobernación, December 11, 1943, both in file 180.1; Rudesindo Monterrosa, Director General de Policía, to Ministro de Gobernación, December 20, 1943, file 312.0, El Salvador, MG, "Antecedentes," 1943; O[verton] G. E[llis], United States vice consul, El Salvador, memorandum, December 22, 1943, enclosure to despatch 1117, December 29, 1943, Decimal File 816.00/1166 1/2, RG 59, NA.

55. Thurston to secretary of state, Telegram 296, December 29, 1943, and despatch 1166, January 11, 1944, Decimal File 816.00/1165 and 1176, RG 59, NA. El Salvador in this period had universal suffrage for men and restricted suffrage for women.

56. Gerhard Gade, United States chargé d'affaires ad interim, El Salvador, to secretary of state, despatch 642, August 4, 1943; Ellis, memorandum, September 9, 1943, enclosure no. 3 to despatch 736, September 10, 1943, Decimal File 816.00/1133 and 1144, RG 59, NA.

57. Intelligence Report, January 31, 1944 (see n. 12 above).

58. Dalton, *Miguel Mármol*, p. 421.

59. McCafferty to secretary of state, telegram 3, January 18, 1934, Decimal File 816.00/935, RG 59, NA; Elam, "Appeal to Arms," pp. 55–56.

60. Dalton, *Miguel Mármol*, pp. 319–20, 372–75, 383–89, 437, 447–53, 464–65, 484; Luna, "Análisis," pp. 118, 120.

61. Figeac, *Libertad de imprenta*, pp. 487–99.

62. Luna, "Análisis," pp. 50–51.

63. Ortiz Mancia, "Memoria general," p. 25.

64. Assistant United States naval attaché, El Salvador, January 31, 1944 (see n. 12 above).

65. Fabio Castillo, interview with author, San José, Costa Rica, October 15, 1976.

66. Luna, "Historia de la Universidad," p. 7. For reports on the content of two student *veladas* in 1943, see Baldwin, Report 135, July 10, 1943, G-2 Regional File 1933-44, El Salvador, file 3020, Box 817, RG 165, WNRC; typescripts headed "Información," San Salvador, July 5 and 17, 1943, enclosed with Francisco Marroquín to Maleady, San Salvador, July 17, 1943, RG 84, San Salvador, 1943, 800, WNRC.

67. Interview with Fabio Castillo, October 15, 1976; Ellis, memorandum, November 4, 1944, enclosure to despatch 2141, November 4, 1944, Decimal File 816.00/11-444, RG 59, NA.

68. J. H. Marsh, United States military attaché, El Salvador, Report 287, December 13, 1941, file 3020, Box 818; Guillermo Moscoso, Jr., assistant United States military attaché, El Salvador, Report 15, August 20, 1942, file 3000-4000, Box 817, G-2 Regional File 1933-44, El Salvador, RG 165, WNRC. The quotation is from Moscoso.

69. Thurston to secretary of state, despatch 216, March 23, 1943, RG 84, San Salvador, 1943, 800, WNRC.

70. Marsh, Report 198, October 4, 1941, G-2 Regional File 1933-44, El Salvador, file 3020, Box 818, RG 165, WNRC; Frazer to secretary of state, despatch 1715, September 22, 1941, and enclosure, "Text of a Manifesto of the 'Juventud Democrática Salvadoreña,' " (translation "from text as published in the *Diario Nuevo*, Sept. 20, 1941") Decimal File 816.00/1082, RG 59, NA.

71. Gilberto Lara to Thurston, San Salvador, February 8, 1943, RG 84, San Salvador, 1943, 843, WNRC.

72. *La Prensa Gráfica*, September 1, 1943; author's interview with Reynaldo Galindo Pohl (president of the Comité Estudiantil Universitario in 1943), Washington, D.C., September 27, 1977.

The labor organizations affiliated with the Antifascist Youth Front were the Sociedad Protectora del Motorista, the Centro Cultural de Motoristas, the Cooperativa de Empleados Municipales, the Alianza Nacional de Zapateros, and the Unión Magisterial Salvadoreña. The Frente Magisterial Democrático also participated, but available information suggests that this organization served less to represent the interests of teachers than as a vehicle for the views of the tireless antigovernment crusader, José Figeac. See Abraham Pineda Q. to Thurston, San Salvador, September 28, 1943, RG 84, San Salvador, 1943, 800; letter from José F. Figeac and José Victor Durán, *El Diario Latino*, May 15, 1944.

For the founding of the Comité de Escritores y Artistas Antifascistas de El Salvador, see Gade to secretary of state, despatch 710, August 31, 1943, RG 84, El Salvador, 1943, 843, WNRC.

73. *La Prensa Gráfica*, September 1, 1943; López Vallecillos, *Periodismo*, p. 311; Luna, "Análisis," p. 120. The authorities were probably right about Vassiliu's political views; Miguel Mármol remembered him as one of a group of young intellectuals who gravitated to the Communist party in the late 1930s. Dalton, *Miguel Mármol*, p. 447.

74. Thurston to secretary of state, despatch 810, September 29, 1943, Decimal File 816.00/1142, RG 59, NA.

75. "Act of Foundation of the 'Acción Democrática Salvadoreña,' " (translation, San Salvador, September 18, 1941) enclosed with Frazer, despatch 1715, September 22, 1943 (see n. 70 above).

76. Marsh, Report 198, October 4, 1941; Frazer, despatch 1715, September 22, 1943 (see n. 70 above for both). Miguel Tomás Molina had served as minister of finance in 1932 and early 1933. McCafferty to secretary of state, despatch 293, August 29, 1933, Decimal File 816.00/928, RG 59, NA.

77. A list of the members of the Central Committee appears at the end of the "Act of Foundation." Information about Pérez, Segovia, and Boza came from the author's interview with Marina Rosales, San Salvador, October 4, 1976. For confirmation of her recollections regarding Boza, see assistant United States naval attaché, El Salvador, Intelligence Report, serial 15-43, December 31, 1943, G-2 Regional File 1933-44, El Salvador, file 3000-3020, Box 817, RG 165, WNRC. Zepeda's name headed the signatories of the dentists' resolution to strike in 1944 (*El Diario Latino*, May 13, 1944). On Cisneros, see Tomás Q. Cuadra, "Homenaje," *La Prensa Gráfica*, September 20, 1944. On Merlos, see Trigueros de Leon, "Educación integral," *La Prensa Gráfica*, January 13, 1940, and Dalton, *Miguel Mármol*, pp. 81, 113.

78. Frazer to secretary of state, despatch 1720, September 23, 1941, Decimal File 816.00/1083, RG 59, NA; Marsh, Report 209, October 11, 1941, G-2 Regional File 1933-44, El Salvador, file 3020, Box 818, RG 165, WNRC.

79. Frazer to secretary of state, despatches 1727, n.d. (date stamp indicates receipt October 1, 1941), and despatch 1740, n.d. (date stamp indicates receipt October 8, 1941), Decimal File 816.00/1084 and 1085, RG 59, NA.

80. Santos Dueñas, *Aurora*, p. 43. The authorities evidently had some inkling of what went on at these gatherings, for the files of the Ministry of Government contain a newspaper notice of a birthday party for David Rosales in a folder marked "PUBLI-

CACIONES/Asuntos Políticos" ("Publications: Political Matters") (El Salvador, MG, "Antecedentes," 1943, file 080).

81. Untitled typescript beginning "La declaración de guerra . . ." (n.p., December 12, 1941) in "Apuntes."

82. "Appeal to Arms," p. 75.

83. Santos Dueñas, *Aurora*, pp. 44–45; Arturo Romero quoted in "Cuarentena para la infección de antidemocracia en El Salvador," *El Diario Latino*, November 15, 1944; "Revolutionary Activities in El Salvador" (San José, Costa Rica, carbon copy with "June 6, 1944" typed on first page), attached to J. Edgar Hoover, director, Federal Bureau of Investigation, letter to Adolf A. Berle, Jr., assistant secretary of state, June 6, 1944, Decimal File 816.00/1456, RG 59, NA. Hoover described "Revolutionary Activities" as "furnished by a reliable confidential source," probably the FBI agent attached to the United States Embassy in San José. It consists largely of a translated report on the insurrection of April 1944 written by Rafael Equizábal (according to Santos Dueñas, a member of the Comité Civil) after he took refuge in Costa Rica.

None of the accounts gives the date of the organization of the Comité Ejecutivo, though they imply that it was 1943. Jorge Bustamante, who became involved in the conspiracy in December 1943, thought contacts between civilian and military conspirators began in 1941 or 1942. Bustamante, interview with author, San Salvador, March 22, 1978.

84. Fortín Magaña's name did not appear in connection with the founding of ADS, but according to Santos Dueñas (*Aurora*, p. 44), he wrote the ADS-inspired petition to the Supreme Court described in the following chapter, and he emerged as one of the most conspicuous members of ADS when it resumed open activity after the fall of Martínez. Rosales, Alvarado, López Harrison, and Segovia all participated along with Fortín Magaña in the delegation that presented the United States Embassy with a copy of the petition to the Supreme Court. W. T[hurston], handwritten note dated October 23, 1943, RG 84, San Salvador, 1943, 800, WNRC.

Lima's role is less clear. A generally unreliable intelligence report referred to him as the head of a group of "lawyers, doctors and other educated men" calling themselves the Partido Democrático. "Current Political Activity in El Salvador" (San Salvador, September 1, 1943), attached to Hoover, letter to Berle, October 18, 1943, Decimal File 816.00/1146, RG 59, NA. The covering letter referred to this document as coming from "a reliable, confidential informant," presumably the FBI agent who served as "legal attaché" in the United States Embassy in San Salvador. This may have been the Partido Social Demócrata, which co-sponsored the demonstration of December 11, 1943 (see Chap. 4), and was described by one intelligence report as "the opposition party." The minister of government evidently thought Lima and Rosales had a hand in the demonstration, for he called them in to inform them that Martínez did not want it to take place. [Signature illegible], Presidente and Secretario, Partido Social Demócrata, to Thurston, San Salvador, December 17, 1943, RG 84, San Salvador, 1943, 800, WNRC; "El Salvador/Political," Ref. 823, December 31, 1943 (handwritten at end, "Source: British Intelligence Report—31 Dec. 43—El Salvador/Political"), G-2 Regional File 1933-44, El Salvador, file 3610, Box 818, RG 165, WNRC.

85. de Suárez, "Vida trágica," pt. 3, *El Diario de Hoy*, July 24, 1965; Ellis, memorandum, April 7, 1944, enclosure no. 1 to despatch 1452, April 11, 1944; Ainsworth, memorandum, January 10, 1944, enclosure to despatch 1167, January 11, 1944; Ellis,

memorandum, March 14, 1944, Decimal File 816.00/1259, 1173, and 1277, RG 59, NA.

86. de Suárez, "Vida trágica," pt. 1, *El Diario de Hoy*, July 10, 1965; Peña Kampy, "*General Martínez*," p. 156; Dalton, *Miguel Mármol*, p. 489.

87. "Revolutionary Activities in El Salvador" (San Salvador, n.d.), attached to Hoover, letter to Berle, May 29, 1944, which described it as a "memorandum received from a reliable and confidential source," presumably the FBI agent who served as "legal attaché" in the United States Embassy in San Salvador, Decimal File 816.00/1418, RG 59, NA; author's interviews with Jorge Bustamante, March 22, 1978, and Victor Lasso, San Salvador, February 18, 1978.

88. "La nutrición y la salud del pueblo salvadoreño," "Legislación social del trabajo?" and "El seguro social y el Congreso de Municipalidades," *La Prensa Gráfica*, September 3, 4, October 9, 12, 14, 16, November 6, 1943.

89. Ellis, April 7, 1944 (see n. 85 above); Krehm, *Democracies and Tyrannies*, p. 13. Arbizú Bosque's imprisonment in January 1944 presumably removed him from participation in the conspiracy. Massey to Thurston, January 7, 1944, file 3600-3610, Box 818, and Massey, Report 221, March 13, 1944, file 3020, Box 817, G-2 Regional File 1933-44, El Salvador, RG 165, WNRC. He and Pérez were identified in Banco Hipotecario de El Salvador, *Memoria de las labores*; Jorge Sol Castellanos in Thurston to secretary of state, despatch 1462, April 13, 1944; Sol's wife as a sister of Pérez in Ellis, memorandum entitled "Political Notes," October 31, 1944, enclosure no. 2 to despatch 2118, October 31, 1944, Decimal File 816.00/1260 and 10-3144, RG 59, NA.

90. Wightman, Report 156, September 17, 1943 (see n. 50 above).

91. Krehm, *Democracies and Tyrannies*, p. 13; Morán, *Jornadas cívicas*, p. 54; Moscoso, BOMID Report 450 (BOMID, Miami, Florida, November 30, 1943), Army Intelligence Project Decimal File, 1941-45, El Salvador 350.05, RG 319, WNRC.

92. Ainsworth, "Interaction" (see n. 10 above); Thurston to secretary of state, despatch 1466, April 14, 1944, Decimal File 816.00/1261, RG 59, NA.

93. Ainsworth, memorandum, December 29, 1943, enclosure no. 2 to despatch 1123, December 30, 1943, Decimal File 816.00/1167, RG 59, NA; Ellis, April 7, 1944 (see n. 85 above); Thurston, despatch 1462, April 13, 1944 (see n. 89 above).

94. Memorandum, April 7, 1944 (see n. 85 above).

95. Maleady, memorandum, May 17, 1944, transcribed in Thurston to secretary of state, despatch 1580, May 17, 1944, Decimal File 816.00/1374, RG 59, NA; Santos Dueñas, *Aurora*, p. 45. The leading members of the Frente Democrático Universitario who appeared in Santos Dueñas's reconstruction of the membership of the Comité Civil were Rafael Equizábal and Oswaldo Escobar Velado. On the FDU, see Chap. 4, p. 49.

96. Maleady, memoranda, September 29, 1943, and February 2, 1944, enclosures to Thurston to secretary of state, despatches 811, September 29, 1943, and 1235, February 3, 1944, Decimal File 816.00/1143 and 1190, RG 59, NA. On the leaflets, see Chap. 4, pp. 46, 49.

97. Interview with Miguel Angel Zepeda, December 17, 1976.

98. Mármol also heard from unidentified sources that Arturo Romero was a party member whom the "CC" (Comité Central) had entrusted with the task of "discovering and unifying the conspiring groups," but this is scarcely credible. It flies in the face

of overwhelming contemporary and retrospective evidence that Alfaro, rather than Romero, functioned as the key coordinator of the revolt. Dalton, *Miguel Mármol*, pp. 469, 486.

99. Baldwin, Reports 100, May 3, 1943, and 111, June 12, 1943 (see nn. 20 and 44 above); Hannah, Report 1155, April 18, 1944 (see n. 5 above). The quotation is from Report 100. Hannah's information came from Agustín Alfaro.

100. Elam, "Appeal to Arms," pp. 58–59; Morán, *Jornadas cívicas*, pp. 53–54; Arturo Romero, quoted in "Cuarantena," *El Diario Latino*, November 15, 1944; Hoover to Berle, April 7, 1944 (described as "information received from a reliable and confidential source . . . furnished in verification of data telephonically related to Mr. Jack Neal of the State Department by an official of this Bureau on April 3 and 4, 1944"), Decimal File 816.00/1263, RG 59, NA; Ellis, April 7, 1944 (see n. 85 above); Hannah, Report 1155, April 18, 1944 (see n. 5 above).

Chapter 4. The Developing Crisis

1. Salazar Valiente, "A veinte años," p. 3.

2. C[harles] P. Baldwin, United States military attaché, El Salvador, Report 112, June 19, 1943, and attached leaflet, Frente Democrático Salvadoreño, "Declaraciones" (n.p., n.d.), G-2 Regional File 1933-44, El Salvador, file 3020, Box 817, RG 165, WNRC.

3. "Manifiesto al pueblo salvadoreño," ("Tomado del folleto conocido como 'Folleto de Pasta Azul' que circuló el 14 de julio de 1943"), Anexo II, Fortín Magaña, *Inquietudes*, pp. 181–88. A copy of this pamphlet is attached to Baldwin, Report 142, July 30, 1943, and a translation is attached to Paul A. Goodin, assistant United States naval attaché, El Salvador, Intelligence Report, serial 1-43, September 24, 1943, G-2 Regional File 1933-44, El Salvador, file 3020, Box 817, RG 165, WNRC.

4. Gerhard Gade, United States chargé d'affaires ad interim, El Salvador, to Edward G. Trueblood, United States chargé d'affaires ad interim, Costa Rica, August 21, 1943, RG 84, San Salvador, 1943, SC800, WNRC.

5. "Al pueblo salvadoreño," carbon copy in "Apuntes." An English translation (Comité Demócrata Revolucionario, "People of Salvador," San Salvador, August 1943) is attached to Goodin, Report 1-43, September 24, 1943 (see n. 3 above).

6. Comité Democrático-Revolucionario [presumably the same as Comité Demócrata Revolucionario, n. 5 above], "Palabras para el ejército nacional" (mimeographed leaflet; San Salvador, September 1943), attached to H. L. Wightman, acting United States military attaché, El Salvador, Report S.I. 13, September 10, 1943, G-2 Regional File 1933-44, El Salvador, file 3000-4000, Box 817, RG 165, WNRC; Comité Democrático-Revolucionario, "Las contribuciones para el Pro-Patria" (mimeographed leaflet; San Salvador, September 1943), RG 84, San Salvador, 1943, 800, WNRC. Quotations are from translations attached to Goodin, Report 1-43, September 24, 1943 (see n. 3 above).

7. Walter Thurston, United States ambassador to El Salvador, to secretary of state, despatch 893, October 22, 1943, Decimal File 816.00/1148, RG 59, NA.

8. Santos Dueñas, *Aurora*, p. 44; "Memorial dirigido a la honorable Corte Suprema de Justicia por un grupo de ciudadanos, solicitandole declare ineficaz un re-

glamento del Poder Ejecutivo que restringe la libertad electoral," October 11, 1943, Anexo IV, Fortín Magaña, *Inquietudes*, pp. 211–22. A typescript of this document bearing the names of 220 signatories appears in RG 84, San Salvador, 1943, 800, WNRC. On the 1941 restrictions, see Chap. 3, pp. 42–43.

9. Assistant United States naval attaché, El Salvador, Intelligence Report, Serial 6-43, November 8, 1943, G-2 Regional File 1933-44, El Salvador, file 3020, Box 817, RG 165, WNRC.

10. Figeac, *Libertad de imprenta*, p. 508; "Re: Current Political Activity" (San Salvador, n.d.), p. 12, G-2 Regional File 1933-44, El Salvador, file 3000-3020, Box 817, RG 165, WNRC.

11. Thurston to secretary of state, despatch 955, November 12, 1943, Decimal File 816.00/1156, RG 59, NA.

12. G[eorge] B. Massey, acting United States military attaché, Report 166, November 16, 1943, G-2 Regional File 1933-44, El Salvador, file 3020, Box 817, RG 165, WNRC.

13. Thurston to secretary of state, despatch 929, November 4, 1943, and enclosure no. 3, "To All Workers" (translation; n.p., n.d.), Decimal File 816.00/1153, RG 59, NA. The Spanish version of this leaflet, "A los trabajadores en general" (carbon copy, n. p., October 31, 1943) appears in RG 84, San Salvador, 1943, 800, WNRC.

14. "Alerta trabajadores del campo, taller y fábrica" (typed copy; n.p., n.d. [handwritten note at top of first page: "Distributed 31 Oct. 1943"]), attached to Massey, Report 166, November 16, 1943 (see n. 12 above).

Rumors that agents of Martínez were fomenting a "Communist" revolt circulated in August 1943 and again in January 1944. "Al pueblo salvadoreño"; Wightman, Report S.I. 10, August 23, 1943, Army Intelligence Project Decimal File 1941-45, El Salvador 000.1, RG 319, WNRC; Massey, Report 190, January 31, 1944, G-2 Regional File 1933-44, El Salvador, file 3020, Box 817, RG 165, WNRC; Thurston to secretary of state, despatch 1238, February 3, 1944, Decimal File 816.00/1191, RG 59, NA. Some members of the opposition, particularly labor militants, may really have feared that Martínez would resort to this tactic, or opponents of the regime may have circulated the rumors for the purpose of scaring workers away from *martinista* demonstrations.

15. Thurston to secretary of state, despatch 1070, December 13, 1943, Decimal File 816.00/1158, RG 59, NA; Oswaldo Escobar Velado and Rafael Equizábal h., to Thurston, San Salvador, December 13, 1943; José F. Figeac and Abraham Pineda h., to Thurston, San Salvador, December 14, 1943; [signature illegible], Presidente and Secretario, Partido Social Demócrata, to Thurston, San Salvador, December 17, 1943, all in RG 84, San Salvador, 1943, 800, WNRC; Massey to Thurston, December 14, 1943, G-2 Regional File 1933-44, El Salvador, file 3600-3610, Box 818, RG 165, WNRC. The quotations are translated from Massey.

In an interview immediately after the resignation of Martínez, José Quetglas referred to a student demonstration on July 14, 1943, as the first action in the movement to overthrow Martínez. *El Imparcial* (Guatemala City), May 9, 1944. However, since no reference to such an event on that day appears in the reports of the United States Embassy, it seems probable that he referred to the December 11 demonstration, possibly confusing the date with that of the "Manifiesto al pueblo salvadoreño" or of the student demonstration of 1940 (Chap. 3, p. 40).

16. Frente Democrático Universitario, "Discurso pronunciado ante la estatua de la

libertad, por el Br. Rafael Equizábal h., a nombre del Frente Democrático Universitario, con ocasión del homenaje a los Estados Unidos de América, el 11 de diciembre de 1943" (typed copy; San Salvador, December 11, 1943), enclosure to Thurston, despatch 1070, December 13, 1943. A copy of this speech also appears in "Apuntes."

17. Fifteen leaflets that appeared from August 1943 to March 1944 are summarized in "Re: Current Political Activity," n.d. (see n. 10 above), pp. 5–7, 26. "Apuntes" contains copies of several of these leaflets, as well as some not mentioned in "Re: Current Political Activity" that probably circulated during the same period.

18. Santos Dueñas, *Aurora*, p. 15.

19. *La Prensa Gráfica* (San Salvador), November 11, 16, 30, 1943, January 1, 19, 29, 1944; September 2, 1943; October 16, 1943; February 2, 1944; Thurston, despatch 1238, February 3, 1944.

20. José Quetglas, interview with *El Imparcial*, May 9, 1944.

21. Letter addressed to "Señor Embajador," San Salvador, October 19, 1943 (marked by hand, "handed to me Oct. 14 [*sic*] by Dr. Rochac"), RG 84, San Salvador, 1943, 800, WNRC. The quotation is from a translation enclosed with despatch 1156, January 8, 1944, Decimal File 816.00/1172, RG 59, NA.

22. José Asencio Menéndez, J. Cipriano Castro, Francisco Lino Osegueda, and Antonio Ramírez Anaya to Ezequiel Padilla, Secretario de Relaciones Exteriores [Mexico], Mexico City, December 20, 1943, enclosure no. 4 to Thurston, despatch 1156, January 8, 1944.

23. Mecham, *Inter-American Security*, pp. 231–33. The quotation is from p. 232.

24. Raleigh A. Gibson, first secretary, United States Embassy, Mexico, to secretary of state, despatch 16729, March 30, 1944, Decimal File 816.00/1224, RG 59, NA; A[rcher] B. Hannah, assistant United States military attaché, Guatemala, Report 1152, April 17, 1944, G-2 Regional File 1933-44, El Salvador, file 3000-3020, Box 817, RG 165, WNRC.

25. Comité Revolucionario Salvadoreño to "Señor Embajador de los Estados Unidos de Norte América," n.p., n.d., transcribed in Comité Revolucionario Salvadoreño to "Muy señor nuestro" [United States consul] (carbon copy; n.p., n.d.), "Apuntes." Two copies of this letter, with minor variations, appear in United States archives: Comité Revolucionario Salvadoreño to H. Gardner Ainsworth, United States vice consul, El Salvador (n.p., n.d. [stamped February 25, 1944]), RG 84, San Salvador, 1944, 800, WNRC, and Salvadoran Revolutionary Committee to Massey, March 13, 1944 (translation), attached to Massey, Report 229, March 20, 1944, Army Intelligence Project Decimal File 1941-45, El Salvador 350.05, WNRC.

26. Romeo Fortín Magaña to Thurston, Ahuachapán, January 1, 1944, enclosure no. 3 to despatch 1156, January 8, 1944 (see n. 21 above); José Quetglas to Thurston, San Salvador, February 26, 1944, enclosure to despatch 1351, March 2, 1944, Decimal File 816.00/1216, RG 59, NA; Agustín Alfaro to Overton G. Ellis, Jr., United States vice consul, El Salvador, March 8, 1944, RG 84, San Salvador, 1944, 800, WNRC. A translation of Alfaro's letter was enclosed with despatch 1494, April 23, 1944, Decimal File 816.00/1277, RG 59, NA.

27. Comité prodemocracia [*sic*] to Cordell Hull, United States secretary of state, Mexico City, January 25, 1944; Thurston to secretary of state, despatch 1239, February 3, 1944; unsigned memorandum dated March 22, 1944 (stamped "Department of State

Office of American Republic Affairs/March 29, 1944"), Decimal File 816.00/1188, 1192, 1242, RG 59, NA; Gibson, despatch 16729, March 30, 1944 (see n. 24 above).

28. Thurston to secretary of state, despatch 1501, April 25, 1944; Hector Herrera to Thurston, San Salvador, April 18, 1944 (translation), enclosure no. 1 to despatch 1501, Decimal File 816.00/1286, RG 59, NA.

29. E[llis] to Thurston, September 9, 1943, enclosure no. 3 to despatch 736, September 10, 1943, Decimal File 816.00/1144, RG 59, NA; Massey, Report 211, February 28, 1944, G-2 Regional File 1933-44, El Salvador, file 3600-3610, Box 818, RG 165, WNRC.

30. Massey, Report 162, November 9, 1943, G-2 Regional File 1933-44, El Salvador, file 3020, Box 817, RG 165, WNRC; Thurston, despatch 955, November 12, 1943 (see n. 11 above).

31. Rudolfo V. Morales, Ministro de Gobernación, to Gobernadores, Circular no. 59, October 26, 1943, file .083, El Salvador, MG, "Antecedentes," 1943; Morales to Director General de Policía, November 19, 1943, número de orden 15636, carbon copy in El Salvador, MG, *Correspondencia despachada, 1943*.

32. Figeac, *Libertad de imprenta*, p. 509; Santos Dueñas, *Aurora*, p. 18. The quotation is from Santos Dueñas.

33. Quetglas to Thurston, February 26, 1944 (see n. 26 above).

34. "Prohibiciones de la censura (hasta el 28 de febrero de 1944)," RG 84, San Salvador, 1944, 891, WNRC.

35. *La Prensa Gráfica*, December 14, 1943, January 18, 25, 1944; *El Diario Latino* (San Salvador), May 29, 1944.

36. Goodin, Naval Intelligence Report, serial 1-43, September 24, 1943; J[oseph] E. M[aleady], United States vice consul, El Salvador, to Thurston, September 7, 1943, and Ellis to Thurston, September 9, 1943, enclosures no. 2 and no. 3 to Thurston, despatch 736, September 10, 1943; Maleady, memorandum, September 29, 1943, enclosure to Thurston to secretary of state, despatch 811, September 29, 1943, Decimal File 816.00/1143, RG 59, NA; *La Prensa Gráfica*, September 7, 1943.

37. Massey, Report 162, November 9, 1943 (see n. 30 above). Another member of the United States Embassy staff commented, ". . . it would probably be difficult if not impossible to arrest all 300 signers. It would probably put the President in a very dangerous position to do so." Assistant United States naval attaché, El Salvador, Intelligence Report, serial 6-43, November 8, 1943 (see n. 9 above).

38. Massey, Report 178, December 28, 1943, G-2 Regional File 1933-44, El Salvador, file 3020, Box 817, RG 165, WNRC; Thurston to secretary of state, despatch 1452, April 11, 1944, Decimal File 816.00/1259, RG 59, NA.

39. Thurston to secretary of state, despatch 910, October 28, 1943, Decimal File 816.00/1151, RG 59, NA.

40. Escobar Velado and Equizábal to Thurston, December 13, 1943 (see n. 15 above); Rafael R. Huezo M. to Thurston, December 14, 1943, RG 84, San Salvador, 1943, 800; Massey, Report 175, December 21, 1943, G-2 Regional File 1933-44, El Salvador, file 3020, Box 817, RG 165, WNRC.

41. The names of the most prominent persons detained appear in several sources. For the fullest list, see "Re: Current Political Activity," n.d. (see n. 10 above), pp. 13–14. For a report by one of the detained see Figeac, *Libertad de imprenta*, p. 265.

42. Interview with Marina Rosales, San Salvador, August 28, 1976; Max P. Brannon to Thurston, San Salvador, December 21, 1943, enclosure to Thurston to secretary of state, despatch 1529, May 3, 1944, Decimal File 816.00/1321, RG 59, NA; Massey to Carl H. Strong, assistant chief of staff, G-2, Panama Canal Department, January 11, 1944, G-2 Regional File 1933-44, El Salvador, file 3600-3610, Box 818, RG 165, WNRC.

43. Thurston to secretary of state, telegram 295, December 28, 1943, Decimal File 816.00/1164, RG 59, NA.

44. Thurston to secretary of state, despatch 1143, January 6, 1944, Decimal File 816.00/1169, RG 59, NA; "Re: Current Political Activity," n.d. (see n. 10 above), p. 14.

45. "Re: Current Political Activity," n.d. (see n. 10 above), pp. 17–18; interview with Jorge Bustamante, San Salvador, March 22, 1978. Bustamante was one of the students involved.

46. "Re: Current Political Activity," n.d. (see n. 10 above), p. 21; "Comments on the Revision of the Constitution," translated in Thurston to secretary of state, despatch 1317, February 23, 1944, which described it as prepared by "Miguel Angel Alcaine, attorney for the Banco Hipotecario." RG 84, San Salvador, 1944, SC800, WNRC.

47. Articles 27 and 56 as translated in "Re: Current Political Activity," n.d. (see n. 10 above), pp. 21–22.

48. Articles 9, 55, 77, and 177.

49. "Re: Current Political Activity," n.d. (see n. 10 above), p. 24.

50. Massey, Report 245, April 18, 1944, enclosure to Thurston to secretary of state, despatch 1484, April 19, 1944; Ainsworth, "The Interaction of Economic and Political Forces in El Salvador" (no. 10/American Embassy, San Salvador, El Salvador, January 13, 1944), Decimal File 816.00/1274 and 1182, RG 59, NA.

51. Maleady, memorandum, February 2, 1944, enclosure to Thurston to secretary of state, despatch 1235, February 3, 1944, Decimal File 816.00/1190, RG 59, NA.

52. Ellis, memorandum, April 7, 1944, enclosure no. 1 to Thurston, despatch 1452 (see n. 38 above); Ainsworth, "Interaction" (see n. 50 above).

53. Massey, Report 245, April 18, 1944; Ainsworth, "Interaction" (see n. 50 above for both).

54. Assistant United States naval attaché, El Salvador, Intelligence Report, serial 7-44-R, January 31, 1944, G-2 Regional File 1933-44, El Salvador, file 3000-3020, Box 817, RG 165, WNRC.

55. "Re: Current Political Activity," n.d. (see n. 10 above), p. 27; Ellis, memorandum entitled "Resignation of Board of Directors of Chamber of Commerce," May 18, 1944, RG 84, San Salvador, 1944, 800, WNRC, and memorandum, April 7, 1944 (see n. 52 above).

56. Memorandum, February 2, 1944 (see n. 51 above).

57. Despatch 1452, April 11, 1944 (see n. 38 above).

58. Maleady, memorandum, quoted in Thurston to secretary of state, despatch 1315, February 23, 1944, Decimal File 816.00/1208, RG 59, NA. On Dalton, see Chap. 3, p. 36.

59. Ellis, April 7, 1944 (see n. 52 above).

60. Roberto Molina y Morales, interview with author, Santa Tecla, March 20,

1978; Baldwin, Report 117, July 3, 1943, G-2 Regional File 1933-44, El Salvador, file 2600, Box 817, RG 165, WNRC.

61. Assistant United States naval attaché, El Salvador, Intelligence Report, serial 7-44-R, January 31, 1944 (see n. 54 above).

62. Luna, "Análisis," p. 72; Gade to secretary of state, despatch 1111, September 9, 1940, Decimal File 816.001/Martínez, Max/73, RG 59, NA.

63. "Leyes de la República," p. 1305; "Alocución del padre Juan Antonio García Artola en la misa campal a la Virgen del Rosario, ayer," *El Diario Latino*, May 22, 1944.

64. Articles 27 and 54.

65. "Episcopado salvadoreño," pp. 1200–1201.

66. Massey, Report 245, April 18, 1944 (see n. 50 above).

67. Elam, "Appeal to Arms," pp. 108–9; Baldwin, Report 100, May 3, 1944, G-2 Regional File 1933-44, El Salvador, file 3020, Box 817, RG 165, WNRC; Massey to Strong, January 11, 1944 (see n. 42 above); assistant United States naval attaché, Intelligence Report, serial 7-44-R, January 31, 1944 (see n. 54 above); Maleady, February 2, 1944 (see n. 51 above).

68. Massey, Report 184, January 10, 1944, G-2 Regional File 1933-44, El Salvador, file 3020, Box 817, RG 165, WNRC.

69. Thurston, despatch 1452, April 11, 1944 (see n. 38 above); Maleady, memorandum, April 9, 1944, enclosure no. 2 to despatch 1452; Massey, Report 240, April 11, 1944, Army Intelligence Decimal File, 1941-45, El Salvador 201.3, RG 319, WNRC; Boaz Long, United States ambassador to Guatemala, to secretary of state, despatch 1069, April 27, 1944, Decimal File 816.00/1290, RG 59, NA; *La Prensa Gráfica*, May 19, 1944 (re: Oscar Armando Cristales); *El Diario Latino*, May 13, 18, 22, 1944 (re: Alfonso Marín, Mario Ernesto Villacorta, Alfonso and Salvador Marroquín); author's interview with Rafael Carranza Anaya, San Salvador, September 23, 1976. Carranza Anaya was an army officer in 1944.

70. Innumerable stories of the April 2 uprising have been written. For contemporary, on-the-spot, but fragmentary and not always accurate, descriptions of the action, see Thurston to secretary of state, telegrams 98, 99, 100, 101, 102, 104, 105, 107, dated April 2, 3, 4, 1944, Decimal File 816.00/1223, 1221, 1228, 1225, 1229, 1233, 1234, 1237, RG 59, NA. The most useful secondary accounts are Thurston, despatch 1452, April 11, 1944 (see n. 38 above); Rufus A. Byers, chief, United States Military Mission to El Salvador, to chief, Military Intelligence Service, War Department, April 10, 1944, file 3000-3020, Box 817; Massey, Reports 236, April 5, 237 and 238, April 6, and 256, April 26, 1944, file marked "Stability Reports," Box 818, G-2 Regional File 1933-44, El Salvador, RG 165, WNRC; de Suárez, "Vida trágica," pts. 4–14, *El Diario de Hoy*, July 31, August 7, 14, 21, 28, September 4, 11, 18, 25, October 2, 9, 1965; Ricardo Mejía, "Breve relato de la revolución del 2 de abril de 1944," *La Tribuna Libre*, May 27–30, June 3, 5–6, 1963; Luna, "Análisis," pp. 107–14; and Morán, "*Jornadas cívicas*," pp. 61–96. Except as otherwise noted, the description of the insurrection in this chapter is based on a comparison of these accounts, which are generally consistent, although they contain differences in detail.

71. Massey, Report 253, April 24, 1944, G-2 Regional File 1933-44, El Salvador, file 3000-3020, Box 817, RG 165, WNRC; Santos Dueñas, *Aurora*, p. 41.

72. According to Massey (Report 238, April 6, 1944 [see n. 70 above]), it broadcast the information "that Dr. Arturo ROMERO was the civilian leader of the movement," and de Suárez quoted Martínez as informing his supporters, "They are saying on the radio here that they are going to name Dr. Romero president." ("Vida trágica," pt. 8, August 28, 1965). However, Thurston reported that "at no time during the uprising was its leadership revealed publicly," and a State Department memorandum based on the report of the British chargé d'affaires in San Salvador said specifically that there had been no "positive declaration that any single person would take over the Presidency." Thurston, despatch 1452, April 11, 1944 (see n. 38 above); W[illiam] P. Cochran, assistant chief, Division of Caribbean and Central American Affairs, United States State Department, "Memorandum of Conversation," April 10, 1944, Decimal File 816.00/1248, RG 59, NA.

Salvadorans who took refuge in Guatemala after the failure of the insurrection told the United States military attaché there that Romero "was actually too young to be of much influence and that there was a possibility that he might be working as a front." Hannah, Report 1152, April 17, 1944 (see n. 24 above). In fact, according to de Suárez, Romero received the titular leadership of the movement in order to free Agustín Alfaro to seek the presidency after Martínez's removal, for Alfredo Aguilar had agreed to command the insurrection on the condition that none of its leaders should become president. "Vida trágica," pt. 3, July 24, 1965. Cf. Massey, Report 247, April 18, 1944 (enclosed with despatch 1484, April 19, 1944, Decimal File 816.00/1274, RG 59, NA): "A commission of six men, three civilians and three military men, were to appoint a provisional president who would assume power during the period between the overthrow of the President and the time for a free election. . . . [He] could not be a candidate for the presidency."

73. Massey, Report 238, April 6, 1944 (see n. 70 above).

74. Krehm, *Democracies and Tyrannies*, pp. 14–15; *New York Times*, April 16, 1944. Thurston reported that planes flying over the city on April 2 did "some bombing (inaccurate)" but said the fire in the center of the city was "apparently started by mortar or shell fire." Despatch 1452, April 11, 1944 (see n. 38 above). Moran agreed. *Jornadas cívicas*, p. 85.

75. Whitaker, "Pan America," p. 46.

76. *New York Times*, April 11, 1944; *El Diario Nuevo*, April 10, 11, 1944; Massey, Report 244, April 17, 1944, enclosure to Thurston, despatch 1484 (see n. 50 above).

77. Thurston to secretary of state, AGM 149, April 12, 1944, Decimal File 816.42/66, RG 59, NA; "Dirección General de la Policía," April 19, 1944, número de orden 450, El Salvador, MG, *Entrada, 1944*; Dalton, *Miguel Mármol*, p. 478.

78. Byers to chief, Military Intelligence Service, April 30, 1944, G-2 Regional File 1933-44, El Salvador, file 3000-3020, Box 817, RG 165, WNRC.

79. Maleady, memorandum, April 9, 1943; Thurston to secretary of state, despatch 1466, April 14, 1944, Decimal File 816.00/1261, RG 59, NA; Massey, Report 239, April 8, 1944, G-2 Regional File 1933-44, El Salvador, file 3000-3020, Box 817, RG 165, WNRC, and Report 253, April 24, 1944 (see n. 71 above).

80. Maleady to Thurston, April 13, 1944, RG 84, San Salvador, 1944, 800; Massey, Report 244, April 17, 1944 (see n. 76 above); Morales to Ministro de Relaciones Exteriores, May 1, 1944, El Salvador, MG, *Correspondencia despachada*,

1944; Thurston to secretary of state, despatch 1462, April 13, 1944, Decimal File 816.00/1260, RG 59, NA.

81. Maleady to Thurston, April 13, 1944, RG-84, San Salvador, 1944, 800, WNRC; Thurston to secretary of state, despatch 1478, April 17, 1944, Decimal File 816.00/ 1270, RG 59, NA; Quetglas, interview with *El Imparcial*, May 9, 1944.

82. This was a Lieutenant Rodolfo Bhános Ramírez, who was convicted of involvement in a "Communist conspiracy" against the government in 1936. A second death sentence imposed in the same case was commuted. *El Diario de Hoy*, November 3, 1936.

83. Author's interviews with Fabio Castillo, San José, Costa Rica, October 15, 1976, and Reynaldo Galindo Pohl, Washington, D.C., September 27, 1977; *El Diario Nuevo*, April 10, 11, 24, 1944; Thurston to secretary of state, despatches 1453, April 12, and 1504, April 26, 1944, Decimal File 816.00/1256 and 1280, RG 59, NA. The lists of persons condemned to death and executed contained in these sources do not mention three officers who, according to Mejía, were condemned to death (though not executed) on April 11: Salvador Salguero, Belizario Peña, and Adalberto Rivera. "Breve relato," June 5, 1944. For a detailed account of the trials and executions, see Morán, *Jornadas cívicas*, pp. 105–27.

84. "El Salvador: No Sanctuary," *Time* 43 (May 15, 1944): 28; Thurston, despatches 1466, April 14, 1944, and 1500, n.d. (stamped "April 25, 1944," presumably on receipt in Washington), Decimal File 816.00/1261 and 1286, RG 59, NA; Rose Harkness, untitled report with dateline "Guatemala, May 4, 1944," quoted at length in Hannah, Report 1183, May 6, 1944, Army Intelligence Project Decimal File, 1941-45, El Salvador, 000.1, RG 319, WNRC. The text of Harkness's report indicates that she had "just reached Guatemala from San Salvador."

85. See, for example, "R.T.S.," memorandum, April 15, 1944, and Ellis, memorandum, April 21, 1944, both in RG 84, San Salvador, 1944, 800, WNRC; Massey, Report 247, April 18, 1944 (see n. 72 above); Thurston to secretary of state, despatch 1534, May 4, 1944, Decimal File 816.00/1323, RG 59, NA.

86. "High-School Revolution," *Newsweek* 23 (May 22, 1944): 66; Thurston to secretary of state, despatch 1515, April 28, 1944, Decimal File 816.00/1295, RG 59, NA; Roberto Mauricio Mendoza, "Como fué la batalla en San Andrés," *El Universal* (Santa Ana), May 26, 1944; Massey, Report 245, April 18, 1944 (see n. 50 above). *El Diario Nuevo* on May 4, 1944, published the government's denial that "hundreds of workers" had been detained and asserted that those who were captured in the action against the Santa Ana contingent had been set free. The Mendoza interview confirms this.

87. "Correspondence: Trouble in El Salvador," *New Republic* 3 (July 10, 1944): 47. A very similar account in *Time*, which identified the victim as Marín, may have inspired the letter in the *New Republic*, for a translation of the *Time* article appeared in the San Salvador press. "El Salvador: No Sanctuary" (see n. 84 above); *La Prensa Gráfica*, May 16, 1944. United States Embassy sources traced the story to the priest who attended Marín. Thurston, despatch 1466, April 14, 1944 (see n. 84 above); "Revolutionary Activities in El Salvador" (San Salvador, n.d. [stamped "May 29, 1944"]), p. 11, attached to J. Edgar Hoover, director, Federal Bureau of Investigation, letter to Adolf A. Berle, Jr., assistant secretary of state, May 29, 1944, Decimal File

816.00/1418, RG 59, NA. The covering letter described "Revolutionary Activities" as a "memorandum received from a reliable and confidential source," presumably the FBI agent who served as "legal attaché" in the United States embassy in El Salvador.

88. Harkness, May 4, 1944 (see n. 84 above); Massey, Reports 254, April 24, 1944, file 3000-3020, and 255, April 24, 1944, file 3020, both in G-2 Regional File 1933-44, El Salvador, Box 817, RG 165, WNRC. The quotation is from Report 255.

89. *La Prensa Gráfica*, May 12, 1944; Venezuela, Chamber of Deputies, "Message of Clemency Addressed to the President of the Republic of Salvador," translated from *El Heraldo* (Caracas), May 2, 1944, enclosure to Frank P. Corrigan, United States ambassador to Venezuela, to secretary of state, despatch 5841, May 2, 1944; Vicente Lombardo Toledano to Martínez, Mexico City, n.d., transcribed in Thurston to secretary of state, despatch 1480, April 17, 1944; Thurston to secretary of state, despatch 1511, April 27, 1944; James W. Gantenbein, United States chargé d'affaires ad interim, Quito, to secretary of state, despatch 1465, April 29, 1944, Decimal File 816.00/1297, 1271, 1293, 1318, RG 59, NA; *New York Times*, April 14, 1944, citing *Panama Star and Herald*, April 13, 1944; "Traducción de un artículo publicado por Star & Herald, Panama, el 15 de abril de 1944: Sensible situación en El Salvador, C. A." (typed carbon copy; n.p., n.d.), "Apuntes"; Pablo Neruda, "Sangre en El Salvador!" *La Tribuna* (San Salvador), June 27, 1944. The quotation is from the *New York Times*.

Another indication of the breadth of interest in the events in El Salvador is that an erroneous report "that Martínez had ordered the execution of a number of newspapermen" gave rise to "formal protests" by two Ecuadoran press associations, while journalists in Ecuador, Venezuela, and Chile wired Martínez on behalf of their imprisoned colleagues. These communications could not have influenced developments in El Salvador, however, since they came after Martínez's resignation. Gantenbein to secretary of state, despatch 1522, May 11, 1944; Corrigan to secretary of state, despatch 5903, May 12, 1944, Decimal File 816.00/1349 and 1353, RG 59, NA; *La Prensa Gráfica*, May 12, 1944.

In this arena of the conflict the activities of Salvadorans in exile may have had some significance. See summary of Quino Caso to José Fidel Gutierrez et al., San José, Costa Rica, April 20, 1944, suggesting actions that Salvadorans in other countries might undertake to influence public opinion. Enclosure no. 3 to unsigned memorandum, United States Embassy, San José, to secretary of state, despatch 1365, May 3, 1944, Decimal File 816.00/1331, RG 59, NA.

90. Thurston to secretary of state, telegram 110, April 10, 1944, Decimal File 816.00/1245, RG 59, NA.

91. Thurston to secretary of state, despatch 1462, April 13, 1944 (see n. 80 above).

Chapter 5. The Civic Strike

1. *Criterio* (San Salvador), May 14, 1944.

2. G[eorge] B. Massey, acting United States military attaché, El Salvador, Reports 242, April 10, 1944, and 255, April 24, 1944, G-2 Regional File 1933-44, El Salvador, file 3020, Box 817, RG 165, WNRC; Report 244, April 17, 1944, enclosure to despatch 1484, April 19, 1944; Walter Thurston, United States ambassador to El Salvador, to secretary of state, despatch 1452, April 11, 1944, Decimal File 816.00/1274 and 1259, RG 59, NA.

3. Quino Caso (pen name of Joaquín Castro Canizales), "Hacia la desobediencia civil," typescript furnished to the writer by Castro Canizales. Summary of intercepted letter from Castro Canizales to Saturnino Rodríguez Canizales, February 3, 1944 (described in covering despatch as "undated report from Legal Attaché, San José, Costa Rica"), enclosure to despatch 1590, May 18, 1944, Decimal File 816.00/1380, RG 59, NA; author's interview with Castro Canizales, San Salvador, December 13, 1976. "ABC" was the name of the leading anti-Machado organization in Cuba.

In his letter to Rodríguez Canizales, Castro Canizales referred to Boza's visit as having taken place in September 1943. However, his written "message" was dated July, and the fact that some of the ideas contained in that message appeared in leaflets that circulated in August and September attests to the authenticity of the earlier date.

Castro Canizales also described his plan in a letter to José Asencio Menéndez. (On Menéndez, see Chap. 3, p. 30, and Chap. 4 n. 22.) Summary of intercepted letter dated April 29, 1944 (described in covering despatch as "obtained from the Embassy's well-informed confidential source"), enclosure no. 4 to "Chargé d'Affaires ad interim," U.S. Embassy, San José, Costa Rica, despatch 1365, May 3, 1944, Decimal File 816.00/1331, RG 59, NA.

The descriptions of the plan contained in these summaries of correspondence differ in significant details from each other and from the text of "Hacia la desobediencia civil." According to the letter to Rodríguez Canizales, Castro Canizales "explained his plan to . . . Boza" as a series of steps that would begin with the organization of "all the opposing forces in a united front" and conclude with "a special day of Passive Resistance or strike of Non Cooperation [*sic*] with the Government. On this day public employees should not go to their offices; workers should not go to their regular jobs; taxpayers should not pay their taxes, etc. . . ." Nonpayment of taxes was also part of the plan as described in the letter to Menéndez. However, in this letter, written five days after the declaration of the university strike in San Salvador, Castro Canizales wrote: "This plan has as its first objective the student's [*sic*] strike, after which will come strikes in all the vital organisms of the country: the railroad men, busmen, business men, school teachers, public employees, officials who don't agree with the government, specialists in certain technical offices, such as banks, Treasury, etc.)," a strategy strikingly similar to that actually adopted by the organizers of the civic strike.

4. See Chap. 4, p. 47. The following passage in "Al pueblo salvadoreño" (carbon copy in "Apuntes") also shows the influence of "Hacia la desobediencia civil":

". . . The Government will fall, not with revolts, but by the force of its errors. The People will be its own liberator. . . .

"Musulini [*sic*], the inspiration of the *Martinista* dictatorship, fell. And a revolution was not necessary. He fell because the system of government had accumulated so many disgraces. That is how General Martínez will fall." The fall of Mussolini was obviously not the clearest of Castro Canizales's examples but was one that would have had immediate significance for contemporary newspaper readers.

5. H. L. Wightman and Desmond Holdridge, assistant United States military attachés, Mexico, Report 3797, May 22, 1944, G-2 Regional File 1933-44, El Salvador, file 3000-3020, Box 817, RG 165, WNRC.

6. "Revolutionary Activities in El Salvador" (San Salvador, n.d. [stamped "May 29, 1944"]), p. 24, attached to letter from J. Edgar Hoover, director, Federal Bureau

of Investigation, to Adolf A. Berle, Jr., assistant secretary of state, May 29, 1944, which describes it as "received from a reliable and confidential source," presumably the F.B.I. agent who served as "legal attaché" in the United States Embassy in San Salvador. Decimal File 816.00/1418, RG 59, NA.

7. O[verton] G. E[llis], United States vice consul, El Salvador, memorandum entitled "Immediate plans of Agustín Alfaro and his associates," May 18, 1944; J[oseph] E. M[aleady], United States vice consul, El Salvador, memorandum, June 9, 1944, both in RG 84, San Salvador, 1944, 800, WNRC.

8. H. G[ardner] A[insworth], United States vice consul, El Salvador, memorandum, May 26, 1944, RG 84, San Salvador, 1944, 800, WNRC. Ainsworth's informant was Ricardo Avila Moreira, a member of the strike committee that functioned apart from the representatives of the Acción Democrática Salvadoreña–Banco Hipotecario group (see Chap. 5, pp. 71–72). He may have had an interest in minimizing the role of the latter.

9. Maleady, June 9, 1944 (see n. 7 above).

10. *El Diario Nuevo* (San Salvador), April 10, 1944.

11. Thurston to secretary of state, despatch 1482, April 18, 1944, Decimal File 816.00/1273, RG 59, NA; Massey, Report 244, April 17, 1944 (see n. 2 above). Romero was actually captured on April 14 and identified two days later. Jesús Somoza h., Gobernador (San Miguel), to Ministro de Gobernación, telegrams dated April 15 and April 17, 1944, folder marked "xx," package number 88, El Salvador, MG, "Antecedentes," 1944.

12. Thurston, despatch 1482, April 18, 1944 (see n. 11 above).

13. "Revolutionary Activities," n.d. (see n. 6 above), pp. 13–14.

Neither of the two former medical students whom the writer asked about these developments could remember the black ties, and both thought the students had stayed away from classes when the university reopened on April 17, which, in Jorge Bustamante's view, was why the rector decided to close the university again. Author's interviews with Victor Lasso, San Salvador, February 18, 1978, and Jorge Bustamante, San Salvador, February 22, 1978.

14. Massey, Reports 255, April 24, 1944, and 264, April 29, 1944, Army Intelligence Project Decimal File, 1941–45, El Salvador 092., RG 319, WNRC; *El Diario Nuevo*, April 21, 22, 1944; Interview with Victor Lasso, February 18, 1944.

15. Written response to author's questions by Sra. de Cisneros, San Salvador, December 1976.

Sra. de Cisneros thought the date of this demonstration was May 6, which may mean that what she remembered was a women's march that according to some accounts took place on May 5. However, since she specifically stated that the group assembled at the penitentiary (rather than the Church of the Rosary, where people gathered on May 5) and associated the action with the prisoners rather than the civic strike, it seems more likely that it was the earlier demonstration.

16. Author's interviews with Fabio Castillo (San José, Costa Rica, October 15, 1976), Reynaldo Galindo Pohl (Washington, D.C., September 17, 1977), and Jorge Bustamante (February 22, 1978); "Revolutionary Activities," n.d. (see n. 6 above), p. 22.

According to Bustamante, the forty-odd delegates were elected by the student body of each participating faculty on April 24 to *approve* the membership of the central committee, which had come into existence during the previous week without benefit of a mandate from the student body as a whole. "Revolutionary Activities" identified Bustamante, Castillo, Castellanos, José Colorado, and another person named Colorado as members of a group entrusted by a forty-two man meeting with the responsibility of naming yet another secret strike committee. However, the testimony of Bustamante, Castillo, and Galindo Pohl as to their own participation in the secret committee can hardly be in error. José Colorado told the writer that he was *not* a member of the central committee. Interview, San Salvador, February 23, 1978.

17. Los hijos del pueblos [*sic*], "Salvadoreños" (typed carbon copy; San Salvador, April 19, 1944), enclosed with letter from Rufus A. Byers, chief, United States Military Mission to El Salvador, to chief, Military Intelligence Service, War Department, April 30, 1944, G-2 Regional File 1933-44, El Salvador, file 3000-3020, Box 817, RG 165, WNRC. A translation of a nearly identical leaflet (Sons of the People, "Salvadorans" [n.p., n.d.]) is enclosure no. 3 to despatch 1512, April 28, 1944, Decimal File 816.00/1289, RG 59, NA.

18. Interview, February 23, 1978.

19. Interview with Jorge Bustamante, February 22, 1978; Mario Luís Velasco, "Manifiesto al estudiantado salvadoreño," *La Prensa Gráfica* and *El Diario Latino*, May 12, 1944.

20. "Al pueblo salvadoreño," as reproduced in *Opinión Estudiantil* (San Salvador), 8ª época, no. 1 (May 20, 1944). The text is also reproduced in Morán, *Jornadas cívicas*, p. 140.

21. "Componente," p. 11.

22. Interviews with Bustamante, February 22, 1978, and March 22, 1978 (San Salvador).

23. Interview with Castillo, October 15, 1976.

24. Interviews with Bustamante, March 22, 1978, and Galindo Pohl, September 27, 1977. A few of the many anonymous leaflets that circulated during the strike did contain incitements to violence, but these were exceptional and probably did not originate with the strike leadership. Thurston to secretary of state, telegram 124, April 27, 1944; Anonymous, "Salvadorans," (n.p., n.d.), translation enclosed with despatch 1512, April 28, 1944, Decimal File 816.00/1278 and 1289, RG 59, NA. See also one of several typed leaflets entitled "Salvadoreños" (n.p., n.d.), in "Apuntes."

25. E. M. E[stes?] (signature unclear), memorandum, May 1, 1944, RG 84, San Salvador, 1944, 800, WNRC.

26. "Al pueblo salvadoreño" (typed carbon copy; n.p., n.d.), in "Apuntes."

This may actually be a compilation of several leaflets, for the full text, which begins by reproducing the announcement of the university strike (n. 20), is three pages long, an unwieldy handout. Cf. translation of a similar but much-condensed leaflet, in "High-School Revolution," *Newsweek* 23 (May 22, 1944): 66. The idea of tax refusal most likely came from Castro Canizales. See n. 3.

27. "One Down," *Interamerican* 3 (June 6, 1944): 8; "El Salvador: No Sanctuary," *Time* 43 (May 15, 1944): 28; José Quetglas, interview published in *El Imparcial* (Guatemala City), May 9, 1944. The quotation is from "One Down."

Quetglas's information was probably secondhand, for he took asylum in the home of the secretary of the Guatemalan Legation shortly after the April 2 uprising and presumably stayed there until he went to Guatemala on May 5. Thurston to secretary of state, despatch 1521, May 1, 1944, Decimal File 816.00/1319, RG 59, NA; Quetglas interview, May 9, 1944.

28. Rose Harkness, untitled report with dateline "Guatemala, May 4, 1944," quoted at length in A[rcher] B. Hannah, assistant United States military attaché, Guatemala, Report 1183, May 6, 1944, G-2 Regional File 1933-44, El Salvador, file 3000-3020, Box 817, RG 165, WNRC. The text indicates that Harkness had just arrived from San Salvador.

29. See Chap. 5, pp. 76–79; Chap. 6, pp. 83–85; "Social," *Ahora*, año 7, no. 82 (May 1944), no pagination. The highest-ranking official to leave his post before the night of May 7 was the president of the Corte de Cuentas (controller general), who presented his resignation to Martínez in person. Confidential interview, San Salvador, 1978.

30. Massey, Report 264, April 29, 1944 (see n. 14 above); interview with Galindo Pohl, September 27, 1977.

31. "Componente"; interviews with Castillo, October 15, 1976, and Bustamente, March 22, 1978.

32. Interview with Galindo Pohl, September 27, 1977; "Componente"; Krehm, *Democracy and Tyrannies*, p. 24 (cf. Krehm's contemporary report that the strike committee was "urging smaller stores to reopen . . . ," William Krehm to William Johnson at *Time* magazine, New York, n.p., n.d. [typed original bearing pencil notation "May 6"], RG 84, San Salvador, 1944, SC 811.11, Krehm, William, WNRC); interview with Bustamante, March 22, 1978; Estudiantes Patriotas, "Pueblo salvadoreño" (typed copy; n.p., n.d.), in "Apuntes." According to Bustamante, Galindo Pohl was in hiding for several days in May and might therefore have been out of touch with some developments in the planning.

33. Interviews with Castillo, October 15, 1976, Bustamante, March 22, 1978, and Galindo Pohl, September 27, 1977.

34. Interviews with Bustamante, February 22, 1978, and Castillo, October 15, 1976. Copies of many leaflets obviously connected with the general strike appear in "Apuntes."

35. Interview with Galindo Pohl, September 27, 1977; Wightman and Holdridge, Report 3797, May 22, 1944 (see n. 5 above).

36. Rose Harkness, May 4, 1944 (see n. 28 above).

37. Santos Dueñas, *Aurora*, p. 46; interview with Galindo Pohl, September 27, 1977; Morán, *Jornadas cívicas*, p. 57.

38. Interview with Bustamante, March 22, 1978.

39. Interviews with Galindo Pohl, September 27, 1977, and Castillo, October 15, 1976. On the Comité Estudiantil Universitario, see Chap. 3, p. 41.

40. Interview with Bustamante, February 22, 1978.

41. Confidential interview, San Salvador, 1978; author's interview with Ana de Sol, San Salvador, March 14, 1978.

42. Interviews with Bustamante (February 22 and March 22, 1978), Castillo (October 15, 1976), and Colorado (February 23, 1978); Massey, Report 269, May 9, 1944, G-2 Regional File 1933-44, El Salvador, file 3020, Box 817, RG 165, WNRC.

43. Author's interview with José Angel Zepeda, San Salvador, December 17, 1976.

44. Interviews with Castillo, October 15, 1976, and Bustamante, February 22, 1979.

45. Thurston to secretary of state, telegram 145, May 6, 1944 and despatch 1560, May 12, 1944, Decimal File 816.00/1306 and 816.504/42, RG 59, NA. The quotation is from despatch 1560, which indicates that a member of the United States Embassy staff was present at the meeting.

46. "AFM," memorandum, May 10, 1944, RG 84, San Salvador, 1944, 800, WNRC.

47. "Estudiantes: La revolución se conquista, no se espera" (typed carbon copy; n.p., n.d.), in "Apuntes."

48. *El Diario de Hoy* (San Salvador), May 9, 12, 1944; *La Prensa Gráfica* (extra), May 10, 1944; "Gesta cívica," no pagination.

49. Interview with Bustamante, February 22, 1978; Ainsworth, May 26, 1944 (see n. 8 above).

50. Thurston, despatch 1560, May 12, 1944 (see n. 45 above).

51. Dalton, *Miguel Mármol*, pp. 478–79. Galindo Pohl identified Amilcar Martínez, the student who served on the commission, as one of the group of forty. Interview, September 27, 1977.

52. Arnoldo Ferreto, "Informe sobre la situación política de El Salvador" (n.p., n.d.), photostatic copy of a document enclosed in an intercepted letter from Ferreto to Antonio Díaz Z. The document and Ferreto are identified in the covering letter, Fay Allen Des Portes, United States ambassador to Costa Rica, to secretary of state, despatch 1587, June 28, 1944, RG 84, San Salvador, 1944, SC800, WNRC.

53. Confidential interview, San Salvador, 1978.

54. Confidential interview, San Salvador, 1978.

The writer found almost no other evidence as to the role of these groups. According to Ambassador Thurston, the strike had affected "few factories" as of May 6. Telegram 145, May 6, 1944 (see n. 45 above). The few may have been textile factories, though the only factory mentioned by any of the strike organizers interviewed was the brewery, whose manager promised on May 6 or 7 to close it the following week. A leaflet dated May 8 listed the brewery (La Constancia) as one of five entities that had been declared on strike. The shoemakers appeared on a list of groups "which are about to go on strike, and whose cooperation is almost indispensable to the movement. . . ." Interview with Bustamante, March 22, 1978; Comité de Huelgas, untitled leaflet (San Salvador: "at 9:30 [A.M.], May 8, 1944"), in "Apuntes"; Estudiantes Patriotas, "Pueblo Salvadoreño." The quotation is from Estudiantes Patriotas. On the bakers, see Chap. 5, pp. 71, 74.

55. Interviews with Bustamante, February 22, 1978, and Colorado, February 23, 1978; Thurston to secretary of state, despatch 1646, May 29, 1944, Decimal File 816.00/1425, RG 59, NA.

According to "Revolutionary Activities" (n.d., p. 21) (see n. 6 above), the market in San Salvador remained open during the strike. However, a contemporary report stated that the market vendors announced their intention to strike (see above, p. 76), and Colorado recalled that the market stalls operated by Palestinian and Chinese proprietors closed *after all the others*. Interview, February 23, 1978. The explanation for this discrepancy is probably that the municipally operated market building remained open, and some vendors appeared from time to time. *El Diario de Hoy* reported on May 9, 1944, that women from nearby districts arrived at the market on May 7, ignorant of what was going on in San Salvador.

56. "Revolutionary Activities," n.d. (see n. 6 above), p. 22.

57. Interview with Galindo Pohl, September 27, 1977; *La Prensa Gráfica* (extra), May 10, 1944; "Gesta cívica" (see n. 48 above). Three sources claimed that churches had closed. "Correspondence: Trouble in El Salvador," *New Republic* 3 (July 10, 1944): p. 47; Dalton, *Miguel Mármol*, p. 479; Cisneros, December 1976. However, no mention of such an unusual occurrence appeared in any other contemporary account of the civic strike, and Bustamante asserted that churches did *not* close. Interview, March 22, 1978.

58. Peña Kampy, "*General Martínez*," p. 166.

59. Interviews with Mario Héctor Salazar, San Salvador, March 20, 1978, and Víctor Lasso, San Salvador, January 16, 1978.

60. Confidential interview with taxi organizer; "Revolutionary Activities," n.d. (see n. 6 above), p. 11.

61. Interview, March 14, 1978. Sra. de Sol was the sister of Guillermo Pérez and wife of Jorge Sol Castellanos. Ellis, memorandum entitled "Political Notes," October 31, 1944, enclosure no. 2 to despatch 2118, October 31, 1944, Decimal File 816.00/10-3144, RG 59, NA.

62. Cesar Ortiz, "AP Special Advance for AMS of Sunday, June 4," (copy of wire, dateline San José, Costa Rica, June 3 [no year], marked at end "sent June 1,") G-2 Regional File 1933-44, El Salvador, file 3000-3020, Box 817, RG 165, WNRC. Punctuation altered for the sake of clarity.

63. Interviews with Galindo Pohl, September 27, 1977, and Bustamante, March 22, 1978. Krehm, *Democracies and Tyrannies*, p. 23; confidential interview, San Salvador, 1978.

64. *El Diario Nuevo*, April 27, 1944; interview with Victor Lasso, San Salvador, January 29, 1978; "Revolutionary Activities," n.d. (see n. 6 above), pp. 14–15. Lasso was an intern at Hospital Bloom in 1944.

65. Maleady to Thurston, April 27, 1944, RG 84, San Salvador, 1944, 800, WNRC.

66. Harkness, May 4, 1944 (see n. 28 above); Krehm to Johnson, n.d. (see n. 32 above); "Empleadas salvadoreñas" (n.p., n.d.), in "Apuntes"; "R.T.S.," memorandum, April 28, 1944, RG 84, San Salvador, 1944, 800, WNRC. The quotation is from R.T.S.

67. Interview with Castillo, October 15, 1976; Thurston to secretary of state, telegram 131, May 3, 1944, Decimal File 816.00/1291, RG 59, NA.

68. Thurston to secretary of state, despatch 1535, May 4, 1944, Decimal File 816.00/1324, RG 59, NA; Herbert Lewy Van Severn et al. (fifty-four names), memorandum beginning "The Medical Corps of the Rosales Hospital . . . assembled in plenary session . . . on May 2nd," translation enclosed with despatch 1535. Original text in *El Diario Latino*, May 10, 1944. A typed copy dated May 2, 1944, appears in an album entitled "Cuaderno de Recortes 'Política Patria' Abril 1938–Sept. 1944." Biblioteca Dr. Manuel Gallardo.

69. E. M. E[ste?], memorandum, May 3, 1944, RG 84, San Salvador, 1944, 800, WNRC.

70. Harkness, May 4, 1944 (see n. 28 above).

71. *El Diario Latino*, May 10, 13, 1944.

72. Thurston to secretary of state, telegram 134, May 5, 1944, Decimal File 816.00/1300, RG 59, NA; *El Diario Latino*, May 12, 1944; Luís V. Velasco et al.,

memorandum beginning "Los infrascritos Médicos y Cirujanos de la Facultad: reunidos en sesión plena el día cinco de Mayo . . . ," *La Prensa Gráfica* (segundo extra), May 12, 1944; Krehm to Johnson, n.d. (see n. 32 above).

73. Krehm to Johnson, n.d. (see n. 32 above); Thurston to secretary of state, telegram 133, May 5, 1944, Decimal File 816.00/1299, RG 59, NA. The quotation is from Thurston.

74. "Revolutionary Activities," n.d. (see n. 6 above), p. 21; Thurston, telegram 133, May 5, 1944 (see n. 73 above); Krehm to Johnson, n.d. (see n. 32 above). The quotation is from "Revolutionary Activities."

75. Cisneros, December 1976.

76. Krehm, *Democracies and Tyrannies*, p. 23; interview with Galindo Pohl, September 27, 1977. Galindo Pohl was in the church.

77. Interview with Bustamante, February 22, 1978.

Cf. Velasco, "Manifiesto": "Day of National Liberation, glorious happy day . . . in which after the solemn Mass where religious liberty was trampled under foot, when all hearts beat in unison, directing their longing toward a single thought: GENERAL STRIKE, GENERAL STRIKE, GENERAL STRIKE . . ." (see n. 19 above).

This gathering and fanning out of people dressed in mourning probably explains reports of a march by women dressed in mourning, which, according to "High-School Revolution," took place on May 2, one month after the April 2 uprising. José Quetglas, obviously not an eyewitness (see n. 27), told an interviewer, "The 15th [*sic*] of this month, a mass had been organized in commemoration of the first month after the uprising [of April 2]; it was going to be celebrated in the Church of the Rosary, . . . but at the last minute the priest appeared[,] saying that the mass had been forbidden; it was beautiful to see five thousand women, dressed all in black, file through the streets of San Salvador in a sign of silent protest." Interview, *El Imparcial*, May 9, 1944.

The writer found no one who remembered such a march except Sra. de Cisneros, whose account appears earlier in the present chapter. Peña Kampy's report that the government gave permission for "a silent and peaceful march of *brazos caídos* in the streets" in commemoration of Labor Day (May 1) and confined security forces to their barracks can only be a garbled version of the events of May 5 and 8. "*General Martínez*," p. 165. If such an authorized demonstration had taken place, some mention of it surely would have appeared in the *martinista* newspapers or the files of the United States Embassy.

78. "Revolutionary Activities," n.d. (see n. 6 above), p. 21.

79. *El Diario Latino*, May 19, 1944.

80. Interview with Reynaldo Galindo Pohl, September 27, 1977; Krehm to Johnson, n.d. (see n. 32 above); "Revolutionary Activities," n.d. (see n. 6 above), p. 22.

81. "Revolutionary Activities," n.d. (see n. 6 above), p. 21.

82. Santos Dueñas, *Aurora*, p. 46.

83. "Revolutionary Activities," n.d., pp. 23–24 (see n. 6 above); interviews with Fabio Castillo, San José, Costa Rica, October 15, 1976, and Jorge Bustamante, San Salvador, February 22, 1978. See Chap. 3, pp. 30, 41–42, and 43 for background on Alvarado, and pp. 39 and 45 on Castaneda Castro.

Luís Escalante remembered attending a large meeting on the day the banks closed (May 5) in the home of Miguel Angel Alcaine, and thought Alcaine had called it. Interview with Escalante, San Salvador, March 29, 1978. However, he may have confused this gathering with the first meeting of the Comité de Reconstrucción Nacional, which Bustamante remembered as taking place in the home of Alcaine. In any case, whether Alvarado or Alcaine hosted the organizing meeting, a close relationship between the CRN and the ADS group became apparent in the negotiating process.

Some doubt exists as to when or by whom Castaneda Castro was named to the Comité de Reconstrucción Nacional. According to "Revolutionary Activities" (p. 23), "confidential source X, whose information has proved to be generally reliable," described Castaneda as one of the original committee members, representing "military men." However, neither Bustamante nor Escalante remembered his attending the first meeting of the committee on May 6, and Escalante thought he might have been invited later because it seemed advisable to have a military man on the committee.

Very little information about the second negotiating committee has come to light. "Revolutionary Activities" (p. 23) listed its members as Joaquín Parada Aparicio, Raúl Estupinian, Napoleón Rodríguez Ruiz, José Pineda, Ricardo Avila Moreira, José Aguilar, José María Méndez, and Manuel Castillo Calvo. The leading members of this group, according to Bustamante, played no role in the general strike but appeared on the scene at the end. However, Ambassador Thurston reported that it "could name seven or eight specific labor groups for which it was acting." Despatch 1560, May 12, 1944 (see n. 45 above). Two of its members received positions in the post-Martínez cabinet.

84. An unsigned note in the files of the United States Embassy indicated that, during the course of the negotiations surrounding the transfer of power, Herrera accompanied Alcaine and Escalante on a visit to Martínez's successor and subsequently to the United States Embassy. (Handwritten note at bottom of Maleady, "List of Names Suggested by 'Velasco' Group for Cabinet Posts," May 9—9:30 P.M., RG 84, San Salvador, 1944, 800, WNRC.)

Moreover, the manifesto of May 6 unmistakably betrayed his authorship. In a letter to Thurston expounding the "scheme" for the solution of El Salvador's problems that he presented to Nelson Rockefeller in March 1944, Herrera mentioned having read Norman Angell's *Let the People Know*, of which he said the "guiding idea" was that " '. . . the most elementary of the rights—the right not to be killed and tortured—may be achieved only by the general fulfillment of an obligation . . . to defend that right on behalf of others. The entire community, the collectivity of all the men, should defend that right . . .' " (Herrera to Thurston, San Salvador, April 18, 1944, translation enclosed with despatch 1501, April 25, 1944, Decimal File 816.00/1286, RG 59, NA.)

The manifesto echoed that paragraph of Herrera's letter: "Certainly it is to be desired that in EL SALVADOR every person should be able to live a life of dignity and decency, with a minimum of material, spiritual and intellectual resources[,] enjoying at least, if it is to be worth living it, the indispensable guarantees that the MOST PRIMARY OF THE RIGHTS OF MAN—THE RIGHT TO LIVE—THE RIGHT NOT TO BE KILLED OR TORTURED, SHALL BE A REALITY, as the great thinker Norman Angell demanded for all humanity." [Names deleted], "Fellow Citizens" (San Salvador, May 6, 1944), translation enclosed in despatch 1545, May 6, 1944, Decimal File 816.00/1347, RG 59, NA.

85. Interview with Bustamante, March 22, 1978; Thurston to secretary of state, telegram 139, May 6, 1944, Decimal File 816.00/1305, RG 59, NA; "Fellow Citizens" (see n. 84 above).

86. Interview with Escalante, March 29, 1978; Thurston to secretary of state, telegram 137, May 5, 1944, Decimal File 816.00/1303, RG 59, NA; telegram 139, May 6, 1944.

87. *El Diario Latino*, May 9, 1944; Thurston, telegram 145, May 6, 1944.

88. Luna, "Análisis," p. 116; Massey, Report 269, May 9, 1944, G-2 Regional File 1933-44, El Salvador, file 3020, Box 817, RG 165, WNRC.

89. Interviews with Galindo Pohl, September 27, 1977, and Castillo, October 15, 1976.

90. Interviews with de Sol (March 14, 1978), Castillo (October 15, 1976), and Bustamante (February 22 and March 22, 1978); Thurston to secretary of state, despatch 1567, May 15, 1944, Decimal File 816.00/1364, RG 59, NA. The quotation is from Thurston.

91. Interview with Mario Hector Salazar, March 20, 1978. Salazar was one of the five who resigned from the Corte de Cuentas.

92. *El Diario de Hoy*, extra, May 9, 1944.

93. Thurston to secretary of state, telegram 148, May 8, 1944, Decimal File 816.00/1309, RG 59, NA; "Revolutionary Activities," n.d., p. 22 (see n. 6 above).

94. *El Diario Latino*, May 24, 1944.

95. "Revolutionary Activities," n.d., p. 21 (see n. 6 above); Somoza to Ministro de Gobernación, May 8, 1944, file 210., "Gobierno Departamental," package no. 92-B, El Salvador, MG, "Antecedentes," 1944; *El Diario Latino*, May 17, 1944.

96. Interview, September 27, 1977.

Chapter 6. The Fall of Martínez

1. Maximiliano Hernández Martínez, interview with *El Imparcial* (Guatemala City), May 12, 1944.

2. Walter Thurston, United States ambassador to El Salvador, to secretary of state, despatch 1584, May 18, 1944, Decimal File 816.00/1377, RG 59, NA; O[verton] G. E[llis], United States vice consul, El Salvador, memorandum entitled "Thoughts on the recent demands made of President Menendez by a group of army officers," May 25, 1944, RG 84, San Salvador, 1944, 800, WNRC. The quotation is from Ellis.

3. G[eorge] B. Massey, acting United States military attaché, El Salvador, Report 244, April 17, 1944, enclosed with Thurston to secretary of state, despatch 1484, April 19, 1944, Decimal File 816.00/1274, RG 59, NA.

4. Ellis, memorandum, April 18, 1944, RG 84, San Salvador, 1944, 800, WNRC.

5. Confidential interview, San Salvador, 1978.

6. *El Diario Nuevo*, April 25, 1944; confidential interview with a high official of the Martínez government, San Salvador, 1978. A member of the National Guard stationed in San Salvador in 1944 independently recalled that his unit was confined to its barracks for some two weeks during the strike to avoid incidents. Conversation with Teodoro Benavides, Elkins Park, Pennsylvania, August 31, 1977.

7. *El Diario Nuevo*, May 4, 1944; "Mentira que hayan libertado reos" (n.p., May 4, 1944), typed carbon copy in "Apuntes." Jorge Bustamante recalled that the government did release many people but only those who had been arrested by mistake. Author's interview with Bustamante, San Salvador, March 22, 1978.

8. Thurston to secretary of state, despatch 1512, April 28, 1944, Decimal File

816.00/1289, RG 59, NA; Gregorio Luna et al., "Los trastornadores protestan" (San Salvador, April 27, 1944), photocopy of leaflet loaned to the author.

9. *El Diario Nuevo*, May 1, 1944.

10. Text in *El Diario Nuevo*, May 6, 1944.

11. Interview with Bustamante, March 22, 1978; *La Prensa Gráfica*, May 17, 1944.

12. Interview with Colorado, February 23, 1978.

13. Thurston to secretary of state, telegram 145, May 6, 1944, Decimal File 816.00/1306, RG 59, NA.

14. Confidential interview, San Salvador, 1978; interview with José Colorado, San Salvador, February 23, 1978.

15. E. M. Este [(?) signature unclear], United States Embassy, memorandum, May 1, 1944, RG 84, San Salvador, 1944, 800, WNRC; interview with Bustamante, March 22, 1978; Thurston to secretary of state, telegram 155, May 9, 1944, Decimal File 316.1123 Wright, Joseph Robert/4, RG 59, NA.

16. Thurston to secretary of state, telegram 139, May 6, 1944, Decimal File 816.00/1305, RG 59, NA.

17. Dalton, *Miguel Mármol*, p. 479. A meatcutter who participated in the strike recalled that police agents arrived at his home to take him to work, and he thought they had rounded up other strikers as well. Confidential interview, San Salvador, 1978.

18. Confidential interview, San Salvador, 1978; interview with Colorado, February 23, 1978; "Revolutionary Activities in El Salvador" (San Salvador, n.d. [stamped "May 29, 1944"]), p. 30, attached to J. Edgar Hoover, director, Federal Bureau of Investigation, letter to Adolf A. Berle, Jr., assistant secretary of state, May 29, 1944, Decimal File 816.00/1418, RG 59, NA. The covering letter describes "Revolutionary Activities" as a "memorandum received from a reliable and confidential source," presumably the FBI agent who served as "legal attaché" in the United States Embassy in San Salvador.

19. Workers Anti-Revolutionary Committee, "Warning to the Capital Striker" (May 6, 1944), translation in "Revolutionary Activities," n.d. (see n. 18 above), pp. 28–29.

20. "Revolutionary Activities," n.d. (see n. 18 above), p. 30; *El Diario de Hoy*, extra, May 9, 1944; *La Prensa Gráfica*, May 27, 1944. Cf. Thurston, telegram 145, May 6, 1944 (see n. 13 above): "The proprietors of smaller establishments are being subjected to direct threats and in some instances violence to oblige them to resume business." Bustamante recalled hearing rumors that stores would be opened by force. Interview, March 22, 1978.

21. Krehm, *Democracies and Tyrannies*, p. 26; "Revolutionary Activities," n.d., p. 29 (see n. 18 above); Thurston to secretary of state, telegram 141, May 7, 1944, Decimal File 816.00/1312, RG 59, NA.

Only very tenuous evidence exists as to what gave rise to these rumors. A high official of the Martínez government recalled hearing that Pro-Patria had recruited a large group of campesinos for a demonstration it subsequently cancelled in response to pleas from various people, including the diplomatic corps. The new arrivals may really have been the army conscripts Krehm reported having seen being "herded into the capital" on May 6. Bustamante thought Martínez originated the story as a "bluff"; had he really mobilized any campesinos the army would immediately have ousted him. Confidential interview, 1978; Krehm, *Democracies and Tyrannies*, p. 25; interview with Bustamante, March 22, 1978.

22. Thurston to secretary of state, despatch 1560, May 12, 1944, Decimal File 816.504/42, RG 59, NA; "W.W.S.," United States Embassy, San Salvador, memorandum, June 7, 1944, RG 84, San Salvador, 1944, Decimal 800, WNRC. The quotation is from W.W.S.

23. *El Diario de Hoy*, extra, May 9, 1944.

24. Thurston to secretary of state, telegram 135, May 5, 1944, Decimal File 816.00/1302, RG 59, NA; confidential interview, 1978. Another informant, possibly in a position to know, recalled that the cabinet, the presidents of the Supreme Court and the Legislative Assembly, and the archbishop of San Salvador held a meeting with Martínez early in May at which they urged an end to the executions and pointed out the serious implications of the strike. Roberto Molina y Morales, interview with author, Santa Tecla, March 20, 1978. This may have been the meeting Thurston heard about on May 5.

25. Thurston to secretary of state, telegrams 140, May 6, Decimal File 816.001/Martínez, Max/74, RG 59, NA, and 141, May 7, 1944 (see n. 21 above).

26. "Revolutionary Activities," n.d., (see n. 18 above), p. 31.

27. Peña Kampy, "*General Martínez*," p. 170.

28. *El Diario de Hoy*, extra, May 9, 1944; interview with Bustamante, February 22, 1978.

29. Roberto Molina y Morales, interview, March 20, 1978; Thurston to secretary of state, telegram 146, May 7, 1944, Decimal File 816.00/1308, RG 59, NA.

30. Confidential interview, 1978; Massey, Report 269, May 9, 1944, G-2 Regional File 1933-44, El Salvador, file 3020, Box 817, RG 165, WNRC.

31. Confidential interview, 1978.

Bustamante remembered hearing that Ponce went to Martínez after his narrow escape at the Palacio Nacional with the assertion that he could break the strike if Martínez would give the order to fire on the crowd, to which Martínez replied that enough blood had been shed. Interview, February 22, 1978. Cf. report that "in a meeting of the Asamblea [Legislativa] in Casa Presidencial prior to Martínez' depositing the presidency, several members urged Martínez to shoot down the strikers without mercy and force open the stores. Martínez refused, saying that enough blood had been shed." Unsigned, untitled document described in covering despatch as "a list of the reports regarding the attitude of the Salvadoran Military which reached the Acting Military Attaché . . . May 15 to 17." Enclosure to despatch 1584, May 18, 1944 (see n. 2 above).

32. Confidential interview, 1978; interviews with Bustamante, February 22 and March 22, 1978, and Reynaldo Galindo Pohl, Washington D.C., September 27, 1977; *La Prensa Gráfica*, January 1, 1944; primera extra and segunda extra, May 9, 1944, as reproduced in *La Prensa Gráfica*, May 12, 1944. Cf. *El Diario Latino*, May 9, 1944, according to which the CRN and the cabinet *discussed* the five candidates mentioned, along with Gomez Zarate.

33. The one informant in a position to know maintained that Martínez recommended the selection of Menéndez to the cabinet, president of the Legislative Assembly, and president of the Supreme Court at their meeting on May 9 on the ground that the army favored Menéndez, and army support would be critical to the success of the new government. Confidential interview, 1978. Martínez may well have discussed the question with military leaders. However, this version of the story, like the report in *El Diario Latino* (May 9, 1944), seems designed to convey the impression that the transfer

of power followed strictly legal procedures; it does not explain the hard bargaining portrayed by *La Prensa Gráfica*.

34. Maleady, memorandum, February 2, 1944, enclosure to Thurston to secretary of state, despatch 1235, February 3, 1944, Decimal File 816.00/1190, RG 59, NA; Rufus A. Byers, chief, United States Military Mission to El Salvador, to chief, Military Intelligence Service, War Department, April 10, 1944, G-2 Regional File 1933-44, El Salvador, file 3000-3020, Box 817, RG 165, WNRC; Ellis, April 18, 1944 (see n. 4 above).

35. Elam, "Appeal to Arms," p. 70; Guillermo Moscoso, Jr., BOMID, Miami, Report 808, May 28, 1944, G-2 Regional File 1933-44, El Salvador, file 3000-3020, Box 817, RG 165, WNRC. Interview with Bustamante, March 22, 1978.

36. *La Prensa Gráfica*, primera extra, May 9, 1944.

37. *El Diario de Hoy*, May 9, 1944.

38. Memorandum signed "Ambassador," May 8, 1944, RG 84, San Salvador, 1944, 800, WNRC; author's interviews with Mario Hector Salazar, San Salvador, March 20, 1978, and Bustamante, February 22, 1978.

39. Massey, Report 269, May 9, 1944 (see n. 30 above).

40. "Revolutionary Activities," n.d., p. 33 (see n. 18 above).

41. *La Prensa Gráfica*, primera extra, May 9, 1944.

42. *El Diario Latino*, May 10, 1944.

43. *La Prensa Gráfica*, segunda extra, May 9, 1944.

44. *El Diario Latino*, May 9, 1944; Poder Legislativo, Decreto número 36, May 10, 1944 [*sic*] *Diario Oficial* (San Salvador), Vol. 136, No. 103 (May 10, 1944). This decree is dated May 10, as are those accepting the resignation of Martínez and designating Menéndez as president, although it is clear from contemporary press reports that the Legislative Assembly's actions took place the day before.

45. *La Prensa Gráfica*, extra, May 10, 1944; *El Diario Latino*, May 10, 1944.

46. Interviews with Bustamante, March 22 and February 22, 1944; Maleady, "List of Names Suggested by 'Velasco' Group for Cabinet Posts," May 9 [1944], RG 84, San Salvador, 1944, 800, WNRC; *El Diario de Hoy*, May 11, 1944.

47. "AFM," memorandum, May 10, 1944, RG 84, San Salvador, 1944, 800, WNRC.

48. Interview with Bustamante, February 22, 1944; *La Prensa Gráfica*, extra, May 10, 1944; *Nuestro Diario* (Guatemala City), May 11, 1944, as reprinted in *La Prensa Gráfica*, May 14, 1944.

49. *El Diario Latino*, May 9, 10, 13, 1944; Thurston to secretary of state, telegram 156, May 10, 1944, Decimal File 816.01/443, RG 59, NA.

50. *La Prensa Gráfica*, extra, May 10, 1944, primera and segunda extras, May 9, 1944; *El Diario Latino*, May 10, 1944; "AFM," May 10, 1944 (see n. 47 above).

51. *La Prensa Gráfica*, extra, May 11, 1944; "Dirección General de Policía," número de orden 526, El Salvador, MG, *Entrada*, 1944.

52. *El Diario Latino*, May 11, 12, 13, 1944; *La Prensa Gráfica*, extra, May 11, 1944; unsigned copy of letter to L. F. Whitbeck, Gerente de los Ferrocarriles Internacionales de Centro América, May 11, 1944, El Salvador, MG, *Correspondencia despachada, 1944*, vol. 5.

53. *El Diario Latino*, May 11, 1944; photo in "Gesta cívica."

Chapter 7. The Question of Intervention

1. Walter Thurston, United States ambassador to El Salvador, to secretary of state, despatch 624, July 29, 1943, Decimal File 816.00/1131, RG 59, NA.

2. See Molina, "Causas," p. xvi. Four of the Salvadorans interviewed in 1976–78 remembered hearing of some action by the diplomatic corps. *El Diario de Hoy* (extra, May 9, 1944) mentioned "members of the Diplomatic Corps" as present at the first meeting between the Cabinet and the CRN on May 8. However, their presence was not mentioned in detailed accounts of the May 8 negotiations that appeared in *La Prensa Gráfica* and *El Diario Latino*.

3. Interview with Luís Escalante Arce, San Salvador, March 29, 1978.

4. [John M.] Cabot, assistant chief, Division of the American Republics, to Philip W. Bonsal, chief, Division of the American Republics, United States State Department, "Memorandum on the Political Situation in El Salvador," December 31, 1943, Decimal File 816.00/1164; O[verton] G[.] E[llis], United States vice consul, El Salvador, memorandum, September 9, 1943, enclosure no. 3 to despatch 736, September 10, 1943, Decimal File 816.00/1144, RG 59, NA. See also Chap. 3, n. 53 on the stated purposes of the constituent assembly.

5. Unsigned memorandum of conversation, enclosure no. 1 to despatch 1156, January 8, 1944, Decimal File 816.00/1172, RG 59, NA; United States naval attaché, Guatemala, Intelligence Report, serial 234-43-R, August 10, 1943, G-2 Regional File 1933-44, El Salvador, files 3000-4000 and 3020 (continuation), Box 817, RG 165, WNRC; "R.T.S.," United States Embassy, El Salvador, memorandum, March 10, 1944, RG 84, San Salvador, 1944, 800, WNRC. The quotation is from the enclosure to despatch 1156.

6. Thurston, memorandum, July 8, 1943, enclosure no. 1 to despatch 577, July 20, 1944, Decimal File 711.16/55; Winnall A. Dalton to Thurston, San Salvador, December 28, 1944, enclosure to despatch 1123, December 30, 1943; Thurston to secretary of state, despatch 1154, January 8, 1944, Decimal File 816.00/1167 and 1171, RG 59, NA; H[.] G[ardner] A[insworth], United States vice consul, El Salvador, memorandum, February 26, 1944, enclosure to despatch 1331, February 28, 1944, RG 84, San Salvador, 1944, 800, WNRC.

7. G[eorge] B. Massey, acting United States military attaché, El Salvador, Report 162, November 9, 1943, and letter to Thurston, December 16, 1943, G-2 Regional File 1933-44, El Salvador, file 3600-3610, Box 818, RG 165, WNRC.

8. Thurston to secretary of state, despatch 1309, February 21, 1944, Decimal File 816.00/1205, RG 59, NA; Massey, Report 205, February 21, 1944, G-2 Regional File 1933-44, El Salvador, file 3020, Box 817, RG 165, WNRC.

Thurston did have a conversation with Martínez about these arrests on December 28, but according to his report of it, he merely mentioned that "friends of some of the detained persons had expressed fear that they might be executed." Thurston to secretary of state, telegram 295, December 28, 1943, Decimal File 816.00/1164, RG 59, NA.

9. Thurston to secretary of state, despatch 1154, January 8, 1944, Decimal File 816.00/1171, RG 59, NA.

10. E. R. Stettinius, Jr., for the secretary of state, to United States diplomatic representatives in Costa Rica, El Salvador, Guatemala, Honduras, and Nicaragua, February

2, 1944, as published in United States Department of State, *Foreign Relations of the United States, 1944* (1967), vol. 7, pp. 1391–92.

11. Thurston, despatch 624, July 29, 1943 (see n. 1 above); Cabot to Bonsal, December 31, 1943 (see n. 4 above). The quotation is from Cabot.

12. *Foreign Relations of the United States, 1943* (1965), vol. 6, pp. 310–12; H. L. Wightman, Report 146, August 17, 1943, G-2 Regional File 1933-44, El Salvador, file 3020, Box 817, RG 165, WNRC.

13. Thurston to secretary of state, despatch 1070, December 13, 1943, Decimal File 816.00/1158, RG 59, NA.

14. Thurston to secretary of state, despatch 1352, March 2, 1943, RG 84, San Salvador, 1944, SC800, WNRC.

15. Thurston to secretary of state, telegram 100, April 3, 1944, Decimal File 816.00/1228, RG 59, NA; Luna, "Análisis," p. 112; de Suárez, "Vida trágica," pt. 14, *El Diario de Hoy*, October 9, 1943. According to Thurston, the diplomatic corps agreed "that it is premature if not unwise to interpose at this stage and that we shall await developments," but it is not clear how that agreement was reached.

16. W[illiam] P. Cochran, assistant chief, Division of Caribbean and Central American Affairs, United States State Department, "Memorandum of Conversation," April 10, 1944, Decimal File 816.00/1248, RG 59, NA.

17. Thurston to secretary of state, despatch 1448, April 5, 1944, Decimal File 816.00/1249, RG 59, NA.

18. Thurston to secretary of state, telegram 109, April 5, 1944, Decimal File 816.00/1244, RG 59, NA.

19. Ellis, memorandum, April 28, 1944, enclosure no. 2 to despatch 1514, April 28, 1944, Decimal File 816.00/1294, RG 59, NA; A[rcher] B. Hannah, assistant United States military attaché, Guatemala, Report 1152, April 17, 1944, G-2 Regional File 1933-44, El Salvador, file 3000-3020, Box 817, RG 165, WNRC; Massey, Report 245, April 18, 1944, enclosure to despatch 1484, April 19, 1944, Decimal File 816.00/1274, RG 59, NA.

20. Massey, Report 264, April 29, 1944, Army Intelligence Project Decimal File, 1941-45, El Salvador, 092, RG 319, WNRC; Thurston to secretary of state, despatch 1474, April 15, 1944, Decimal File 816.00/1267, RG 59, NA.

21. Thurston to secretary of state, despatch 1514, April 28, 1944 (see n. 19 above); J[oseph] E. Maleady, United States vice consul, El Salvador, memorandum, April 28, 1944, enclosed with despatch 1514.

22. Massey to AUDIOR, number 12364, April 25, 1944, RG 319, NA, G-2 Message File, Records of the Army Staff.

23. "Jack" [Cabot] to Thurston, May 9, 1944; [Thurston] to John M. Cabot, May 12, 1944, RG 84, San Salvador, 1944, 800, WNRC.

24. Thurston to secretary of state, despatch 1503, April 26, 1944, Decimal File 816.00/1288, RG 59, NA. The entire Salvadoran air force (consisting of some six planes) participated in the April 2 insurrection.

25. Cochran to "Miss Bush," April 13, 1944; Cordell Hull, United States secretary of state, to Thurston, Instruction 556, April 26, 1944, Decimal File 816.001 Martínez, Max/72, RG 59, NA.

26. Thurston to secretary of state, telegram 129, May 1, 1944; unnumbered tele-

grams marked "not sent"; Hull to Amembassy, San Salvador, telegram 130, May 8, 1944, all in Decimal File 816.001 Martínez, Max/73, RG 59, NA.

27. "GG" (Gerhard Gade [?], United States Embassy, San Salvador), memorandum, May 4, 1944, RG 84, San Salvador, 1944, 800, WNRC.

28. Thurston to secretary of state, telegram 137, May 5, 1944, Decimal File 816.00/1303, RG 59, NA.

29. Hull to Amembassy, San Salvador, May 6, 1944 (copy, headed "Telegram Sent"); Thurston to secretary of state, telegram 139, May 6, 1944, Decimal File 816.00/1303 and 816.00/1305, RG 59, NA.

30. Peña Kampy, "*General Martínez*," p. 169.

31. Thurston to secretary of state, telegram 144, May 7, 1944, RG 84, San Salvador, 1944, 320 Wright, Joseph Robert, WNRC.

32. Memorandum signed "Ambassador," May 8, 1944, RG 84, San Salvador, 1944, 800, WNRC; *El Diario Latino*, May 13, 1944; Krehm, *Democracies and Tyrannies*, pp. 26–27.

33. Memorandum signed "Ambassador," May 8, 1944, RG 84, San Salvador, 1944, 800, WNRC.

Dalton's account of ex-President Meléndez's role would be interesting if true, but it appears to have been a fictitious pretext for Trabanino's visit to Thurston. On Dalton, see above, Chap. 3, p. 35.

Chapter 8. The May Strike in Perspective

1. Walter Thurston, United States ambassador to El Salvador, to secretary of state, despatch 1584, May 18, 1944, Decimal File 816.00/1377, RG 59, NA.

2. Interview with Jorge Sol Castellanos, San Salvador, April 13, 1978.

Sources

The Martínez era has yet to receive the scholarly attention it deserves. The valuable studies by Everett Alan Wilson ("The Crisis of National Integration in El Salvador, 1919–1935"), Alejandro Marroquín ("Estudio de la crisis de los años treinta en El Salvador"), and Rafael Guidos Vejar ("El ascenso del militarismo en El Salvador") cover only Martínez's first term as president. The only serious work that deals with the entire lifespan of the regime is David Luna, "Análisis de una dictadura fascista Latinoamericana, Maximiliano Hernández Martínez 1931–44." Although several good reconstructions of the April 2, 1944, uprising exist, published accounts of the general strike (in Luna, "Análisis"; William Krehm, *Democracies and Tyrannies of the Caribbean*; and Francisco Morán, *Las jornadas cívicas de abril y mayo de 1944*) are sketchy. Luna and Morán also contain obvious inaccuracies.

The present study is based on reports in the contemporary Salvadoran press and in the *New York Times* and United States news weeklies, as well as on archival materials and interviews with participants.

Four record groups in the United States National Archives proved invaluable: the General Records of the Department of State (Record Group 59); Records of the Foreign Service Posts of the Department of State (Record Group 84); and two overlapping military intelligence files—the G-2 Regional File, 1933–44 (Record Group 165), and the Army Intelligence Project Decimal File, 1941–45 (Record Group 319).

In addition to the observations of various members of the United States Embassy staffs, these files contain correspondence and other materials (such as leaflets) received from residents of El Salvador, as well as transcriptions and translations of significant documents. Of particular interest is a series of detailed reviews of political developments in El Salvador, copies of which appear in various record groups. Although these memoranda were unsigned and sometimes filed without any identifying data, all can probably be attributed to the Federal Bureau of Investigation agent who served as "legal attaché" in the embassy. They undoubtedly incorporated information received from his embassy colleagues as well as his own sources, and since the ambassador routinely received copies, they were reflected in the latter's reports to the State Department.

In El Salvador, both the Biblioteca Nacional and the library of the Museo Nacional in 1976 contained excellent newspaper files and a significant sampling of periodical literature from the Martínez era. The private Biblioteca Dr. Manuel Gallardo in Santa Tecla houses a wealth of both published and unpublished sources on Salvadoran history; of particular value for the present study was a unique collection of leaflets and other memorabilia contained in an album marked "Apuntes de Política Patria: Dic 1941/44[,] Dic 1954/Feb. 1955." Some relevant material also appears in a second album, "Cuaderno de Recortes 'Política Patria' Abril 1938–Sept. 1944."

The Archivo General de la Nación as of 1978 contained no material from 1943–44 except a few folders of routine business records from the Ministry of Education. The other ministries presumably still had whatever files they had preserved from this period. The writer was able to consult only those in the Ministry of Interior (successor to the Ministry of Government). The Ministry of Government materials from 1943 and 1944 included, for each calendar year, two registers of correspondence, *Entrada de correspondencia* and *Salida de correspondencia*; carbon copies of outgoing correspondence bound in a set of volumes called *Correspondencia despachada*; and a large collection of folders called "antecedentes," containing incoming correspondence, copies of replies, and other miscellaneous material, arranged in a decimal subject file and stored in numbered packages. These files shed considerable light on the bureaucratic processes of the Martínez administration but contained disappointingly little about the movement to overthrow the president, probably because such sensitive information was either never committed to writing or not left in the files. The writer also checked the archives of the Archdiocese of San Salvador in 1976, but the only files available for 1944—a small box of correspondence between parish priests and the office of the Archbishop ("Correspondencia Vicaria")—proved to be of no interest for the present study.

Interviews with participants provided much of the detail regarding the organization of the general strike and the final hours of the Martínez regime. A few key informants asked not to be identified; their statements in the text are attributed to "confidential interviews," with the year and place of the interview.

Unpublished Documents

Washington, D.C., United States National Archives Building
- Record Group 59, General Records of the Department of State Decimal Files:
  - 1930–39—Selected documents on El Salvador (816.).
  - 1940–44—816.00 and cross-referenced material (El Salvador).
  - 1944–815.00 and cross-referenced material (Honduras); 817.00 (Nicaragua).
- Record Group 319, Records of the Army Staff, G-2 Message File.
- Records of the Office of Strategic Services, Research and Analysis Branch.

Suitland, Maryland, Washington National Records Center, National Archives
- Record Group 84, Records of the Foreign Service Posts of the Department State, San Salvador: 1943, 1944.

Record Group 165, Records of the War Department General and Special Staffs, Records of the Office of the Director of Intelligence: G-2 Regional File, 1933–44, El Salvador.

Record Group 319, Records of the Army Staff, Records of the Office of the Assistant Chief of Staff, G-2 Intelligence: Army Intelligence Project Decimal File, 1941–45, El Salvador.

San Salvador, El Salvador, Ministerio del Interior, Sección de Archivos

"Antecedentes": 1943, 1944.

Correspondencia despachada: 1943, 1944.

Entrada de correspondencia: 1943, 1944.

Salida de correspondencia: 1943, 1944.

Santa Tecla, El Salvador, Biblioteca Dr. Manuel Gallardo

Album marked "Apuntes de Política Patria[:] Dic 1941/44[,] Dic 1954/Feb. 1955."

Album marked "Cuaderno de Recortes 'Política Patria' Abril 1938–Sept. 1944."

Miscellaneous, from private individuals

Caso, Quino. "Hacia la desobediencia civil: Mi mensaje al pueblo salvadoreño." San José, Costa Rica, July 1943.

Luna, Gregorio, et al., "Los trastornadores protestan." San Salvador, April 27, 1944. Photocopy.

Published Documents

Banco Hipotecario de El Salvador. *Memoria de las labores de la institución desde el 1º de julio de 1943, hasta el 30 de junio de 1944* presentada por la Junta Directiva a la Junta General de Accionistas el 28 de agosto de 1944, 9º Ejercicio. San Salvador, n.d.

——— [de El Salvador], Junta Directiva, *Lo ocurrido en el Banco Hipotecario de El Salvador (Libro blanco)*. Publicación de la . . . ordenada por la Junta General de Accionistas en sesión del 22 de agosto de 1945, vol. 1 ("Segunda Parte"). San Salvador, 1946.

El Salvador. *Constitución política de la República de El Salvador, decretada por la Asamblea Nacional Constituyente el 20 de enero de 1939*.

———. *Constitución política de la República de El Salvador, decretada por el Congreso Nacional Constituyente de 1886*.

———. *Diario Oficial* (San Salvador), various numbers, 1932–44.

———. Asamblea Nacional Constituyente [1944]. *Reformas a la constitución política de la República de El Salvador*.

Fortín Magaña, Romeo. *Inquietudes de un año memorable, 1944*. San Salvador: Talleres Gráficos Cisneros, [1945].

García, Miguel Angel. *Diccionario histórico enciclopédico de la República de El Salvador; Universidad Nacional: Homenaje en el primer centenario de su fundación*. Vol. 4, *Recopilación de documentos para su historia, 1890–1947*. San Salvador: Imprenta Nacional, 1956.

Las jornadas de mayo: Texto completo de todos los documentos que condujeron al movimiento liberador de Colombia el 10 de mayo de 1957. Bogotá: Ediciones Documentos Colombianos, 1957.

Ortiz Mancia, Alfredo. "Memoria general de la Universidad de El Salvador, correspondiente a los años 1944 y 1945." In *Memoria de las labores de la Universidad Autónoma de El Salvador durante los años 1944 y 1945. La Universidad, órgano de la Universidad Autónoma de El Salvador*. San Salvador: Talleres Gráficos Cisneros, n.d.

U.S. Department of State. *Foreign Relations of the United States*, 1943, vol. 6, and 1944, vol. 7. Washington, D.C.: U.S. Government Printing Office, 1965 and 1967.

Interviews

Benavides, Teodoro. Elkins Park, Pennsylvania, August 31, 1977.

Bustamante, Jorge. San Salvador, February 22 and March 22, 1978.

Carranza Anaya, Rafael. San Salvador, September 23, 1976.

Castillo, Fabio. San José, Costa Rica, October 15, 1976.

Castro Canizales, Joaquín. San Salvador, December 13, 1976.

Cisneros, sra. de. San Salvador, December 1976 (written response to author's questions).

Colorado, José. San Salvador, February 23, 1978.

Crespo Sánchez, Salvador. San José, Costa Rica, October 1976.

Escalante Arce, Luís. San Salvador, March 29, 1978.

Galindo Pohl, Reynaldo. Washington, D.C., September 27, 1977.

Lasso, Victor. San Salvador, January 16, 29, and February 18, 1978.

Luna, David. San José, Costa Rica, October 1976.

Magaña, Ernesto Mauricio. San Salvador, March 1978.

Rosales, Marina. San Salvador, August 28 and October 4, 1976.

Salazar, Mario Hector. San Salvador, March 20, 1978.

Sol, Ana de. San Salvador, March 14, 1978.

Sol Castellanos, Jorge. San Salvador, April 13, 1978.

Zepeda, José Angel. San Salvador, December 17, 1976.

Newspapers

Criterio (San Salvador), May 14, 1944.

El Diario de Hoy (San Salvador), November 3, 1936, and May 8–12, 1944.

El Diario Latino (San Salvador), May 9–30 and November 2–17, 1944.

El Diario Nuevo (San Salvador), October 27, November 3, and November 11, 1943; January 1–May 6, 1944.

El Gran Diario (San Salvador), April 1–May 12 and October 27–December 30, 1944.

El Imparcial (Guatemala City), May 9, 12, 1944.
El Nacionalista (San Salvador), June 6, 1935.
New York Times, April 4, 5, 8–11, 13–16, 20, 22, and May 4, 7–12, 1944.
Opinión Estudiantil (San Salvador) 8ª época, no. 1 (May 20, 1944).
La Prensa Gráfica (San Salvador), January 3–April 30, 1940; September 1, 1943–November 18, 1944.
La Tribuna (San Salvador), June 27, 1944.
El Universal (Santa Ana, El Salvador), April 7–May 26, 1944.

Articles

Ainsworth, H. Gardner. "Government Measures for Improvement of Living Standards in El Salvador." *Monthly Labor Review* 57, no. 2 (August 1943): 233–36.
Anderson, Charles W. "El Salvador: The Army as Reformer." In *Political Systems of Latin America*, edited by Martin Needler, pp. 53–72. Princeton, N.J.: D. Van Nostrand Co., 1964.
Arias Gómez, Jorge. "Datos históricos del proceso de reforma universitaria en El Salvador (1918–1963)." *Opinión Estudiantil*, época 21, no. 15 ("1ª quincena de julio de 1968"): 3.
Castro Ramírez, Manuel (discurso del . . .). "Camino de la esperanza." *La Universidad* (San Salvador) (1944): 13–17.
"Un componente de la huelga de mayo habla para esta revista: El br. Reynaldo Galindo Pohl, hace importantes revelaciones." *Repertorio Salvadoreño* (San Salvador) 2ª época, año 6°, no. 6 (July 15, 1946): 11.
"Correspondence: Trouble in El Salvador." *New Republic* 3, no. 2 (July 10, 1944): 47.
de Súarez, Carmen Delia. "La vida trágica de un hombre representativo." *El Diario de Hoy*, July 10, 16, 24, August 7, 14, 21, 28, September 4, 11, 18, 25, October 2, 9, 16, 1965.
"El episcopado salvadoreño solicita de la Asamblea Nacional Constituyente algunas reformas." *Revista Interdiocesana*, año 5 (January–February 1944): 1200–1201.
Galindo Pohl, Reinaldo [Reynaldo]. "Discurso pronunciado por . . . a nombre de la Asociación General de Estudiantes Universitarios (A.G.E.U.S.)." *La Universidad* (1944): 19–23.
Grieb, Kenneth J. "The United States and the Rise of General Maximiliano Hernández Martínez." *Journal of Latin American Studies* (Cambridge, England) 3, pt. 2 (November 1971): 151–72.
Guandique, José Salvador. "Noción y aspectos de la clase media en El Salvador." In *Materiales para el estudio de la clase media en América Latina*, edited by Theo. Crevenna, vol. 4, *La clase media en Panamá, El Salvador, Honduras, y Nicaragua, seis colaboraciones*, pp. 113–19. Washington, D.C.: Pan American Union, 1950.
"Haunted Theosophist." *Time* 43, no. 16 (April 17, 1944): 40.
"High-School Revolution." *Newsweek* 23, no. 21 (May 22, 1944): 66.
"La historia de una gesta cívica." *Ahora* (San Salvador) año 7, no. 82 (May 1944), no pagination.

Larín, Arístides Augusto. "Historia del movimiento sindical de El Salvador." *La Universidad*, año 96, no. 4 (July–August 1971): 135–79.

"Las leyes de la República de El Salvador respecto a la Iglesia." *Revista Inter-Diocesana*, año 5 (January–February 1944): 1202–8; (March–April 1944): 1258–62; (May–June 1944): 1300–1305.

López, Matilde Elena. "¿'Masferrer' socialista utópico, reformista o revolucionario?" *La Universidad*, no. 5 (September–October 1968): 101–8.

López Vallecillos, Italo. "La insurrección popular campesina de 1932." *Abra* (San Salvador) 2, no. 13 (June 1976): 3–18.

———. "Reflexiones sobre la violencia en El Salvador." *E.C.A.* (*Estudios Centroamericanos*) (San Salvador), año 31, no. 327–328 (January–February 1976): 9–30.

Luna [de Sola], David [Alejandro]. "Análisis de una dictadura fascista, Maximiliano Hernández Martínez 1931–44." *La Universidad*, año 94, no. 5 (September–October 1969): 39–130.

——— de Sola, David Alejandro. "Las bayonetas en El Salvador." *Vida Universitaria* (San Salvador), época 2, (March–April 1963): 10.

——— [de Sola], David A. "Un heróico y trágico suceso de nuestra historia." In *El proceso política centroamericano (Seminario de Historia Contemporánea de Centro America)*, 49–65. San Salvador: Editorial Universitaria, 1964.

——— [de Sola], David [Alejandro]. "Historia de la Universidad de El Salvador." Departamento de Relaciones Públicas y Promoción Universitaria (San Salvador). *Boletín Universitario*, [no. 4] (July–August [1971]): 3–8.

Marroquín, Alejandro D. "Estudio de la crisis de los años treinta en El Salvador." In *América Latina en los años treinta*, by Luís Antezana E. et al., 113–90. Mexico City: Instituto de Investigaciones Sociales, UNAM, 1977.

Mejía, Ricardo. "Breve relato de la revolución del 2 de abril de 1944." *Tribuna Libre* (San Salvador), May 27–30 and June 3, 5, 6, 1963.

Molina, Miguel Tomás. "Causas que motivaron un acontecimiento político jurídico de nuestra historia contemporánea." In *Democracia y socialismo (seguido de otros breves estudios)*, by Romeo Fortín Magaña, xi–xx. San Salvador, 1953.

Monteforte Toledo, Mario. "Sociología del liberalismo en Mesoamérica." *Cultura* (San Salvador), no. 19 (January–March 1961): 9–19.

"One Down." *Inter-American* 3, no. 6 (June 1944): 8.

Salazar Valiente, Mario. "El Salvador: Crisis, Dictadura, Lucha . . . (1920–1980)." In *América Latina: Historia de medio siglo*, coordinated by Pablo González Casanova, vol. 2, 87–138. Mexico City: Siglo Veintiuno Editores, 1981.

———. "A veinte años del 2 de abril." *El Universitario* (San Salvador), año 2 (April 2, 1964): 3.

"El Salvador: No Sanctuary." *Time* 43, no. 20 (May 15, 1944): 28.

"Setenta horas de ayuno en la Policía Judicial." *Repertorio Salvadoreño*, 2ª época, año 6° (July 15, 1946): 9.

"Social." *Ahora*, año 7, no. 82 (May 1944).

Stanisfer, Charles L. "Application of the Tobar Doctrine to Central America." *The Americas* 23 (January 1967): 251–72.

"Uruguay." *Latin America Regional Report/Southern Cone Report* (August 3, 1984): 3.

Whitaker, Arthur P. "Pan America in Politics and Diplomacy." In *Inter-American Affairs, 1944*, edited by Arthur P. Whitaker, 4–74. New York: Columbia University Press, 1945.

Books

Abad de Santillán, Diego. *La F.O.R.A.: Ideología y trayectoria del movimiento obrero revolucionario en la Argentina*. 2d ed. Buenos Aires: Editorial Proyección, 1971.
Alexander, Robert J. *Organized Labor in Latin America*. New York: Free Press, 1965.
Anderson, Thomas P. *Matanza: El Salvador's Communist Revolt of 1932*. Lincoln: University of Nebraska Press, 1971.
Baloyra, Enrique A. *El Salvador in Transition*. Chapel Hill: University of North Carolina Press, 1982.
Bell, John Patrick. *Crisis in Costa Rica: The 1948 Revolution*. Austin: University of Texas Press, 1971.
Berardo García, José. *La explosión de mayo*. Cali, Colombia: Imprenta Departamental, 1957.
Browning, David. *El Salvador: Landscape and Society*. Oxford: Oxford University Press, Clarendon Press, 1971.
Dalton García, Roque. *Miguel Mármol: Los sucesos de 1932 en El Salvador*. San José, Costa Rica: Editorial Universitaria Centroamericana, 1972.
———. *Poemas*. San Salvador: Editorial Universitaria de El Salvador, 1968.
Durham, William H. *Scarcity and Survival in Central America: Ecological Origins of the Soccer War*. Stanford: Stanford University Press, 1979.
Feltham, Percy M., Jr. *The Textile Industry in El Salvador*. New York: United Nations Technical Assistance Programme, 1954.
Figeac, José F. *La libertad de imprenta en El Salvador*. San Salvador: Imprenta Funes, 1947.
Gallardo, Ricardo. *Las constituciones de El Salvador*. 2 vols. Madrid: Ediciones Cultura Hispánica, 1961.
González y Contreras, Gilberto. *El último caudillo: Ensayo biográfico*. Mexico City: B. Costa-Amic, Editor, 1946.
Guidos Vejar, Rafael. *El ascenso del militarismo en El Salvador*. San Salvador: UCA Editores, 1980.
Johnson, John J. *Political Change in Latin America: The Emergence of the Middle Sectors*. Stanford: Stanford University Press, 1958.
Jones, Chester Lloyd. *The Caribbean since 1900*. New York: Prentice-Hall, 1936.
Krehm, William. *Democracies and Tyrannies of the Caribbean*. Westport, Conn.: Lawrence Hill, 1984.
Londoño Marín, Abelardo, and Flavio Correa Restrepo. *"Soldados sin Coraza" (Historia de una revolución)*. Medallín, Colombia: Editorial Bedout, 1957.
López Vallecillos, Italo. *El periodismo en El Salvador: Bosquejo histórico-documental*. San Salvador: Editorial Universitaria, 1964.
Luna [de Sola], David Alejandro. *Manual de historia económica de El Salvador*. San Salvador: Editorial Universitaria, 1971.
Macaulay, Neill. *The Sandino Affair*. Chicago: Quadrangle Books, 1967.

Magaña Menéndez, Gustavo. *Estudios sociales, políticos y económicos (homenaje pótumo)*. [San] Salvador: [Universidad de El Salvador], 1950.
Mecham, J. Lloyd. *The United States and Inter-American Security, 1889–1960*. Austin: University of Texas Press, 1961.
Menjívar, Rafael. *Formación y lucha del proletariado industrial salvadoreño*. San Salvador: UCA Editores, 1979.
Morán, Francisco. *Las jornadas cívicas de abril y mayo de 1944*. San Salvador: Editorial Universitaria, 1979.
Munro, Dana G[ardner]. *The Five Republics of Central America: Their Political and Economic Development and Their Relations with the United States*. Edited by David Kinley. 1918. Reprint. New York: Russell & Russell, 1967.
Ochoa Mena, H. *La revolución de julio: La caída de la tiranía militar en Chile*. Santiago, Chile: Imp. "Cisneros," 1931.
Olmedo, Daniel. *Apuntes de historia de El Salvador*. 3d. ed. Barcelona: Tip. Cat. Casals Caspe [1952].
Parada, Alfredo. *Etapas políticas: Historia de El Salvador*. Vol. 1. San Salvador, 1950.
Peña Kampy, Alberto. *"El general Martínez": Un patriarcal presidente dictador*. [Mexico City]: Editorial Tipográfico Ramírez, n.d.
Reynolds, David R. *Rapid Development in Small Economies: The Example of El Salvador*. New York: Praeger, 1967.
Rodriguez, Mario. *Central America*. Englewood Cliffs, N.J.: Prentice-Hall, 1965.
Santos Dueñas, Tiburcio. *Aurora del dos de abril de 1944*. San Salvador: "Editado por El Pica-Pica. Imprenta y encuadernación 'La República,' " 1944.
Vidal, Manuel. *Nociones de historia de Centro América (especial para El Salvador)*. 8th ed. San Salvador: Ministerio de Educación, Dirección General de Publicaciones, 1969.
Wallich, Henry C[hristopher], and John Adler, with the collaboration of E. R. Schlesinger, Florence Nixon, and P. J. W. Glaessner. *Public Finance in a Developing Country: El Salvador, a Case Study*. Cambridge: Harvard University Press, 1951.
White, Alastair. *El Salvador*. New York: Praeger, 1973.
Wood, Bryce. *The Making of the Good Neighbor Policy*. New York: Columbia University Press, 1961.
Woodward, Ralph Lee, Jr. *Central America: A Nation Divided*. 2d ed. New York: Oxford University Press, 1985.

Theses and Dissertations

Alas, Leonilo Armando. "Comercio exterior y la inflación en El Salvador, durante el período de 1931 a 1952 inclusive." Thesis, Universidad de El Salvador, 1954.
Astilla, Carmelo Francisco Esmerelda. "The Martínez Era: Salvadoran-American Relations, 1931–1944." Ph.D. diss., Louisiana State University and Agricultural and Mechanical College, 1976.
Clamp, Christina Anne. "The Overthrow of Jorge Ubico: A Case Study of Nonviolent Action in Guatemala." B.A. thesis, Friends World College, 1976.

Elam, Robert Varney. "Appeal to Arms: The Army and Politics in El Salvador, 1931–1964." Ph.D. diss., University of New Mexico, 1968.
Guardado, Gregorio. "Las ideas económico-políticas en El Salvador (breve ensayo de crítica económico-política de la historia de 'El Salvador')." Doctoral thesis, Universidad Autónoma de El Salvador, 1946.
Parkman, Patricia. "Insurrection Without Arms: The General Strike in El Salvador, 1944." Ph.D. diss., Temple University, 1980.
Petersen, John Holger. "The Political Role of University Students in Guatemala: 1944–1968." Ph.D. diss., University of Pittsburgh, 1969.
Pleitez de Gómez, Morales, Lilian Aracely, Gladys Alvarado Salguero de Batres, and Sonia Elizabeth Rivas de Escobar. "Federación unitaria sindical de El Salvador: Desarrollo histórico, organización y luchas." Thesis, Escuela de Trabajo Social (San Salvador), 1975.
Wilson, Everett A. "The Crisis of National Integration in El Salvador, 1919–1935." Ph.D. diss., Stanford University, 1970.

Index

About the Author

Patricia Parkman devoted a total of thirteen months to research on the Martínez era in El Salvador in 1976 and 1978. She holds a doctorate in Latin American history from Temple University and was a postdoctoral fellow at the Program on Nonviolent Sanctions in Conflict and Defense, the Center for International Affairs, Harvard University, from 1984 to 1987. She is co-author, with Christopher Kruegler, of "Identifying Alternatives to Political Violence: An Educational Imperative," *Harvard Educational Review*, February 1985 (reprinted in Joseph J. Fahey and Richard Armstrong, *A Peace Reader: Essential Readings in War and Justice, Nonviolence and World Order* [Mahwah, New Jersey: Paulist Press, 1987]).